A Fleeting Empire

A FLEETING EMPIRE

EARLY STUART BRITAIN AND THE
MERCHANT ADVENTURERS TO CANADA

ANDREW D. NICHOLLS

McGILL-QUEEN'S UNIVERSITY PRESS
MONTREAL & KINGSTON · LONDON · ITHACA

© McGill-Queen's University Press 2010

ISBN 978-0-7735-3778-1

Legal deposit third quarter 2010
Bibliothèque nationale du Québec

Printed in Canada on acid-free paper that is 100% ancient forest free
(100% post-consumer recycled), processed chlorine free.

This book has been published with the help of a grant from the Research
Foundation, Buffalo State College.

McGill-Queen's University Press acknowledges the support of the Canada
Council for the Arts for our publishing program. We also acknowledge the
financial support of the Government of Canada through the Canada Book
Fund for our publishing activities.

Library and Archives Canada Cataloguing in Publication

Nicholls, Andrew D. (Andrew Dean), 1965–
A fleeting empire : early Stuart Britain and the merchant
adventurers to Canada / Andrew D. Nicholls.

Includes bibliographical references and index.
ISBN 978-0-7735-3778-1

1. Kirke's Expedition, 1627-1629. 2. Québec (Quebec)–History–Capture,
1629. 3. Canada–Discovery and exploration–British. 4. Great Britain–
Politics and government–1603–1649. 5. Canada–History–To 1663 (New
France). I. Title.

FC330.N53 2010   971.01'14   C2010-903008-7

This book was designed and typeset by studio oneonone in Sabon 10.2/14.5

For Laura ...

Contents

ILLUSTRATIONS

Acknowledgments

As the reader will soon discover, this work stems from a long-standing interest in several overlapping stories. Bringing them all together in this book has been a project many years in development, and I owe thanks to a number of people who have helped it to fruition.

Shirley Whittington, then Public Information Officer at Sainte-Marie among the Hurons, encouraged me to write my first article on the Kirke Brothers for the site's magazine in 1995. That, as they say, got the ball rolling. Courtesy of an invitation from my friend Dr David Allan to speak at St Andrews University in 2001, I was able to test and expand my research on Lord Ochiltree. Dr Allan and his colleague Dr Roger Mason offered many useful suggestions for further elucidating the Ochiltree element of the story. As these threads started to come together, I entered into a most fruitful correspondence with Dr John G. Reid of St Mary's University. The reader will see how important his work has been in shaping this book. I want to thank him for the encouragement and expertise he offered me while I worked on it and several articles that preceded it.

Closer to home I have benefited from the interest and assistance of many others, not least from my wife, Laura, and my parents, Dean and Elaine Nicholls. Much of this book was written while I was on sabbatical in the fall of 2007 and spring of 2008. Never underestimate the value of friendship and exercise when writing! Bosworth (the beagle) got me out for a walk every morning at 10:30 precisely! He's a great companion.

Friends, colleagues, and a decade's worth of students at Buffalo State College and elsewhere, have heard and critiqued various parts of this material, and I have enjoyed and appreciated their input. An unexpected pleasure and adventure was the chance to present my research to the officers of HMCS *Toronto*, while sailing between Norfolk, Virginia, and New York, in May 2008. That remains a wonderful memory, and I want the officers and crew of that fine ship to know how much it meant for me to live among them for a few days and experience life at sea.

Several people read all or parts of the manuscript as it evolved and offered useful feedback and comments during the writing process. I would especially like to acknowledge Paul Delaney, Dennis Ford, Jamie Hunter, Paul Marttin, and Ted Schmidt. The manuscript benefited greatly from suggestions of the two anonymous referees engaged by McGill-Queen's University Press.

Writing a book requires a great deal of tangible assistance, and considerations large and small. My two department chairs through this process, Drs E.O. Smith, Jr and David Carson, were helpful and kind in a variety of ways that benefited the work. Drs Lawrence Flood and Mark Severson, deans of the School of Natural and Social Sciences at Buffalo State College during these years, provided both encouragement and financial support for research and publication. I further wish to acknowledge the financial assistance provided by the Buffalo State College Provost's Incentive Program, and by Ted Turkle and the Research Foundation.

Finally, my thanks to Jonathan Crago, Joan McGilvray, and Jane McWhinney, all of McGill-Queen's University Press. Jonathan has been a constant advocate and friend through this process; Joan steered me through all the production-related elements that were essential to this book; and Jane copy-edited the manuscript with skill, grace, and wit. It has been my pleasure to work with all of them.

Introduction:
On Filling the Gaps

On the front cover of *Building the Canadian Nation*, the history text my mother used in high school, is a collage: a lone Indian in a canoe is surrounded by images of a Viking longboat, a prairie farmer driving a wagon piled with wheat, a North West Mounted Police officer, a locomotive, and drawings of Second World War–era military hardware. Looking at it, one would assume that the history it recounted had entailed many things, and that not all were benign. As with all survey texts, its intention was to be as comprehensive as possible, and it had to conform to a particular narrative defining a Canadian nation. But, as many history instructors, students, and readers will attest, the survey approach also makes gaps inevitable.

In the account of the founding of New France and what used to be known as the "heroic period" of Canadian History – when intrepid missionaries lived among the indigenous peoples, and in several cases died as martyrs for the cause of Christianity – one such gap appeared. In describing the early career of Father Jean de Brébeuf and the aftermath of his arrival in New France, the author, George Brown, noted: "For three years he worked among [the Hurons]. Then Quebec was taken by the English in 1629 and until the French returned the work came to an end."[1]

My mother cannot recall if she questioned this interruption to the otherwise dominant theme (the study of indigenous peoples aside) of early Canadian history – the development of New France – but I remember my own first fleeting awareness of this story. In the book we used at Parkview Public School in Midland, Ontario, in the late 1970s, whose title I no longer know although I can still in my mind's eye see its royal blue cover, we learned a little more: the Kirke brothers, who were English privateers, seized and held Quebec in 1629 until it was returned to the French according to the provisions of a treaty in 1632. In my high school and first undergraduate Canadian History courses, the Kirke brothers were sometimes mentioned but they were never explained. That pattern is present in most survey texts of Canadian history – if they mention the Kirkes at all. The privateer brothers are ghosts who make only a fleeting appearance and are gone.

Their story would likely never have meant any more to me had I not in the mid-1980s worked as a summer interpreter and later as a staff supervisor at Sainte-Marie among the Hurons in Midland, the reconstructed historic site of the French Jesuit mission headquarters in Huronia. In discussing the history of that site, especially in the wake of Pope John Paul II's 1984 visit to Sainte-Marie and the adjacent Martyrs' Shrine, the Kirke brothers suddenly re-emerged, not least because much of our interpretation involved Brébeuf and, by necessity, his sudden departure from Huronia in 1629, courtesy of the Kirkes and their capture of Quebec.

By 1995 I had begun doctoral studies in British History at the University of Guelph, and I was invited to write an article for the site's magazine. I chose to research the Kirke brothers' story a little further. Because my doctoral dissertation dealing with the impact of the 1603 union of the English and Scottish crowns led me to Glasgow that winter, I began to explore the ways in which the appearance of the Kirkes at Quebec in the late 1620s stemmed from the foreign and wartime policies of King Charles I, and even more, from the aspirations of one of his courtiers, Sir William Alexander, who held the original charter for Nova Scotia.

Even a cursory reading of the relevant *Calendars* of English State Papers and the *Registers of the Privy Council of Scotland*, to name just two accessible printed primary sources, showed me that the events and personalities involved in the taking of Quebec and the planting of Nova Scotia represented much more than exotic footnotes for Charles and his English and Scottish governments. Connections I made as a result of the Glasgow visit later permitted me to broaden the scope of my study and

The Taking of Quebec by The English

N. Vander Gucht, "Taking of Quebec by the English." The
earliest-known artist's conception of the fall of Quebec to the
Kirke brothers. The artist erroneously portrayed Quebec as
an established European-style city.

to incorporate a previously almost unknown figure in the story, James
Stewart of Killeith, fourth lord Ochiltree. So began a course of research
that has lasted for more than a dozen years and culminated in this work.

Others have appreciated the difficulty I experienced in trying to situ-
ate this story in the broad framework of early Canadian History, or in
my case, also into early modern British History. Bernard Allaire, whose
essay dealing with the Kirke brothers' seizure of Quebec appears in the
wonderful collection celebrating four hundred years of continuous

French presence in North America in 2004, understood the problem of incorporating that story into a wider history of New France or Canada. He called the incident "a pyrrhic victory for one side, a humiliating defeat for the other," and noted: "The siege and occupation of the settlement of Quebec (1629–32) during the French-English Wars is a subject most historians have more or less swept under the carpet. Although the basic facts can be found in the textbooks, the information is too fragmentary to be useful. The minute we try to look more closely, questions spring up on all sides."[2]

The story of the Kirke brothers, Sir William Alexander and his dream of founding a "New Scotland," and the European war that brought them into conflict with subjects of the king of France in North America in the late 1620s does not fit easily into one particular historical category. I suspect this may be why it has not received a comprehensive treatment until now.[3] In attempting the more intense study that could demonstrate the importance of the incidents that took place in the later 1620s and early 1630s in what is now part of Canada, several questions arise, as Allaire has suggested. Is this one story? Or are there several stories here, whose intersections are merely coincidental? Can these stories be linked together as a narrative, or do they demand an analytical study that draws upon and augments existing paradigms in the discipline? Should it be categorized as Canadian history, as British history? Or does this study of the European overseas ventures shaped by emerging political, economic, and military models fall more appropriately under the more encompassing rubric of Atlantic History?

In preparing A Fleeting Empire, I found that the historical events and figures previously treated in isolation were in fact intimately related, and that the many threads could be synthesized as one narrative. Furthermore, the relationship among the elements of the story, when properly explained, can give us new perspectives on lesser-known aspects of early British initiatives on the North American mainland.[4] The tale also sparks a compelling counterfactual possibility, in that a very different history of North America would have emerged had Charles I in the early 1630s more aggressively pressed the claims his agents had won for him on the St Lawrence and in Nova Scotia. Explaining why he did not do so is also one of this book's aims.

The narrative cannot proceed smoothly, however. In trying to construct the broader historical context I found it essential first to profile the backgrounds and aspirations of the main protagonists in turn. Strict chronology can therefore not be our structural guide. The story will flow chronologically at times, but take a step backward when a new theme or character emerges. My hope is that forewarned is indeed forearmed, and that this narrative style will not cause the reader undue confusion. The book will unfold as follows.

Chapter 1 traces the early history of New France, emphasizing in particular the importance to the French of alliances with various indigenous peoples, notably members of the Huron Confederacy. It examines Samuel de Champlain's efforts to make Quebec the recognized base of operations for the Canadian fur trade and offers a profile of the region that would be contested by French and British interests in the period from 1627 to 1632. I also trace the first missionary endeavours, with a nod to the factors that led to my interest in the wider story. An account of the early career in Canada of Father Jean de Brébeuf and his forced evacuation from the Huron country in 1629 serves as an opening "bookend." The decision to begin the book with this event reflects both my first acquaintance with the broader story, and the presentation it has traditionally received in Canadian History survey texts such as the one alluded to earlier and those that other interested scholars like Allaire have examined.

In the second chapter, I present a corresponding overview of English trading and exploration initiatives in the North Atlantic world to 1603. In the Elizabethan years, although such initiatives and events seemed to indicate a sense of national interest and destiny in relation to navigational and commercial ventures, they are better understood as having been privately or locally motivated. England's earliest colonial ventures, particularly on Newfoundland and in Virginia, were relatively modest overseas achievements into first decade of James VI/I's English reign. For that reason, Sir William Alexander's aspirations for his colonial charter need not be seen as overly romantic or unrealistic in the context of the times.[5]

In chapter 3 we look at James VI/I's desire to achieve political unity among his British kingdoms in the wake of regal union in 1603.

Although this theme may at first appear to be unrelated to the story at hand, we shall see that James encouraged inter-kingdom co-operation as a means of extending central authority into remote regions of the British Isles.[6] I suggest that important connections may be drawn between these domestic efforts and the king's personnel who enacted them, and early commercial and colonial ventures in North America. This chapter also illustrates the ways in which personal relationships made at James's court sparked interest in overseas ventures for key courtiers. A major protagonist of our story, Sir William Alexander of Menstrie, was among these courtiers.

In the following chapter, Alexander's career begins to receive the reinterpretation this work offers. Rather than being seen as failure who was out of his depth in attempting to plant a colony, Alexander deserves to be acknowledged as a rising political figure in the political world of early Stuart Britain. Service to his sovereign, whether as advisor, political operative, or diplomat, was therefore his major imperative; colonial ventures represented at best secondary investments of both his time and his resources.

Chapters 5 and 6 begin the chronological narrative that constitutes the primary thread of this story. We will see how the death of James VI/I and the ascension of Charles I occasioned a much more bellicose foreign policy for the British kingdoms, and eventually, war with both Spain and France. As the new king was financially and logistically incapable of prosecuting these wars with his own forces, the use of proxies such as mercenaries on the European continent or privateers on the high seas was a crucial element of this specific wartime policy – which Alexander himself sought to implement among his state responsibilities. This wartime strategy meant that Alexander could hardly gainsay the successes that English privateers (the Kirke brothers) seemed on the verge of achieving in 1628, even though they potentially compromised his charter claims in the New World. The partnership that resulted was thus another means of protecting potential claims and profits, at the same time as prosecuting the king's war. Much would depend on what would actually be achieved on the St Lawrence and in Nova Scotia in 1629.

It is for this reason that in chapter 7 we must make one last chronological detour, to introduce and contextualize another key figure in this story, James Stewart of Killeith, fourth lord Ochiltree. His enlistment as the leader of a separate Anglo-Scottish colony on Cape Breton Island in 1629 shows that trade and plantation were not the only purposes the new Merchant Adventurers to Canada (the Alexander-Kirke consortium) had been charged to pursue. The Cape Breton colony was unique at this juncture of early British overseas efforts in that an immediate strategic imperative was among its *raisons d'être*. Ochiltree's career also presents another example of an individual who, having performed quasi-military services to the crown on the peripheral edges of the British kingdoms, was forced by his depleted coffers and political fortunes to turn to overseas ventures as a way to regain royal favour.

Chapters 8 through 11 carry the story through to its narrative conclusion. The Kirkes took Quebec in 1629, at the same time that Ochiltree planted his colony on Cape Breton Island, and Alexander's son, Sir William Alexander junior, established the first incarnation of "New Scotland." And yet, this set of apparent British triumphs in what had otherwise been a disastrous war was not destined to last. Charles I's haste to make peace with France on the terms most beneficial to him meant that the new North American gains would be bargained away. Ochiltree's political misjudgments at this juncture, coupled with Alexander's own acquiescence, provided Charles with all the cover he needed to ensure that Quebec and Nova Scotia would not be stumbling blocks in his pursuit of larger interests.

The restitution of New France meant the resumption of ante-bellum activities at Quebec. French interests renewed their trade, Samuel de Champlain returned as de facto governor of New France, and Father Jean de Brébeuf went back to Huronia. And so, with this closing bookend to our story, we come back to our point of departure, where we may pick up the thread of the customary narrative of Early Canadian History.

But can these events be seen as something other than simply a collection of anecdotes from early Canadian history? Where does this study fit in the context of broader historiographic patterns?

In my view, the account that follows has a place in the three mentioned sub-branches of historiography – Canadian/Early North American,

British, and Atlantic History – and that in linking them together, we gain new insights into the interrelationship of European aspirations and North American options in the early modern period. My goal here is, to borrow Nicholas Canny's phrase, to provide "a transatlantic, if not transnational dimension" to a story that has mostly been treated as a sidebar of early Canadian History.[7]

In the past several decades, a variety of historians, anthropologists, economists, political scientists, and geographers have sought to broaden our understanding of such topics as the interaction of peoples, patterns of trade, colonization, emigration, slavery, and the homogenization of political and military systems in comparative terms, by treating the entire Atlantic World (roughly 1400–1850) as a single region.[8] A stimulating result of this unified perspective has been to allow us to look beyond present-day national labels when dealing with the Atlantic World.

This study dialogues with those approaches in the following ways. First, it asserts the primacy of European events and experiences in explaining what Europeans were doing in North America in the late 1620s and early 1630s. To that extent, the Atlantic Ocean is portrayed as a distinct theatre in the narrative, an entity that was understood in contemporary maritime culture, economic and commercial aspirations, and strategic decisions.[9] Most important for our purposes is the role it played in the wartime strategy adopted by Charles I's governments – how it affected decisions to employ privateers or fostered merged interests in the 1627–29 war with France.

Where nomenclature is concerned, labels like "Canadian" or "American" as they pertain to the way history is now taught are not helpful or descriptive for this period. Although the word "Canada" appears in my title and the events analysed here took place in what became Canadian provinces between 1867 and 1949, the areas in question were distinct unto themselves. "Canada" slowly began to enter the European *lingua franca* through Jacques Cartier's accounts of his voyages to North America between 1534 and 1542, but the word was used imprecisely, most often to denote the area from the Gulf of St Lawrence upriver to the Island of Montreal. For that reason, the St Lawrence River was often referred to in the sixteenth and seventeenth centuries as "the Great River of Canada," with little relation to the land itself.

This lack of specificity would fuel confusion and sometimes-competing claims when monarchs granted exaggerated licenses for trade or colonization, without really knowing the lands at all. "Canada" should not be read as a clearly defined territory, therefore, much less as a forerunner of the country that would eventually bear that name. The same qualification is needed in discussions of Alexander's chartered territories. His patent covered the present-day Maritime Provinces of Canada and much of the modern state of Maine, and stretched north to the shores of the St Lawrence. The French who settled there first called the region "Acadie," while British interests used "Nova Scotia" and "New Scotland" almost interchangeably.

Similarly, we will see that supposedly established national designations and declensions like "British," "English," Scottish," and "French" must be used carefully for this period. National origins did not always correspond with national loyalties. Identity could derive as easily from one's region, class, religion, or vocation as from a state. Although it would require a separate study, another underlying premise of this book is that many mariners of the period comprised a multi-lingual, multi-racial, multi-faith community unto themselves.[10] What is more, as two of the most distinguished proponents of this broader approach have noted, states such as the British kingdoms and France were themselves works in progress in the early seventeenth century, and crowned heads and royal administrations tended to be limited in terms of what they could effect, especially across a vast ocean.[11] Nevertheless, important developments that were taking place within the British kingdoms during these years provide a crucial context for this story.

Although the north Atlantic and northern North America are our primary theatres of focus, this work owes a substantial debt to new understandings of "British History" that have emerged in the past generation. Beginning with J.C. Beckett's 1966 book, *The Making of Modern Ireland*, and energized and given disciplinary definition by J.G.A. Pocock in his seminal 1975 article "British History: A Plea for a New Subject," a paradigm has now developed that emphasizes the interconnected nature of the history of the British Isles themselves, and by extension, of the wider English-speaking world.[12] While England, Scotland, Ireland, Wales, and more localized regions within these territories (to name just the largest constituent parts of the British Isles – and, for administrative purposes, the English-speaking ones– in what Pocock has called an "Atlantic archipelago") remain the focus of individual study, this more holistic approach has generated new and stimulating analyses of the eventual formation of a British state. It has also given us insight into ways the peoples of that state responded as economic, social, political, military, religious, and personal aspirations and pressures propelled them beyond their borders.[13]

This analysis from a British perspective forms a critical lens through which to view the broader narrative of events in the early decades of the seventeenth century. Our consideration of this period begins with the early Stuart monarchy itself, the most important contemporary institutional projection of a new British identity. After 1603 Scotland and England (and by extension Wales and Ireland) shared a ruler. Regal union did not produce a political union, however, and as kings, James VI/I and Charles I were, to cite Jenny Wormald, frequently in the position of acting as "kings of all, but kings of each."[14] The potential therefore always existed for actions undertaken with reference to one kingdom and its constituent interests to clash with contrary or divergent orders issued for another. With no institutional mechanism for addressing these conflicts, save their regal authority or the interventions of a comparatively small circle of court advisors, the early Stuarts were obliged to deal with these situations in a decidedly *ad hoc* fashion.[15] As Peter Donald, Allan Macinnes, Conrad Russell, and others have demonstrated, in the case of Charles I especially, this situation was a recipe for serious inter-kingdom tension, which was exacerbated by the king's determined wielding of his prerogative powers. Ultimately it would lead to rebellion and civil war throughout the British Isles.[16]

In the 1620s, however, the hybrid Anglo-Scottish composition of the courts of the early Stuarts offered many hopeful examples of growing inter-kingdom connections. One tangible role of the royal court was to bring Englishmen and Scotsmen together in a variety of initiatives, and this blending of actors helped create contacts, networks, sponsorships and partnerships that could be described as truly British in nature. This was especially the case for overseas ventures. Alexander, a Scot, became interested and involved in the possibilities of colonial plantation[17] through his friendship with English courtiers like Sir Ferdinando Gorges, one of the original patentees of New England, and Sir George Calvert and Lord Falkland, early colonisers of Newfoundland. Shared British kingship did more as well. The early Stuarts' aspirations for peace and unity in their combined realms also helped foster techniques and personnel that would ultimately prove useful in British overseas initiatives.

Regal union after 1603 also permitted the governments of the constituent kingdoms to pursue tangible new ways of extending central authority to the peripheries of the British Isles – regions that had often resisted central power. Chapter 3 explores these experiments, paying particular attention to the similarities of method and manpower employed by the crown in asserting its authority in the Highlands and Islands of Scotland, in Ireland, and in overseas ventures such as Newfoundland in the early seventeenth century.[18] Conceptually, and thanks to the aforementioned personal connections he had made at court, Alexander was well aware of these methods and precedents when he conceived of a "New Scotland" and convinced James VI/I to charter it in 1621. Furthermore, he understood the priority his king assigned to order within his dominions, and with an eye to recent Anglo-Scottish plantation ventures in Ulster, he asserted the value of colonies to this end: "Thus Ireland which heretofore was scarcely discovered, and only irritated by others, proving to the *English* as the *Lowe Countries* did to *Spaine*, a means whereby to waste their men, and their money, is not really conquered, becoming a strength to the State, and a glorie to his Majesties gouernment, who hath in the setling thereof excelled all that was commended in any ancient Colonie."[19]

The experience of asserting metropolitan authority and interest in the marchlands and peripheries of the British Isles is now treated as a formative component for understanding contemporary overseas colonial ventures, thereby drawing "British" and "Atlantic" historiographical approaches together. The works of scholars J.P. Greene, Allan Macinnes, Jane Ohlmeyer, and Ned Landsman, to name just a few, have given some of the clearest frameworks within which to view the aspirations of would-be colonists, traders, and the monarchs who licensed them.[20]

Within such frameworks, Alexander can be seen as a colonial factor who capitalized both on court connections and on his ruler's metropolitan aspirations. Furthermore, in committing his hopes to paper and publishing his *Encouragement to Colonies* to generate support for Nova Scotia, he joined a growing European community of overseas enthusiasts who broadcast their dreams via promotional literature.[21]

Alexander nonetheless receives new consideration in this work, vis-à-vis these broader frameworks. Traditionally, he has been analysed as a would-be coloniser first and foremost, and judged according to his evident failures in those ventures.[22] This study reverses the British and Atlantic focuses, arguing that political service to his sovereigns in a domestic context and the patronage with which he was rewarded on an ongoing basis were Alexander's priorities. His colonial aspirations were ultimately secondary to his loyalty, and when the right inducements were offered, he was willing to sacrifice his colony to keep common cause with his king. We shall return to this in due course.

Up until the summer of 1628, Alexander's efforts to promote his colony had mostly been unsuccessful. But his royal masters never wavered in offering what fulsome and creative support they could to the nascent venture. This was true even to the point of their risking discord among the nobility of the British kingdoms through the creation of a new order of Scots peerage, the Knights Baronet of Nova Scotia, for those willing to subscribe to Alexander's proposed colony. Therefore, on the drawing board at least, Nova Scotia offers both a contemporary and a retrospective difference from parallel British ventures in North America such as Newfoundland, Virginia, and New England. The proprietors of those colonies were never empowered by the crown to offer this sort of social inducement to subscribers.[23] Retrospectively, the early Stuarts' efforts on behalf of Alexander's scheme also stand in contrast to a general pattern of royal indifference to colonial ventures that present-day scholars have profiled for the early seventeenth century.[24]

In the summer of 1628, Alexander's colonial aspirations, and the royal support they had achieved, were suddenly challenged by an unforeseen set of circumstances. The exigencies of war had caused Charles I to issue letters of marque to a family of merchant sailors, the Kirke brothers, mandating them to act as privateers under his authority as king of England. Their successes against French installations in what is now Canada in the summer of 1628 created a problem, however, as Alexander viewed the Kirkes' conquests as an impingement on the terms of his colonial patent. Two different thrusts of governmental policy – one in support of colonization, the other tied to the prosecution of the war – thus created a conflict with an Anglo-Scottish dimension. Past practices, however, provided a possible solution.

The king, concerned members of his court, and emerging mechanisms for fostering Anglo-Scottish co-operation in overseas ventures were all marshalled in an effort to salve the conflicting claims of the Kirkes and Alexander in 1628–29. The creative use of the king's authority, in both its personal and institutional understandings, thereby created a synthesis of British interests embodied in a new partnership between the Kirkes and Alexander, which became known as the Merchant Adventurers to Canada.[25]

Although at first glance this newly formed entity might appear to be nothing more than a solution for a comparatively minor court squabble, in reality, it was more. The British kingdoms were at war with France (and Spain) in early 1629, and the war had been going badly. Kevin Sharpe, who has provided a masterful analysis of these years and their importance in framing the king's fateful decision to dispense with his English parliament in 1629, noted the king's mood and view of the war: "The retreat from war was for Charles more necessity than desire. In his view the failures of the years 1625–28, military failures and failures to fulfil promises to allies and friends, stained with dishonour and shame his first actions as king. The words dishonour and shame come naturally onto the page because Charles often employed them during these years and evidently more often experienced them."[26] In such a climate of gloom, any victory, no matter how obscure the source or remote the theatre, was bound to be seized upon and celebrated.

The Kirke brothers' privateering successes along the St Lawrence in 1628, and the assumption that they would capture Quebec itself in 1629, had taken hold in the public imagination, and were almost the only successes to which Charles's governments could point in the dismal war. For that reason, finding a compromise between the overlapping claims of Alexander and the Kirkes was more than the desired removal of an irritant; it became a wartime imperative. Once their partnership was forged, however, a new projection of colonial initiative – and military strategy – became possible.

If successful in their endeavours, the Merchant Adventurers to Canada would open up enticing possibilities that served commercial, colonial, and military priorities. For the short term, that military victory suited the king's needs. The Merchant Adventurers would then be free to pursue a mercantile agenda (control of the Canadian fur trade) and make profits that would benefit the private interests underwriting this new company. Alexander would personally use this partnership as a further spur for planting colonies in his territory chartered as Nova Scotia, an initiative he had been attempting unsuccessfully since 1621. Finally, and perhaps most enticingly for Charles and his advisors, if successful, the combination of these eventualities would tangibly increase his area of claimed dominion in North America, so as to virtually eliminate a French presence.

If projections of metropolitan power into the peripheries of the British Isles and the operation of peer networks and connections at court are two components for analysing extensions of British interests into the Atlantic World, then the enlistment of personnel to lead and man such ventures is a third. As John Reid has demonstrated, a dichotomy existed between the promoters and financial backers of overseas ventures on the one hand, and the operational heads of such endeavours overseas, on the other. Furthermore, he has shown that both British and French initiatives in North America featured connections and chains of command that reflected established hierarchical, kin, and client networks that were common within the home kingdoms.[27]

Much was expected of those who became operational leaders of these ventures. They had to possess sufficient social standing to maintain communications with their backers, particularly when these were ranked among the most powerful in the kingdom, and they needed the power to assume acknowledged command over the personnel of their venture, be they sailors, colonists, traders, or soldiers. Furthermore, it was generally expected that they would already have direct experience with military command and with the exercise of duty in their king's name. They had to be trustworthy as well, because the vast distances of time and space meant that formal orders were often vague, leaving great latitude for individuals to make their own decisions.

In Alexander's case, this latitude enabled him to choose his son, Sir William Alexander junior, to lead his colonists out to Nova Scotia. Like the Kirke brothers, the younger Alexander had enjoyed success operating under a letter of marque as a member of Charles I's proxy forces in the war against France. This model profile and prior experience for a colonial or commercial leader are especially important in the consideration of yet another key protagonist in this story, James Stewart of Killeith, fourth lord Ochiltree. It is with Ochiltree that the synthesis of British commercial, colonial, and military agendas becomes particularly evident.

Ochiltree had all the prerequisites for command and then some; peerage, military and political experience in the king's name, previous participation in a colonial venture, and above all, a desire to win accolades. He was well placed to lead a hastily assembled colonial effort on Cape Breton Island that would provide a geographic and strategic link between Quebec and Nova Scotia, and which would be able to exercise sufficient coercive force to assert his king's new claims in the region.

Ironically, however, almost nobody related to the Alexander-Kirke-Ochiltree efforts in the spring of 1629 realized that diplomacy had already intervened and that the war was over. Having brokered a compromise between Alexander and the Kirkes, the British king was now forced to make an unpleasant choice of his own; would he preserve his proxies' achievements in North America and all that these might entail, or use them as bargaining chips to win lasting peace with France? That he chose the latter alternative was a sign of his prioritizing more immediate and understandable foreign policy goals that these New World territories now facilitated.[28] Charles could not afford to let the possibility of peace slip away.

Sir William Alexander (earl of Stirling by 1633) made his master's decision considerably easier by opting to accept increased powers and privileges at home in return for acquiescing in the surrender of his long-standing colonial ambitions. This dynamic in turn underlines the revision Alexander receives in this study. Nova Scotia might be lost, but Alexander would be well looked after. His options were, of course, made infinitely clearer because he knew what his king wanted, and as an agent of his government he understood and supported Charles's foreign policy priorities. Others were not so fortunate. The Kirke brothers gained very little from their partnership with Alexander, and were left with less attractive options than those opened for their erstwhile Scottish associate, even though they continued to serve Charles I as best they could.

Lord Ochiltree had likewise sought to please his king, and had made tangible sacrifices related to the 1629 operations. As long as a resumption of colonial initiatives in Nova Scotia remained a possibility, Charles was even ready to provide assistance to Ochiltree. But herein lies another nuance of this study. As John Reid has shown, Charles was sincere in his diplomatic efforts to protect the integrity of Alexander's chartered territory generally, and the Nova Scotia colony specifically, in diplomatic negotiations with the French up to 1632. What is added here is the assertion that Ochiltree, through disastrous political manoeuvrings of his own in 1632, provided Charles and Alexander with a cover for abandoning Nova Scotia, to the benefit of both the king's agenda and Alexander's finances.

———————

I hope in this study to address many of the questions to which Allaire alluded, and which I recall from my first acquaintance with these incidents. The appearance of the Kirkes before Quebec, and their ultimate seizure of France's most important installation in the New World, was more than a random act, and must be seen as an aspect of a deliberate wartime strategy on the part of Charles I and his governments. The wider possibilities for exacting benefits from this privateering venture were tied to Britain's other colonial ventures in North America, most specifically Alexander's project of a New Scotland. These ventures were in turn animated by past practices and assumptions that had been useful in extending metropolitan authority into peripheral regions of the British Isles. Personnel who had either performed such services to the crown, or who had similar experiences, would be employed in these overseas ventures. When parallel initiatives that had been licensed by the Stuart monarchs under different national crown authorities came into conflict, mechanisms developed at the hybrid Stuart courts were invoked to forge a partnership. Not only did this strategy settle a quarrel among potentially competing interests but the resulting partnership also opened the possibility of a more aggressive prosecution of the war with France in the New World theatre, and the extension of British hegemony along almost all of North America's northeastern coastline. That a peace was reached, and that Charles I quickly opted to return Quebec to the French, but reserved his decision on Nova Scotia, is well known. What this study shows is the part British domestic politics and court patronage ultimately played in bringing about the abandonment of Nova Scotia.

It is my further hope that my assertions will enrich and inform Early North American/Canadian History and early Modern British History, and, through the case studies and linked narrative they offer, prove useful to those interested in wider Atlantic approaches. As Allaire also suggested, however, the disparate nature of the sources involved sometimes means that absolute certainty, particularly on points of detail, is all but impossible. This is mainly true of such details as precise sailing dates, nautical routes, and exact points where landfall was made. Where I have had to privilege inference over judgment, it is usually because of contradictory documentary evidence. In all such cases I have tried to summarize or to quote sufficiently from the documents in question for readers to make comparisons and weigh my conclusions accordingly.

This is a story about a diverse North Atlantic World as it existed in the early seventeenth century. Some of its major figures crisscrossed the ocean numerous times, while others never left Europe. It recounts collisions of interests, faiths, and aspirations, and the main protagonists' frequent deep disappointment and frustration related to the "strange nations" of their fleeting trans-Atlantic empire. I am fortunate in that the convergence of the lives and themes that constitute this book permits me to begin in a place that is not strange to me at all – the place where I was born.

A FLEETING EMPIRE

Though seeming but by accident to us,
Yet in the depths of heavenly breasts first bred,
As arguments demonstrative to prove
That weaknesse dwels below, and pow'r above.
Loe, prosperous *Caesar* charged for a space,
Both with strange nationes, and his countreys spoyles.
Even when he seem'd by warre to purchase peace,
And roses of sweet rest, from thorncs of toils.

SIR WILLIAM ALEXANDER,
The Tragedy of Julius Caesar (1607)

And if those who are employed do not manage affairs with care
and vigilance, as well as with fidelity, voyages are
rendered useless, and those who advance their money lose
courage when their plans are defeated, and they are often
disappointed of the hopes they had entertained.

SAMUEL DE CHAMPLAIN (1632)

1

The Huron Mission and the Promise of New France

Three years ago you came here to learn our language, in order
that you might teach us to know your God and to worship and
serve him ... And now ... you are abandoning us.
SAMUEL DE CHAMPLAIN, on the departure of Brébeuf (1632)

The arrival of spring can be agonizingly slow in the lands around the
Great Lakes. Nature teases the land and water with subtle tricks. Ice will
break close to shore but a shift in the breeze or prevailing currents will
quickly make waterways impassable again, as chunks of broken pack ice
drift inward. A mild and sunny day that melts the snows of late March
and early April can rapidly reverse its effects overnight when the tem-
perature drops. Spring snowstorms are not infrequent and a damp chill
seems to hang in the air well into May. The sky is sometimes clouded
for days at a time. Yet, the return of migratory birds or the emergence of
animals from hibernation signals that the season of rebirth is approaching. In spite of its delays, fits, and starts, spring in the Great Lakes region,
as everywhere else, is a time of hope and renewal.

For the five clans of the Huron Confederacy who lived in lands
adjacent to Georgian Bay, the massive appendage to Lake Huron that is
sometimes considered a Great Lake on its own, spring meant a return
to planting corn, beans, pumpkins, and squash in the fields outside their
palisaded villages. It was mainly women who performed this work, while
men prepared for spring hunts and fishing expeditions. Another group,

carefully selected, girded themselves for a more gruelling task, an annual odyssey that had changed their world. Over time this journey had brought them transformative iron pots and knives, fishhooks, glass beads – and, for some, fire arms. This great transition in the material culture of the Huron clans rested on the fruits of a lucrative alliance.[1]

For more than a generation by 1629, these people had been the favoured trading partners of the French, whose primary base of operations in North America was at the narrowing of the St Lawrence River at Quebec, more than eight hundred miles from the country of the Hurons.[2] The alliance had begun to take shape in 1609, just a year after Samuel de Champlain had decided to relocate the headquarters of the sieur de Monts's monopoly for the Canadian fur trade from Port Royal on the Bay of Fundy to a new inland location further to the north and west. Although the nomadic Algonquin and Montagnais people who travelled through the region around Quebec provided excellent furs for the traders, their sources were limited and competition was fierce. The sedentary Hurons, by contrast, held promise as middlemen in an exchange of furs for European trade goods that soon penetrated far into the North American interior.[3]

Champlain had earned this partnership for the French. The Montagnais had facilitated his first contacts with these distant peoples, and none of the aboriginal groups were entirely certain what to make of the short, bearded Frenchmen, with their hulking ships at anchor in the St Lawrence, their strange ways, and their wondrous goods. But Champlain would prove himself, and in the process gain great advantages – and incur great risks – for the French.

In 1609 he accompanied a Montagnais, Algonquin, and Huron raiding party into the lands of the Mohawk, one of the five nations of the Iroquois Confederacy, the traditional enemies of the Huron Confederacy. In their major engagement, Champlain fired his arquebus, killing one Mohawk captain immediately, and wounding another so severely that he also soon died. As Champlain later recorded:

> The Iroquois were much astonished that two men should have been killed so quickly, although they were provided with shields made of cotton thread woven together and wood, which were proof against

their arrows. This frightened them greatly. As I was reloading my arquebus, one of my companions fired a shot from within the woods, which astonished them again so much that, seeing their chiefs dead, they lost courage and took to flight, abandoning the field and their fort, and fleeing into the depths of the forest, whither I pursued them and laid low still more of them.[4]

To his Huron companions, Champlain had proven his worth as a warrior and as an ally.[5] Promises of further co-operation were exchanged, and to seal their friendship, Champlain sent a young Frenchman, Étienne Brûlé, to live with the Algonquins and learn about the natives' lands and languages. In return, Champlain became the guardian of a Huron youth named Savignon, who was sent to Quebec, and later in 1610 accompanied Champlain to France, for the same purpose.[6] A unique partnership in the annals of North American history, which would witness so much conflict between natives and newcomers, had begun. Significantly, it featured practices, points of contact, and rituals that, as often as not, would force the French to bend to native sensibilities. When trade took place, native expectations that commercial exchange would be accompanied by festivals, dancing, feasts, and speeches had to be met.[7]

Champlain's emerging strategy was therefore twofold. In the short term, the Huron alliance offered a potential bonanza of inland furs for the merchant traders who made Quebec their base of operations. Theirs was an intense competition because, although traders at Quebec were technically privileged to be there under the terms of the sieur de Monts's original monopoly, unlicensed merchants continued to sail to Canada and engage in fur trading ventures as well. At Tadoussac, where the Saguenay River flows into the Gulf of St Lawrence, illicit trading had been going on for years; after the loss of de Monts's monopoly in 1609, free trade in furs was permitted until 1613.[8] By making Quebec the centre through which furs from the interior of the continent were bartered, Champlain hoped to ensure that volume, quality, and chartered trade in furs passed through a single controlled location. He soon fostered an additional layer of protection for the legal traders by arranging for the native flotillas to meet the French still further upriver from Quebec, at Cap de la Victoire on the Island of Montreal. However, if the first objective of insulating the legal fur trade from interlopers was mostly pragmatic, Champlain's second objective was much more far-reaching in its intent.

In its earliest years, Quebec could hardly have been called a colonial installation at all. Traders were eager to obtain their furs and return to France so that they could realize immediate profits. They were not at all keen to establish permanent residences themselves, or to facilitate settlement by others.[9] In spite of the fact that licensing terms for participation in the fur trade usually made specific reference to the encouragement of settlers, most French traders were not interested in backing massive re-settlement in the New World. Therefore, almost out of necessity, Champlain pursued an alternative strategy. Even though immigration from France should continue to be encouraged as aggressively as possible, he hoped that the traits and characteristics he had seen among his Huron allies could lead to something more significant than an alliance based merely on trade or military considerations. Sometime around 1613, he began to foresee the possibility of deeper connections based on religious confraternity.[10] As early as 1611 he had made a commitment to a party of Hurons and Algonquins who had agreed to accompany him on a northern expedition: "If I discovered the country to be good and fertile, I promised to establish several settlements there, whereby we should have communication with one another, and live happily in the fear of God, whom we should make known to them. They were much pleased with this proposal, and urged me to see to it, saying that they on their part would do their utmost to bring it about."[11]

This determination grew for Champlain during an extended visit to the country of the Hurons in 1615–16, when he witnessed their culture first hand. Based on farming, it was a relatively sedentary existence in villages that remained in place for a decade or longer. It featured an epistemology that accorded all things a spirit, spoke of a creator, offered a creation legend, venerated the dead, and promised life after death.[12] For Champlain, these beliefs meant that the Hurons could benefit from the presence of Christian missionaries, thereby allowing religion to add texture to the alliance. Christianity might also leaven the many practices of the natives that Champlain found to be barbaric, particularly the torture and cannibalization of prisoners of war.[13] In his

Huron longhouses. During his 1615 visit to Huronia, Champlain estimated a population of 30,000, settled in palisaded villages.

letter to Louis XIII that formed the preface of his memoirs for 1615–18, he was very clear in stating his purpose: "And since they are by no means so savage but that in time and through intercourse with a civilised nation, they may be refined, you will likewise see here what a great hope we entertain of the result of such long-continued and painful toil as for fifteen years we have sustained, in order to plant in this country the standard of the cross, and to teach them the knowledge of God and the glory of His holy name ... so that with the French speech they may also acquire a French heart."[14] But, as with the solidification of Quebec as the primary French base in North America, the process of cultural and religious outreach to the Hurons and other native peoples moved slowly.

Initially, Champlain had lacked the clear authority needed in Quebec to establish links with the Hurons, who crossed the pragmatic lines of trade and opposition to a common enemy, the Iroquois. De Monts's monopoly had lapsed in 1609, and through the next three seasons, merchant traders from a variety of Norman and Breton ports, primarily Saint-Malo, Dieppe, Caën, La Rochelle, and Rouen, set sail for Tadoussac,

or other points along the St Lawrence, to co-opt as much of the fur trade
as they could. These efforts represented more than commercial competition among individuals. In some cases it was syndicate against syndicate; in others, interests from one port against another. A third dimension
was added by religion, as some trading interests were headed by Roman
Catholics, while others were backed and led by French Protestants
(Huguenots).[15] Given France's long and protracted religious and dynastic struggles through the second half of the sixteenth century, it is not
surprising that old hatreds and animosities were stoked and kept alive
even in mercantile circles. Although a "New France" would eventually
take hold in North America, in the early seventeenth century that territory was less the scene of any national enterprise than it was a field of
competition for a diverse, multi-faith, multi-ethnic stew of divided and
more than often conflicting loyalties.[16] What set Champlain apart was his
willingness to see the aboriginals as partners for more than trade and his
ability to establish networks of support for his vision in both European
and North American contexts.

After the cancellation of de Monts's monopoly, overall authority for
Canada in France had passed in turn to two important noblemen: first to
the comte de Soissons, and next, to the king's cousin the prince de Condé.
The former died before he could assert any influence on behalf of the
colony; and the latter simply followed the old practice of parcelling out
trading rights to any parties willing to pay, thereby ensuring that the St
Lawrence basin remained a cockpit of competing parties.

Champlain returned to France frequently during these uncertain years
and he effectively exploited his connections and the growing reputation
he derived from publishing accounts of his exploits. Most significantly,
he addressed noble and clerical delegates to the 1614 meeting of the
Estates General, the body representing the three estates of the realm that
was occasionally called upon to advise the king.[17] From these contacts
he obtained permission and funding to bring to Quebec a party of four
Recollet (Franciscan) priests. Their task would be to establish spiritual
order in the colony and to undertake missionary work among the native
peoples.[18] This missionary initiative had an equally important corollary in that it fired the imagination of pious donors in France, who over
time might prove willing to underwrite further religious initiatives. It

remained to be seen, however, whether the native peoples would accept the missionaries.

On his return to Quebec in 1615, Champlain soon had an opportunity to test the role that religion could play in drawing the natives closer to his vision for the colony. One of the Recollets, Father Joseph Le Caron, embarked almost immediately for the country of the Hurons. In August of that year, Champlain also joined a Huron party returning to their villages from their trade on the St Lawrence, and with Le Caron presiding, oversaw the celebration of the first Catholic mass to take place in what is now the province of Ontario.

That Champlain should have gone to Huronia is not surprising, given his evident love of adventure and exploration. Since his arrival in the New World in 1603, he had explored the North American coastline from Massachusetts to Newfoundland. In the interior, he had followed the tributary river systems leading into the St Lawrence both to the south, in the 1609 military expedition that took him into the heart of what is now eastern New York State near the lake that bears his name, and to the north, most notably in 1613 in search of the rumoured northern sea. The 1615 venture was his most ambitious to date, however, carrying him more than eight hundred miles inland from Quebec along the system of rivers, lakes – and more than fifty portages – that formed the spine of the Hurons' route to meet with their French partners. Turning northwest from the St Lawrence at Cap de la Victoire, his flotilla followed the Ottawa River and the Mattawa into Lake Nipissing, and from there, the French River into the seemingly oceanic stretches of Georgian Bay, a body of water so immense that Champlain christened it "la Mer Douce" – the freshwater sea.[19]

During this visit, not only did Champlain explore much of the Huron country but he also accompanied a war party across Lake Ontario in an unsuccessful expedition against the Onondaga, another of the five nations of the Iroquois Confederacy. For his troubles he took two arrows in a leg, and was forced to winter over in Huronia, a circumstance that permitted him, in the company of Le Caron, to visit the Tobacco and Neutral peoples of what is now southwestern Ontario.[20] Clearly, all the components for a strong Franco-Huron alliance were in place. What was missing, however, was clarity of purpose for New France.

At the end of 1616, Champlain once more returned to France, where he did his utmost to put operations in the colony on a sounder footing. In the interim since Champlain's last visit to France, the prince de Condé had become involved in plots against his cousin Louis XIII, and was now in prison. Vice-regal authority for New France passed to the duc de Montmorency in 1619, and Champlain had to move swiftly to win over this new patron. Mercantile competitors sabotaged his efforts briefly, but in a series of letters to Montmorency and the king, he laid out a bold blueprint for the colony that recommended a massive influx of new settlers, soldiers to protect them, the creation of social and legal structures modelled on those of France, and the recruitment of more than a dozen Recollet fathers to minister to the French population and expand missionary initiatives among the native peoples. He gave assurances that profits from furs, timber, fish, and other natural resources would bring immediate and lucrative returns for investors; and, most important, he pledged to continue explorations into the North American interior in pursuit of the ever-elusive trade route to China.[21]

With the backing of the French Chamber of Commerce, and with a special commission from the king to oversee the administration of the colony, Champlain returned to New France in 1620. For the next four years he worked to improve living conditions at Quebec, maintain and extend alliances with the natives, and arbitrate disputes among licensees for the fur trade. During a brief visit to France in 1625, the duc de Ventadour, who had since assumed the shifting vice-regal position from Montmorency, confirmed him in his authority. When Champlain returned to Quebec in the spring of 1626, he was also greeted with the news that at least one other component of his long-standing plans had taken a step forward. Missionary activities, particularly among Champlain's key allies, the Hurons, were about to resume at an accelerated pace.

Ever since Le Caron's excursion to Huronia in 1615–16, confidence in the possibility of mass conversions to Christianity on the part of these people had grown. Like Champlain, Le Caron had crossed the Atlantic several times between 1616 and 1625, and had received increasing authority over his peers, funds to start a school at Tadoussac and a seminary at Quebec, and encouragement from his superiors in the Recollet order for the missionary work that was taking place, mainly along the

St Lawrence. In 1623–24, in the company of Father Nicholas Viel and Brother Gabriel Sagard, Le Caron was once more in Huronia, where he wrote a description of native life and customs that was intended to encourage support for missionary initiatives.[22] The great problem facing the Recollets, however, was that they were a mendicant order with few financial resources to support sustained missionary efforts. The Society of Jesus, by contrast, had established a tradition of successful missionary ventures almost from the time of its inception in 1540. In France the Jesuits enjoyed access to numerous wealthy and powerful patrons who were eager to underwrite and support intensified missionary ventures in Canada. One such person was precisely the new viceroy, the duc de Ventadour, who, in conjunction with an influential and pious courtier, the marquise de Guercheville, made it possible for three Jesuit priests and two lay brothers to sail for Quebec in 1625.[23] The following July, two of these Jesuits, fathers Anne de Noüe and Jean de Brébeuf accompanied the Recollet father Joseph de la Roche Daillon to the country of the Hurons. It was an excursion that encapsulated all the hopes and frustrations inherent in missionary work.

Almost from the start, Champlain had appreciated the value of missionary efforts in New France. His own faith impelled him to lay the groundwork for the salvation of peoples whom he considered heathen, but experience had taught him that priests made better emissaries for the natives than did traders or adventurers, who trafficked in liquor, enjoyed the favours of native women, and in some cases "went native" themselves. He had encouraged missionary instruction wherever and whenever he could, and in the case of the Hurons, had made it quite clear that they were to act hospitably when priestly visits were made in 1615–16 and again in 1623–24. For their parts, however, the missionaries faced considerable social, linguistic, and epistemological challenges. Le Caron and his confrères had found that the innate curiosity of the natives, coupled with their desire to maintain good trading relations with the French, was not enough to create conditions conducive to religious instruction. The would-be missionaries would have to live with, and largely as, their native charges did.

For some, this cultural immersion meant attaching themselves to nomadic bands of Montagnais or Algonquins, and risking abandonment or starvation in the winter if hunting was unsuccessful. For others, inhabiting a smoky Huron longhouse, home to as many as ten extended families, might be their lot. The main diet of the longhouse people, particularly when fish and game were unavailable, was a thin mixture of corn meal, water or saliva, and ashes, called "sagamité."[24] In any such scenario, the priests encountered cultural mores they believed were depraved: sexual license, easy termination of marriage, lack of privacy or any concept of private property, torture and cannibalism, and an overall way of life that struck them as dissolute and lazy. And yet, to gain the trust and adherence of their flocks, they had to endure these conditions cheerfully.

Language, of course, was a great barrier in this work. The native tongues were very different from European languages, particularly in terms of structure and syntax.[25] Le Caron and Sagard had made the most systematic early efforts to untangle the variances they had heard within the languages they had been exposed to, but the confusing clusters of vowels and consonants within the various dialects meant that they were only partway toward meaningful comprehension. Nor were they helped by the natives who sometimes deliberately taught their pious visitors guttural and blasphemous terms. Even worse for the missionaries were the merchant traders who, fearing rivals for native attentions or wishing to avoid censure for their unscrupulous trading habits like the sale of liquor, either refused to teach them any vocabulary or copied the natives in their linguistic jokes.[26] The result was that both sides probably communicated in what has been described as a sort of pidgin language, featuring both native and French idioms.[27] Missionary success among the native peoples thus required men who combined deep faith and religious zeal with immense physical stamina and innate intelligence and curiosity. In 1625, just such a man arrived in Quebec.

Father Jean de Brébeuf was born into a farming family in Condé-sur-Vire in Normandy in 1593. His early priestly studies took him to port centres like Caën and Rouen, which were key embarkation points for traders to North America, and which, by the time of his ordination, were hotbeds of speculation about the secular and religious potential of New France.[28] Brébeuf was a physical giant, and in spite of an early period of ill health, by the time he was assigned to Quebec in 1625, his size and gentle temperament seem to have struck his superiors as crucial assets for the nascent mission.[29]

It was not long after his arrival in Quebec that Father Brébeuf made contact with his new charges. Although he was unable to set off immediately for Huron country, from October 1625 through March 1626 he followed and lived among a band of nomadic Montagnais who wandered in the region north of the main French settlement. In these months, he received his initial intensive exposure to a native language, and experienced the rigours of this form of missionary work.[30] After surviving the winter with the Montagnais, Brébeuf and a second Jesuit, Father Anne de Noüe, were chosen to accompany the veteran Recollet missionary, Father Joseph de la Roche Daillon, on the latter's journey back to Huron country with the returning trade flotilla in July. On this trip Brébeuf proved himself to his guides through his physical exertions in paddling the canoe and carrying immense burdens over portages, and by accepting the spartan campsite conditions with cheerfulness. He soon earned the Huron name "Échon," which is popularly thought to have meant "he who pulls a heavy load."[31] First, however, considerable challenges had to be overcome.

In the autumn of 1626, Daillon was instructed to apply himself to the conversion of the Neutral nation, who lived to the south and west of the Huron lands. This change not only deprived the Jesuits of their experienced and seasoned colleague but it also sowed dissent among the Hurons, who believed that Daillon's mission to the Neutrals was part of a French conspiracy to expand the trading alliance. Left alone in Huronia, Brébeuf and de Noüe had to overcome Huron suspicion and jealousy in order to make a start on their own missionary initiatives. Sadly, de Noüe proved incapable of learning even a modicum of the Huron tongue, and in the spring of 1627, Brébeuf was forced to send him back to Quebec. Daillon had by then returned from his own harrowing venture to the Neutrals, but he too would return to Quebec in 1628.[32]

For nearly three years, however, Brébeuf was able to live among, learn from, and minister to the Hurons. Although no complete record of his initial stay in Huronia survives, it is evident that the qualities he had shown since his arrival in North America, particularly his willingness to

offer physical as well as religious service, gained him an important following within the Huron Confederacy.[33] Unbeknownst to Brébeuf, however, events elsewhere were conspiring to force him to abort missionary
work, just when his efforts seemed to have begun to pay dividends.

Back on the banks of the St Lawrence, New France was still anything
but a thriving colony. Its population in 1627 consisted of a mere seventy-
two people clustered below the new Fort Saint-Louis, which occupied
the high ground beyond the bluffs overlooking the St Lawrence. In
addition to the stone *habitation* that was the principal residence of the
community, Quebec boasted a few storehouses, nearby dormitories for
the Récollet and Jesuit missionaries, and the farm of the late Louis
Hébert, a former apothecary who had been raised to the nobility, and
whose land provided Quebec's only domestic agriculture. The settlement
served a tiny and transient European population that remained focused
on the fur trade, not the peopling of a new colony.[34]

France's other holdings in North America included the older, but even
more fragile settlement in Acadia, which in 1628 was occupied by just
twenty men.[35] Beyond this, New France was little more than a few scat-
tered wharves and trading posts stretching from Miscou Island in the
Gulf of St Lawrence, along the river to Tadoussac and Cap Tourmente,
and below Quebec to Trois-Rivières and Cap de la Victoire. Apart from
Quebec, only Cap Tourmente and Acadia had any year-round residents.
In total, the French population in these locations numbered just 107 in
1627, of which only twenty could be considered permanent settlers. In
essence, they provided a French commercial presence in North America
that compared quite unfavourably to the combined 2,610 English and
Dutch settlers who were simultaneously planting more extensive colonies
to the south.[36]

Although these shortcomings were recognized, several factors still
militated against improving this situation and consolidating France's
holdings. The most notable among them were confusing divisions of
authority, competing commercial interests, and a corresponding lack
of interest in the lands, apart from their value as a source of furs. Acadia
was considered part of a seigneury controlled by the marquise de

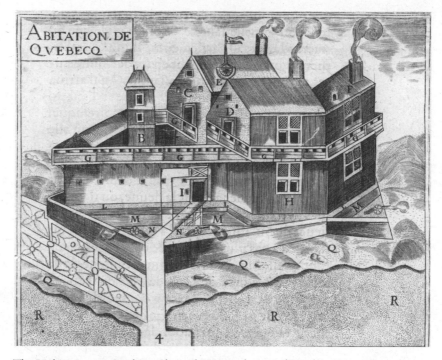

The Habitation at Quebec. Champlain's rendering of Quebec circa 1613

Guercheville, with trading rights held by agents of another merchant, the late Charles de Biencourt. The other sites in the St Lawrence were under the vice-regal control of the duc de Montmorency, who in 1621 had entered into a partnership with a Huguenot trader, Guillaume de Caën of Dieppe. While de Caën and his cousin Émery (a Catholic) were in formal control of trade and settlement in the St Lawrence, Champlain had also been confirmed in his lieutenancy at Quebec, a position he had basically held since 1608.

The resulting conflicts of interest formed an ongoing basis of the colony's weakness. While the de Caëns were responsible, as a condition of their charter from Montmorency, to increase settlement and provide for an expanded clerical presence, their motives were commercial and their religious proclivities made them anything but zealous in the cause of Catholic missionary work. In the commercial realm, they underwrote the continued practice of trading with the Indians in various locations, rather than concentrating activities at Quebec, the policy Champlain had promoted since founding the settlement. Indeed, Champlain recorded in

his memoirs that much of the weakness of New France in these years
was traceable to a wilful lack of co-operation among its patrons.[37]

In 1628, however, it appeared that the colony would receive much-
needed infusions of capital and personnel. The previous spring, Louis XIII
and his chief minister, Cardinal Richelieu, had approved the creation of
a new monopoly company known as the Company of One Hundred
Associates, which would be the central agent of commerce and administration in New France. Furthermore, the company's charter promised
advantageous treatment for investors and potential colonists alike, and
declared a new commitment to both missionary work and the spiritual
needs of the colonists, who henceforth would be Catholics only.[38]

With an optimistic eye to the future, the company promised to: "transport to the said colony of New France, two to three hundred men of all
trades during the ensuing year 1628, and to increase their number up to
four thousand of both sexes during the fifteen years next following [and]
to provide them with shelter and foodstuffs, and to furnish them generally with all things necessary to sustain life during the first three years
only, at the end of which time, the said Associates may be released from
this obligation if they choose, by granting to them (the settlers) sufficient
lands for their subsistence."[39] In all, the creation of the Company of One
Hundred Associates seemed to offer a true beginning for New France,
and the hard-pressed settlers at Quebec were buoyed by the news that
some twenty supply ships carrying food, new settlers, and 150 pieces of
ordnance, could be expected from Dieppe that summer.[40] What was not
known was that international tensions were about to ruin everything for
the French at Quebec.

In 1627 Charles I, king of England, Scotland, and Ireland, had
declared war on his brother-in-law, Louis XIII of France. It was a
rash decision. The two kings had formerly been allies, their liaison
symbolized by Charles's marriage to Louis's sister, Henrietta Maria, in
the spring of 1625. But a combination of issues that we will shortly
explore facilitated the British king's jingoism. For the moment these may
be summarized as complaints that his wife's dowry remained unpaid, that
France was mistreating its Huguenot population, and that Cardinal
Richelieu had misled Charles's chief advisor, the duke of Buckingham, in

diplomatic negotiations. Charles's kingdoms were, however, ill equipped to fight a major European power.[41]

England's parliament had already shown great reluctance to provide open-ended funding for another war, the ongoing conflict with Spain; both England and Scotland lacked permanent standing armies; and the military force in Ireland served to garrison a kingdom where rebellion was constantly feared. The royal navy, for its part, was cash-strapped and incapable of undertaking sustained operations.[42] Given this limitation, the crown looked to proxies to help with the prosecution of the war, most notably privateers who could harry French military and commercial vessels.[43] One such group of English privateers, the Kirke brothers, were about to alter plans for and at Quebec.

In the early spring of 1628, a flotilla led by Captain David Kirke set sail from the port of Gravesend in the Thames estuary and made for the St Lawrence basin. There, they proceeded to capture merchant vessels and booty, and went on to seize the trade outpost of Tadoussac. By July, Kirke had the St Lawrence completely closed to French shipping and was bearing down on Champlain and his fledgling trading post at Quebec.[44] During the remainder of the summer, Kirke laid siege to the installation. Despite severe shortages of food and other supplies, however, Champlain resolutely refused to surrender. He knew that Cardinal Richelieu's Company of One Hundred Associates was about to re-supply and defend Quebec, and that if he and his party could just hold out a little longer, relief would come. As autumn approached, Kirke realized that the siege of Quebec would have to be abandoned until the following year.[45] Nonetheless, in London, the exploits of the Kirke brothers received wide public acclaim. Although the operations of 1628 had not seen the Kirkes' final taking of Quebec, it was clear to everyone concerned what the New Year would hold.

It was in light of these circumstances that word was sent to Huronia instructing Father Brébeuf to abandon his missionary activities. Échon would have to return to Quebec and face the uncertain future with his fellow countrymen. For the many natives who had come to love and venerate him, this was a particularly sorrowful development, as Champlain recorded: "What is this? They said to him. Are you deserting us? Three years ago you came here to learn our language, in order that you might teach us to know your God, and to worship and serve him, having come for that special object, as you testified to us. And now that you know our language more perfectly than anyone else who ever came among us you are abandoning us."[46]

It was the spring of 1629, the season of rebirth and regeneration. Perhaps Brébeuf's faith in the ways of his Lord, and the promise of renewal, convinced him that he was not leaving Huronia forever. He told his followers that "by the grace of God, he would come to them again, and bring whatever was necessary for teaching them to know God and serve him."[47] And yet, this Norman priest, who had first practised his vocation in Caën and Rouen, and who knew the ways of merchants and seamen, and the fragile nature of the outpost at Quebec, must also have realized that the many complexities of the Old World and its politics were about to engulf the New World, and his order's mission. There were many reasons why privateers licensed by King Charles I would appear as the nemesis of New France in 1628 and 1629, and they had been several generations in the making.

2

Early English and British
Expeditions in the
North Atlantic Theatre

No King, nor Kingdome hath ... more Peaceable Means ... whereby,
to become, In wealth, far passing all other: In Strength, and Force,
INVINCIBLE: and in Honorable estimation, Triumphantly Famous,
ouer all, and aboue all other.

JOHN DEE (1577)

Sir Humphrey Gilbert's scheme was grand: The English West Country
soldier of fortune, sailor, and geographer had become convinced in the
1560s that his sovereign, Queen Elizabeth, could join the front ranks
alongside Europe's most powerful monarchs, and that England itself
could achieve vast commercial wealth and prestige by capitalizing on a
northwest trading passage to Asia. The fact that he was only speculat-
ing on the existence of such route (to be found, he believed, north of
Labrador) – and that he had no idea whether he could actually enter it
or sail through it if he managed to get there – did not concern him in
the least. The time had come, he decided, for a bold assertion of English
navigational skill, with great rewards to be won, and Elizabeth's rivals
to be vanquished in the Asian trade. In a pamphlet on the subject, he
asserted metaphorically: "The Queenes Maiestie, hauing so good op-
portunitie, and finding the commoditie [the North West Passage], which
thereby might ensure to the common welth: woulde cutte them of, and
enioye the whole traffique to her selfe, and thereby the Spaniardes and

Portingals, with their great charges, would but beate the bushe, and other men catche the birds."[1]

Gilbert's proposal came at the beginning of a remarkable epoch in early English ventures in the North Atlantic world, and elsewhere. Between 1575 and 1630 some thirty different English mercantile companies were established, many of which had large enough subscription lists, and eminent enough rosters of directors and stockholders, to suggest an emerging and coherent sense of national enterprise.[2] As a group these consortia transformed England's focus on overseas trade from a local concentration on the wool trade with the Netherlands, to a truly global set of enterprises that featured commerce with the Far East, Russia, Africa, and the Mediterranean World. This transformation also meant that the Atlantic Ocean would soon become a reconceived entity, more a highway for commerce than a barrier to be feared or avoided.[3] Correspondingly, the era also gave rise to a new and influential generation of publicists for English maritime exploits.

Most notably, that group included the Welsh alchemist, mathematician, and mapmaker John Dee (1527–1608), an ardent believer in the notion of a global *British* empire, protected by a strong and publicly funded "Pety Navy Royall," that would guard the waters and fisheries of the British Isles at home, shield foreign trade, and extend *Britain's* honour and holdings abroad. As Dee wrote: "No King, nor Kingdome hath, by Nature and Humayn Industry (to be used) any, more LAWFVLL, and more Peaceable Means (made euident) whereby, to become, In wealth, far passing all other: In Strength, and Force, INVINCIBLE: and in Honorable estimation, Triumphantly Famous, ouer all, and aboue all other."[4] Dee's dedication of his *General and rare memorials pertaining to the perfect art of navigation* (1577) to Sir Christopher Hatton, one of Elizabeth's most influential courtiers, indicated a growing political interest in the kingdom's maritime potential. These aspirations also appeared allegorically in the so-called Sieve Portrait of Elizabeth (c. 1583), showing the queen seated in front of a globe dominated by English ships.[5]

The notion that England should pursue a glorious maritime destiny was also echoed prominently by the clergyman, Oxford don, and one-time chaplain to the English ambassador to France, Richard Hakluyt the younger (c. 1553–1616),[6] and later, by the cleric and travel writer Samuel

Purchas (1577–1626). Hakluyt's great skill lay in collecting and publishing accounts of English overseas explorations and ventures. His most famous volumes, *The principal navigations, voyages, traffiques & discoveries of the English nations* (1589 and 1598–1600) compiled the memoirs of those who had first plied the world's oceans in the service of England's sovereigns. And yet, while these volumes have often been seen as examples of early English imperial propaganda, Hakluyt perceived highly practical and commercially beneficial aspects to overseas ventures, not the least of which would be achieved through colonization in North America. Hakluyt's ambitions were for England alone, however.

Samuel Purchas, writing a bit later, also seemed well placed to influence people in power; he enjoyed access to the court of King James VI/I through his patron, George Abbot (Archbishop of Canterbury 1611–33). In his best-known works – *Purchas, His Pilgrimage* (1611), *Purchas, His Pilgrim* (1619), and *Purchas His Pilgrimes* (1625) – he foresaw a more diverse expansion. His elucidations of seamanship and discovery were twinned with calls for a truly *British* co-operation among the Protestant peoples of the British Isles, especially across the Atlantic Ocean, calls that would have resonated with his king, who had only assumed the English throne in 1603 on Elizabeth's death.[7] The dynamics created by the union of the English and Scottish crowns under the Stuart dynasty would have far-reaching and important ramifications for efforts in the New World, and are pivotal to understanding the context of the Kirke brothers' presence before Quebec in 1628.

Sir Humphrey Gilbert, for his part, did not get his opportunity to prove himself across the Atlantic until 1583. By then, his experiences of fighting in Ireland, where Elizabeth's government was attempting, mostly unsuccessfully, to pacify the Catholic Old English and Irish populations, had made him an even more ardent believer in what he conceived to be the queen's – and England's – destiny. What fired his imagination now was military colonization in Newfoundland and a search for gold or silver mines, to be coupled with the use of that island as a base of operations for exploiting the North West Passage. He set sail, carrying the hopes and investments of some very powerful backers. Not for the first time in the history of England's North Atlantic ventures, however, the mission ended in disaster.[8]

When he arrived off Newfoundland to claim the island for Elizabeth, Gilbert found more than thirty vessels already fishing off the coast. He then forced the Spanish, Basque, French, English, and Portuguese skippers he assailed to accept fishing licenses from the English government in return for provisions for his own men. After making landfall he held a brief ceremony near what is now St John's Harbour, proclaiming the island to be English. For three weeks his men explored the island and took soundings. He then set sail toward the south, perhaps making for Cape Breton or Sable Island. Autumn gales were now upon his squadron, however, and two ships were sunk off the American coast. Gilbert and the remainder of the party tried to re-cross the Atlantic, and reportedly made it to the vicinity of the Azores, where he and his crew, and their ship, the *Squirrel*, were lost in heavy seas.[9]

Although Gilbert was gone, his efforts had captured a reorientation in English thinking about the wider world.[10] His earlier references to the Spanish and Portuguese in his pamphlet, and his expressed desire to see his kingdom supersede them in garnering new trading opportunities or in exploiting the riches of the New World, reflected a century-old strain of English frustration with the navigational presumptions of the Iberian kingdoms. Portugal and Spain had, of course, been the first European kingdoms to mount extensive voyages of exploration in pursuit of new trading routes in the later fifteenth century.[11] England might have played a lead role in that exploration, and men like Gilbert believed the time had come to make up for opportunities lost.

———————

Ironically, prior to 1492, Christopher Columbus, the Genoese sailor who had inadvertently done the most to first open the western hemisphere to Spanish influences, had tried to convince both King Henry VII of England, and King Charles VIII of France, to finance his scheme of finding a trade route to the east by sailing west. Both monarchs had declined to back him. As is well known, Columbus eventually found his backers in Queen Isabella of Castile and her more reluctant husband, King Ferdinand of Aragon, and their newly united Spanish monarchy.[12] By 1494, however, King John II of Portugal had become fearful about the implications of Columbus's "discoveries," and his assertions that he had reached India. By Portuguese reckoning, these claims were an inadmissible intrusion on their king's rights, as Portugal claimed exclusive control over the Indian trade via the southerly approach – around the horn of Africa – that had been achieved by his subject Bartholomew Diaz in 1488.

The Treaty of Tordesillas (1494) eventually settled Portugal's African and Indian interests, and ratified Spain's claims in the western Atlantic. Under its terms, Pope Alexander VI approved a line of demarcation that stretched between the poles, and originated some 370 leagues west of the Cape Verde Islands. With Spanish and Portuguese interests now mollified, these two maritime powers could concentrate on exploiting their spheres of influence, secure in the knowledge that the pope had sanctioned them.[13]

This knowledge, coupled with concerns over the sweeping rights that were asserted by Spain and Portugal in the Treaty of Tordesillas, brought Henry VII to the realization that England, too, needed to conduct overseas ventures of her own. Accordingly, in March 1496 he signed letters patent empowering another Genoese mariner, Giovanni Caboto (John Cabot in his English styling), to undertake trans-Atlantic explorations.[14]

Cabot's results were mixed. An initial voyage in 1496 had to be aborted because of bad weather, but in June 1497 he landed on the eastern coast of North America. His report that he had reached Asia was sufficient to convince Henry to back another voyage in the spring of 1498. Unfortunately, this time Cabot and his party were lost, and never heard from again. The English crown's desire to back overseas discoveries again waned.[15] Cabot's son Sebastian tried to sustain interest in finding alternative trading routes to Asia, but with the accession of Henry VIII in 1509, royal attention shifted to continental military and mercantile priorities.

Nevertheless, enterprising sailors out of the port of Bristol continued to cross the Atlantic to Newfoundland (which they initially called Hy-Brazil), as they had done possibly as early as 1480. Thereafter, Bristol commercial interests had joined the fleets, mainly French and Basque, who quietly harvested from the immense cod stocks on the Grand Banks, and likely established drying and salting stations on the island of Newfoundland.[16]

None of these ventures, however, marked any sort of national undertaking that could be tied to sponsorship or policy on the part of the English crown.[17] England's major commercial interests lay in the export of raw woollens and woollen cloths to the European continent, mostly under the auspices of the mighty trading firm founded in 1407, the Merchant Adventurers. By the mid-sixteenth century the Merchant Adventurers controlled some three-quarters of the kingdom's trade, and its London directors and investors pursued policies focused on profit, not voyages of discovery. When Henry VIII tried to establish a national exploration company in 1521, the London merchant community effectively squashed it.[18] With a few exceptions, sustained interest in explorations on the other side of the Atlantic on the part of English royalty would have to wait until the next century with the reign of Henry's daughter, Elizabeth.

Other European and English powers and interests were active in the North Western North Atlantic during the early and mid-sixteenth century, however. The opening decades of the sixteenth century, especially the reign of Francis I (r. 1515–47), witnessed a waxing in the power and influence of the French crown. Although his real priorities lay in containing (not always successfully) the continental ambitions of his Habsburg rivals, Spain and the Holy Roman Empire, Francis also showed an interest in trans-Atlantic exploration. Seamen from Normandy and Brittany had probably crossed to Newfoundland as early as 1500, and the first official sponsorship of a voyage of exploration occurred in 1524 when Francis engaged the Florentine mariner Giovanni da Verrazzano to search for a passage to Asia. Verrazzano's first voyage featured an exploration of the North American coastline from the Carolinas to the region of the modern state of Maine and the Canadian Maritime Provinces, and proved definitively that a formidable land mass stood between Europe and a trans-Atlantic route to Asia. Verrazzano persisted, however, and two more voyages, in 1527 and 1528, saw him trying his luck in more southerly waters, this time off Brazil, and in the Caribbean. But, his 1528 voyage ended in disaster when he and several members of his crew were captured and eaten by cannibals in the Antilles.[19]

The next French expeditions to the New World were much better coordinated and represented a clearer expression of royal interest in the

A view of Percé. The striking entryway into the St Lawrence River.

potential of new overseas lands. Jacques Cartier's explorations of 1534, 1535, and 1541–42 are often seen as the real beginning of European interest in the territory that would eventually become New France. But, Francis I's decision to sponsor the expedition had little to do with aspirations for settlement or the conversion of natives, two major elements of the eventual history of New France. His primary goal was to discover the elusive trade route to the east or, at the very least, to acquire mineral riches such as the Spanish crown was extracting from its possessions in Mexico and Peru.[20] Nonetheless, Cartier's penetration of the St Lawrence River, his dealings with the native peoples of the region, and his explorations upriver as far as the island of Montreal helped set the stage for fishing and fur-trading ventures from France at the close of the sixteenth century and the opening of the seventeenth.[21]

Documented English interest in the Atlantic theatre is not completely absent for this period either. In early 1536 a London merchant named Richard Hore organized funding for, and led, an expedition consisting of two ships, the *William* and the *Trinity*, to Newfoundland. Hore's group, which is said to have included a number of aristocratic "tourists," seems to have skirted the coast of northern Cape Breton Island before heading for southern Newfoundland, where they fished and hunted. There is also some speculation that they may have entered the Strait of Belle Isle and coursed part of this waterway separating Newfoundland from Labrador. What seems much less likely is that the company faced starvation and turned to cannibalism, as was alleged in *post-facto* accounts of the voyage published by the younger Hakluyt. The party had most certainly returned to England by late September or early October 1536, and for his pains, because his creditors claimed the voyage had not met their terms, Hore faced legal action before the English Admiralty Court.

An interesting sidebar to Hore's story is that he had engaged a Breton mariner named Alayne Moyne to act as pilot for his flagship, presumably because Moyne had knowledge of the route Cartier had followed in those waters two years earlier.[22] This employment confirms something we will return to throughout this study: the international nature of the Atlantic World's maritime community of sailors and merchants. As the cases of Columbus, Cabot, and Verrazzano also show, maritime personnel were pragmatic in terms of the services they offered, and their availability constantly cut across national lines. In addition to noting the diversity of individuals who participated in such ventures during this period, it is also important to differentiate further the characteristics that separated court-sponsored operations from those that might better be described as private or localized ventures.

As we have already noted, it was during Queen Elizabeth's reign that crucial changes in England's seafaring ways took place. First of all, the dominance that the Merchant Adventurers had exercised over English trade began to wane as new consortia, composed mainly of London-based interests formed companies with the specific charges to seek commercial opportunities in new areas. The Muscovy Company (1555) opened trading relations with Russia and eventually with Persia; and in 1581 the Turkey Company provided English access to the Levant through the Mediterranean Sea.[23] A legal trade through Spanish ports had existed courtesy of dynastic marriage alliances since the early Tudor period, but with deepening of religious tensions in Europe in the wake of the Reformations and their religious wars – and specifically with the slow crawl toward war between England and Spain that dominated the 1570s and early 1580s – the goals of mariners were altered. Where Englishmen like John Hawkins had once traded in Spanish ports like Seville, or in the Canary Islands, with the sanction of King Philip II of Spain, they now circumvented his licenses for trading and slaving, and carried out trans-Atlantic ventures of their own. For many of these seamen, the profits to be made from selling slaves in the Caribbean, or trading in luxury goods like gold, ivory, and pepper in Europe, outweighed the dangers of interdiction by Spanish authorities.[24] They also took another lesson from these ventures: Spain was vulnerable in the New World, and this realization yielded both illicit profits in peacetime and a new strategy of disrupting Spain's overseas ports and shipping as war approached.[25]

Ever since the mainly Protestant and Dutch Northern Netherlands had rebelled against Spanish authority in 1567, some of Elizabeth's advisors and subjects had urged war against Spain in the name of Protestant solidarity. Others had noted the economic vulnerability that would result for England if key ports in the Netherlands came under Spanish occupation. When Pope Pius V issued the papal bull of excommunication against Elizabeth in 1570, many more people became worried that a victory for the king of Spain across the Channel would eventually threaten England's very shores, to say nothing of hazarding the queen's personal safety. Still Elizabeth hesitated. Fears over Catholic uprisings at home, and bankruptcy or worse if war on the side of the Dutch went badly, caused her to delay open warfare until 1585.[26]

In the intervening years many English seamen had taken matters into their own hands and joined with French Huguenot privateers in harrying Philip's treasure fleets in what amounted to acts of undeclared war. This was the age of the fabled Elizabethan seadogs, and in addition to Hawkins, men like Richard Grenville, Francis Drake, and Walter Raleigh added to an impression of England's growing assertiveness and skill at sea. And yet, in spite of considerable and honoured achievements like

Drake's circumnavigation of the globe (1578–81), which also brought in
a rich return for the queen and Drake's other investors from the treasure
he had captured, most of these exploits were more symbolic than practical. As far as the development of comprehensive English policies toward
ventures in the northwestern North Atlantic was concerned, things continued to move haltingly. Private profiteering interests had proven bolder
than government initiative.

The Newfoundland fishery, for example, had grown progressively in
importance during the sixteenth century. By the time Gilbert attempted
the first abortive English attempt at colonization on the island in 1583,
not only were Newfoundland waters being harvested by fishermen from
a variety of different European kingdoms but many of these entre-
preneurs had also established drying stations and temporary quarters
onshore. Anything more resembling settlement was fraught with difficulty, however. The climate was inhospitable and the land was poor for
agriculture. The local Beothuk Indians, who had little to trade, frequently
raided the storage sheds that some Europeans left ashore at the end of
their season's fishing.[27]

Altogether, Newfoundland seemed an unpromising location for
permanent or semi-permanent settlement in spite of the practical calls
for it made by the likes of the Bristol merchant Anthony Parkhurst, who
argued that year-round stations would allow for improved equipment
storage, permanent salting facilities, and better overall protection of the
fishery.[28] Such calls were in vain, for the short term, at least. When
Gilbert's half-brother Sir Walter Raleigh tried his hand (unsuccessfully)
at planting colonies, he did so much further to the south, at Roanoke
Island off the coast of what is now North Carolina but was then considered part of the entire Chesapeake Bay region that Raleigh had christened "Virginia." Significantly, the Roanoke colony was established with
an eye toward the south, rather than the north, because Raleigh envisioned
it as a base of operations against Spanish shipping in the Caribbean.[29]

As is well known, Roanoke's fate is shrouded in mystery. Raleigh first
sent colonists out in 1585, but Drake repatriated them to England in
1587. Yet another party, made up of several extant families, was deposited in 1588. However, the crisis in England caused by the threat from
the Spanish Armada prevented any further contact with the colonists,

and when English suppliers reached Roanoke in 1590, they found the colony deserted with no trace of its inhabitants to be found.[30]

In spite of renewed calls in favour of colonization from writers like Hakluyt, major trans-Atlantic efforts ceased in the 1590s owing to the ongoing war with Spain and corollary hostilities in Ireland, known there as the Nine Years' War. When Elizabeth was succeeded by James VI of Scotland in 1603, England could still boast no permanent plantations on the other side of the Atlantic.

The new king saw himself as a peacemaker and quite sensibly noted that he had no personal quarrel with Philip III, who had himself just succeeded his father as king of Spain. Accordingly, in 1604 James brought the long conflict with the Spanish crown to an end, and the following year issued a proclamation against privateering.[31] Commercial interests could once more be directed into trading ventures and planting settlers in the New World in expectation of rewards from the resources to be had there.[32] Jamestown in Virginia was the first settlement be established, in 1607, and in 1610, another effort was made to place settlers in Newfoundland, this time under the direction of the Bristol merchant John Guy.

Jamestown did not flourish at first. Its sponsors, the investors who formed the Virginia Company in 1606 and had projected major returns to accrue through trade in sugar and tobacco, would spend eighteen fruitless years waiting for profits to materialize. The 144 colonists who formed the first wave of settlement were completely unsuited to the task that lay before them, believing they would grow rich without needing to perform the hard labours necessary to construct shelter and obtain food. Only the stern discipline imposed on the plantation by Captain John Smith staved off disaster, and Jamestown continued to be a fledgling colony, threatened by internal divisions, bleak prospects for anyone wishing wealth, and a damaging war with the local Algonquins in 1622. In 1624 the Virginia Company collapsed, and the English Privy Council was forced to assume control of the colony for the crown.[33]

Conflicting French and English claims in North America also caused friction in the first decades of the seventeenth century and sometimes led to significant diplomatic exchanges. British authorities had been aware of France's claims in North America from as early as November of 1603 when the sieur de Monts's patent for inhabiting "Acadia, Canada, and other places in New France" was deposited by Henry IV's ambassador at the court of James VI/I in London.[34] Notwithstanding these wide claims, which defined a "New France" that stretched as far south as Florida, the Virginia Company planted its settlers on Chesapeake Bay in 1606, and in 1607 established the supposedly more secure colony at Jamestown. The English also encountered the French directly in the New World because fishermen from both nations claimed rights to the Grand Banks off Newfoundland, and maintained fishing stations on the island.

Actual conflict erupted in the New World in 1613 when a squadron of English vessels from Jamestown led by Captain Samuel Argall attacked the French settlement at Port Royal and killed several men, including a Jesuit lay brother, and took other members of the French party to Virginia as prisoners.[35] This action drew a heated protest from the admiral of France, the duc de Montmorency, who personally demanded justice from James along with restitution for the French patroness of the colony, the marquise de Guercheville. Furthermore, he reminded the English king that the boundaries of New France had been established for over eighty years, and requested that the Council of Virginia declare its boundaries.[36] The English did not accept any of his demands, and private interests continued to assert themselves along the American coastline.

One of these was veteran soldier and courtier Sir Ferdinando Gorges. He had been involved with draft plans to plant a colony in what is now generally known as New England since 1606.[37] His interest in the area stemmed from conversations he had held with Captain George Weymouth, who had coursed the coastline in 1606 and had returned to England accompanied with five captured Indians. Gorges assumed the guardianship of three of them, helped to teach them English, and in the process, learned more about their country. In optimistic hopes of settling the region, Gorges next helped form two companies, one based in London, and the other in Plymouth, to encourage investment and settlers.[38] The partnership did not endure, however, and progress in encouraging settlement was painfully slow. By 1619 the Plymouth and London interests were in competition with one another and Gorges was forced to defend his [Plymouth] rights before the House of Commons.

Following more licensing changes, a reconstituted Council of New England was formed under Gorges' direction.[39] It was from this firm and its council that a group of separatists from the Church of England, who had tried and failed to find a desirable religious climate in the Netherlands and Virginia, obtained post-facto permission to settle near what is now Cape Cod. They had arrived at their new home, which they named Plymouth, aboard the *Mayflower* in November 1620.[40] Although Gorges and the Council of New England had initially been ignorant of the Pilgrims' encroachment, they were glad to reach an agreement permitting the settlement.[41] Gorges had good reasons to foresee renewed troubles with the French – and to be glad of any English presence in the region.

Much further to the north, Newfoundland's early development featured more diverse sets of interests than were present in company-controlled Virginia, or than would be seen in New England until the 1630s. John Guy had already enjoyed a political and business career of some note in his native Bristol, and it was through these connections and others he made in London that he was appointed the first governor of Newfoundland in 1610. Under the auspices of the new London and Bristol Company, and with Guy in command, a settlement was established at Cuper's Cove (now Cupids Cove), habitations constructed, and parts of the island explored.[42] Guy was able to enlarge the settlement's population in 1612, but problems associated with the colony arose almost immediately.

A long-standing irritant for colonial proprietors and colonists on the island was the animosity they faced from English West Country fishermen and the crews of London-based or Dutch "sack" ships (vessels that went to Newfoundland with ballast in their holds, and returned with cargos of purchased fish for sale in England or in continental markets).[43] For these two groups, colonists represented rivals that were difficult to tolerate, particularly when commodity prices fluctuated.[44] Additional irritants – personal quarrels among the colonists themselves or with visiting fisherman, pirate raids, and the governor's long absences from the summer of 1613 into 1614 – also hampered growth. With a keen eye to

the future, Guy recognized that the colony needed to diversify its activities beyond the fishery. Accordingly, he drafted plans to establish such
things as glass and iron works, and to encourage the settlers to engage
in trading naval stores and furs. Profits remained frustratingly elusive,
however, and by 1615 John Guy had fallen out with his London backers and a new governor, Captain John Mason, was appointed.[45]

Mason likely owed his appointment to the success he had enjoyed in
1610 as part of a squadron that had participated in a large show of government force in the Western Isles of Scotland. That background will be
addressed in the next chapter, but for our immediate purposes, Mason's
appointment brought two important developments for Newfoundland.
First, he undertook a series of sounding expeditions around much of the
island that helped him produce Newfoundland's first map. This became
part of a pamphlet he published in 1620 entitled *A Brief Discourse of the
New-found-land.*[46] His governorship also coincided with the planting of
three new British ventures on the island. The Bristol interests who had
been brought into the Newfoundland Company by John Guy seem also
to have been alienated by their London partners, and in 1617 they received a charter and lands as a new company, the Merchant Venturers.
Their settlement, Harbour Grace, in an allotment they called Bristol's
Hope, appears to have been a relatively successful, though small, project that prospered by using Bristol connections in Spain and Portugal as
markets for their fish.[47]

Welsh academic William Vaughan, who had purchased land from
the Newfoundland Company in 1616, founded the second venture.
Vaughan's early motive was to use the colony as an experiment in clear-
ing Wales of its vagrant population, and in the general encouragement of
commerce. Although nothing is known about the abilities, or even the
initial numbers, of colonists that Vaughan sent out to his settlement at
Renewse in 1617, Richard Whitbourne, the governor Vaughan appointed
in 1618, found his charges barely surviving in subsistence conditions.
The enterprise only lasted until 1619, when Vaughan sold part of his
grant to Sir Henry Cary and Sir George Calvert.[48]

Cary was a soldier of fortune, an early officer of the Virginia Company
and the North West Passage Company, which had backed Henry Hudson's ill-fated 1610 voyage.[49] He was also a courtier and an English Privy

Counsellor, who was created Viscount Falkland in 1621. His standing with James VI/I was affirmed in 1622 when he was named Lord Deputy of Ireland. In Newfoundland, his territories were diffuse and did not share contiguous boundaries. The more southerly portion was a narrow strip of land, just six miles from north to south, but running east to west some fifty miles (albeit, interrupted by St Mary's Bay), and featuring the west coast fishing ports on the Avalon Peninsula of Fermeuse and Renewse. More than a hundred miles to the north, on Trinity Bay, and containing Cape Bonavista, was a much larger allotment acquired from the Newfoundland Company.[50] In 1623 a small settlement was established there under the leadership of Governor Sir Francis Tanfield. It appears to have been unsuccessful, however, and had been abandoned by 1628.[51]

George Calvert, who was elevated to the peerage as first baron Baltimore in 1625, was a former English secretary of state and, like Cary, had served the crown in Ireland in the years after James's ascension to the English throne. The two men may have attended Oxford at the time William Vaughan was there in the 1590s, but it is speculated that the latter's brother, John Vaughan, may have known Calvert in Ireland. Whatever the origins of their relationship, Calvert's purchase from William Vaughan lay in the centre of the Avalon Peninsula, running some 50 miles from north to south, and over 100 miles east to west; and containing the ports of Aquafort and Ferryland in the south, and Petty Harbour in the north.[52]

Initially, both Falkland and Calvert envisioned their colonies as expedients for the English government's policy of pacifying Ireland. According to their schemes, families from the Catholic Old English population of Ireland would be encouraged to emigrate, leaving their old lands to be occupied by Protestant Anglo-Scottish settlers in Ireland. The king's British security would thus be enhanced, and a grateful Catholic population would find new opportunities to serve their king and assert his sovereignty across the Atlantic. For his part, Calvert converted to Catholicism in 1625 and as Lord Baltimore, repaired to his lands in Ireland. The political difficulties occasioned by his conversion further inspired him to see his colony as a place of refuge for English Catholics as well.[53] In 1627 he made it known that he intended to focus even more directly on his trans-Atlantic project by residing at Ferryland, the settlement he had begun in Newfoundland.[54]

By the end of James VI/I's reign in 1625, the British presence in the North Western North Atlantic had clearly grown and become more diverse. Had Gilbert still been alive, he might have seen his own embryonic dreams of English expansion being realized through a number of ventures. Although the fishery and associated industries continued to form the economic basis of British initiatives, plantation settlements were being attempted under different groups, in different parts of Western Newfoundland. Also significant was the fact that participation in these ventures cut across ethnic lines, with English, Welsh, Scottish, and Irish participants all a part of the mix of British peoples who were crossing the Atlantic. And yet, it is difficult to be precise about the numbers of people this involved. In 1620, the English Privy Council received a petition stating: "By twelve years' quiet possession, under His Majesty's patent, Newfoundland has become a hopeful country, employing yearly 300 ships with 10,000 British seamen, and thereby relieving 20,000 more poor people of the western parts of England, who wholly depend thereon for their maintenance ... The King's subjects, both of England and Scotland, are now joined together in hopes of making a more settled plantation there."[55]

As the petition suggests, features surrounding the British presence in the North Western North Atlantic constituted an extension of political realities in the British Isles themselves. The idea that English and Scottish interests would co-operate was certainly something that was bound to cater to the king's desires for unity and harmony among his peoples. More practically, however, the petitioners noted the need for greater governance, settlement, and defence, in order to sustain the British position in Newfoundland. They appear to have been pleased with John Mason's performance as governor because they also asked that his authority be extended. Numerous foreign fishermen still plied the waters off Newfoundland, and the French were seemingly more deeply ensconced on the St Lawrence. The Stuart dynasty may have made claims of sovereignty in the New World, but these claims were highly compromised by factors of distance, communication, and qualified or tempered allegiances. Furthermore, the settlements that had been planted in North America were generally haphazard affairs, featuring little cohesion or discipline on the parts of the new colonists. The few settlers who had taken up residence in North America had not, in general, acted co-operatively, like bees in a hive, as contemporary literature on the subject of planting colonies suggested they would.[56]

Still, English maritime advances in Elizabeth's reign had, since the union of the crowns, been accentuated by real plantation efforts overseas, some commercial successes, and multi-ethnic involvement on the part of subjects from all three of James's kingdoms. To better understand how this "British" dimension to what had previously been solely English enterprises unfolded, we must next turn to the Scotsman who ascended the English throne in 1603.

3

KING JAMES VI/I AND THE CHALLENGE OF ANGLO-SCOTTISH CO-OPERATION

... a thing of great consequence to our Nation not only at present, but like to bee much more beneficiall when the plantation there shall increase which God grant to his owne glorie and the good of our Common-Wealth.

CAPTAIN JOHN MASON (1620)

The death watch had been underway for weeks, although for some observers its implications had been a source of concern for many years. In the lengthening days of March 1603, Queen Elizabeth, the "Virgin Queen," "Gloriana," and the last of the Tudors, lay dying. Her reign had marked England's emergence as a Protestant and maritime power, but it had also featured vulnerabilities. One of the greatest stemmed from the queen's long-held determination to maintain and maximize her own personal authority by avoiding marriage and risking a dilution of her powers to a consort. So, she had presented the public aspect of virginity and helped to create the illusion that she was married to her kingdom. The strategy had been successful for the most part, but it had left her childless and left the English throne without a clear heir. Elizabeth had consistently and resolutely refused to name a successor, and to be discovered discussing or corresponding on the subject was a serious breach of protocol that could mean ruin for an indiscreet courtier.[1]

The queen's insistence on making her succession a taboo subject notwithstanding, for prudent and foresighted advisors like her secretary

Sir Robert Cecil, the question could not be left to chance. For him, and those like him whose priorities were to maintain the stability of the kingdom, protect the Protestant faith, and safeguard his own position and interests there was but one legitimate heir out of the dozen or so potential candidates with claims, and that was Elizabeth's distant cousin King James VI of Scotland.[2]

James's claim to the English throne came via his great-grandmother, Henry VIII's sister Margaret Tudor (thus, Elizabeth's aunt), who had married King James IV of Scotland in 1509. Although Henry's final will and the English parliament's *Act of Succession* formally excluded candidates from the house of Stuart from inheriting the English crown, the subsequent politics of Reformation Europe and the narrowing of the field of candidates with blood claims had revived Stuart hopes.[3] Elizabeth was certainly mindful of the fact that James's Catholic mother, Mary, Queen of Scots, was a potential rival for her throne as long as she lived, and wittingly or not, Mary was the focus of numerous plots that, if successful, would have ended with Elizabeth's assassination. The loss of her own throne in 1567 had forced Mary to seek exile in England, where, over time, she became a virtual political prisoner, and was finally executed for connivance in a plot against Elizabeth in 1587.[4]

James, who had been proclaimed king of Scotland as an infant in 1567, never knew his mother, and was reared under a succession of regents and advisors who used the young king's person as a guarantor for their own powers. That meant James also became the focus of plots, intrigues, and even kidnappings during his youth. One of the few consistencies he grew up with was a stern and austere education in the Protestant faith, served to him by Presbyterian tutors like George Buchanan and Andrew Melville. The latter was fond of reminding the king that his authority in Scotland was secondary to that of Jesus Christ (and his trustees in the Presbyterian clergy), and on one memorable occasion, that, though James was king, he was merely "God's silly vassal."[5]

By the time of his mother's execution in England in 1587, however, James was beginning to emerge from the shadows of his guardians, and thereafter he asserted himself more forcefully. As the 1590s dawned, it could accurately be said that he was ruling as well as reigning in Scotland, although any projections of power were tempered by the comparative poverty of his nation and the difficulties that existed in making the royal will operative throughout a rugged kingdom divided into Lowland and Highland zones by topography, corresponding Anglo-Scots and Gaelic language areas, clan loyalties, and differences in religion. The prospect that he might one day succeed Elizabeth on the English throne, and thereby expand both his personal wealth and power, was thus an enticing one for James, but the queen's reticence in naming an heir forced him to bide his time.

Eventually, Sir Robert Cecil provided the assurances James had sought from England, and as Elizabeth's death approached, they maintained a secret correspondence. When Sir Robert Carey, the English envoy, arrived at the Palace of Holyrood House in Edinburgh on 27 March 1603 with the news that James was now also King James I of England, the new dual monarch made little effort to feign surprise.[6] But what did it mean to be simultaneously the ruler of two kingdoms that had shared a long history of enmity?

James harboured no doubts on this subject and almost immediately began the work of turning the regal union into a political union, with England and Scotland to be formally merged as a new kingdom, to be called Great Britain. His ambitions were destined for frustration. Although the king used the mechanisms he controlled to assert a new styling of himself as "King of Great Britain," and in spite of the fact that his own communiqués to his peoples proclaimed a new nation, the political classes in his kingdoms, particularly in England, were dubious, and they ultimately opposed his project. Commissions from both kingdoms were formed in 1604 to study the union question, but they got nowhere. By 1607 James's dream for Anglo-Scottish union was effectively derailed by the English parliament.[7] Thereafter, although he would resolutely proclaim peace and unity among his peoples as the badge of the now British Stuart dynasty and would occasionally assert policies that suggested encompassing rule, James was forced to use secondary measures to draw his peoples closer together.[8]

Providing for the overall security of the British Isles was one such task that could foster inter-kingdom co-operation. The pacification of England's satellite, the kingdom of Ireland, through Anglo-Scottish (Protestant) settlement offered a second, related opportunity in the early seventeenth century. Opening up English overseas ventures to Scottish investors and participants marked a third way of encouraging greater co-operation among some of his peoples. These three initiatives were intertwined, and their interrelationship needs further exploration.

Even if he had never succeeded Elizabeth I and become king of England, James VI of Scotland was well aware of the regional challenges of the British Isles and the limited force of government authority in some of its more remote areas. In an effort to ingratiate himself with England's queen and her government, he had in 1586 signed the Treaty of Berwick, which had committed the Scottish crown to co-operative defence measures in the British Isles alongside England, including those related to the security of Ireland.[9] James and his government had priorities closer to home as well.

The reality that James's rule in Scotland was far from absolute struck at his prestige not just because it compromised his authority as king, but also because it meant irregularities across the kingdom as far as the rule of law, the practice of religion, the collection of revenues, and titles to and protections for lands were concerned. Addressing these irregularities meant more to the king and his key advisors on the Privy Council than simply bolstering James's image. They believed they had a divinely authorized responsibility to make Scotland a godly, and well-ruled state. Nowhere, it seemed to many of them, was their task more pressing than in imposing law and order in those regions of the kingdom that seemed ungovernable: the Borders region that separated England and Scotland, the Highlands and Western Islands, and, to a lesser extent, the Northern Islands of Orkney and Shetland.

Although James and his Scottish government had made attempts to address concerns in these areas before 1603, the union of the crowns offered new circumstances and opportunities for the assertion of royal power. One of the early successes of the immediate post-regal union period was the establishment of joint Anglo-Scottish patrols for the

Borders, which within a few years had succeeded in reducing cattle thiev-
ing, clan feuds, and other forms of banditry in the hinterland between the
two kingdoms.[10]

The Highlands and Islands posed a different set of problems, not
least because of their remoteness from the Scottish capital at Edinburgh,
and because many of the clans of these regions had significant military
capabilities of their own. These complexities were exacerbated by co-
operation between related Scottish and Irish clans, who enjoyed easy
maritime communication across the Irish Sea, and who were mercenary
in their loyalties.

Like his great-grandfather James IV, who had suppressed the Mac-
Donald Lordship of the Isles in 1493, James VI especially considered the
powerful clans of the Highlands and Western Islands throwbacks to a
barbaric "Gaeldom" that had to be curtailed. For the most part, he and
his advisors recognized that a central authority could not force allegiance
on its own. But, efforts at asserting control were often contradictory. At
times they rested on diluting Gaeldom through efforts to plant supposedly more civilized Lowlanders in the region, and at others they worked
through powerful client nobles like the Campbell earls of Argyll in the
southwest, the Gordon earls of Huntly in the northeast, and later, the
Mackenzie earls of Seaforth in the northwest.[11] In recent years historians have come to see in these efforts in Scotland and Ireland important
precedents for the ways in which early colonial enterprises overseas were
conceived and handled.[12]

James's policy of establishing order through plantation predated the
union of the crowns.[13] In *Basilikon Doron*, the advice manual he wrote
for his eldest son and heir, Prince Henry, in 1599, James predicted that
plantations in the Outer Hebrides would: "within short time ... reform
and civilise the best inclined among them, rooting out or transporting
the barbarous and stubborn sort, and planting civility in their rooms."[14]
Specific attempts to achieve these migrations were not always promising, however. Efforts to establish a colony of adventurers from Fife on
the Isle of Lewis, the largest of the Western Isles, in 1599 and 1605 were
failures, as was a proposal to relocate Lowlanders on the peninsula
of Kintyre.[15] James even contemplated a major military solution to the
perceived Highland problem prior to 1603, but the costs, the logistical

difficulties, and the reputations of the king's potential adversaries seem to have curtailed him.[16]

Still, the clan politics of the region did provide the crown with some surprising opportunities to assert its authority. In one of the most interesting twists in the convoluted histories of the Irish province of Ulster, and the Highlands and Western Islands of Scotland, in the late sixteenth century, James, in 1596, was able to strike at the power base of one of his adversaries in the Western Isles, Angus Macdonald of Dunyveg, with the guarantee of support from Macdonald's own Ulster clansman, James MacDonnell of Antrim. The king of Scotland remembered MacDonnell's loyalty when he ascended to the English throne in 1603, and showed his gratitude by giving MacDonnell's son and heir, Randal MacDonnell, the securest title to his lands among all the Ulster chiefs.[17] This vignette illustrates the way in which James was able to profit from the shifting nature of loyalties, rewards, and policies in the region.

James's reward to MacDonnell had coincided with another piece of good luck that came to the king along with his new English crown – the completion of the Nine Years' War in Ireland. When James came to the English throne, he immediately inherited greater peace in Ireland than had existed in a generation, and when the most important Ulster chieftains, the earls of Tyrone and Tyrconnell, balked at the terms of allegiance demanded by the crown and fled to Spain in 1607, all of Ireland was suddenly opened to new schemes for pacification via English and Scottish settlements. As the 1586 Treaty of Berwick had foreshadowed, the British Isles as a whole now constituted a theatre that required both co-ordinated security and co-operative efforts that crossed national lines. The king's desire for tangible efforts toward the unity of his peoples seemed on the verge of being met.

We can, for example, see multi-kingdom coordination starting to emerge from the Scottish government's efforts to bring the chieftains of the Western Isles to heel between 1608 and 1610. The government perceived three distinct problems in this region: idiosyncrasies in the culture of clan society which permitted violence; a hesitance on the part of clan chieftains to offer sufficient levels of allegiance to the king; and an unwillingness (or inability) on their parts to present titles to their lands, and thus provide the crown with the rents and revenues it expected.[18]

None of these were new concerns, but regal union now provided a novel and perhaps more effective means for dealing with them.[19]

In 1608 the Scottish Privy Council dispatched a maritime expedition, first against the MacDonalds and their stronghold at Dunyveg Castle on Islay, and then onto the Isle of Mull. The man charged with leading the expedition was Andrew Stewart, third lord Ochiltree. He was an old favourite of the king's and, more important, a veteran of recent efforts to bring order and settlement to the Borders region.[20] Plantation was no longer the aim where this expedition to the isles was concerned, however; Ochiltree represented the leading edge of an effort to coerce clan chiefs into swearing obedience to the king. The exercise bore all the trappings of the new sort of co-operative British enterprise that James desired. Ochiltree, the Scottish commander, would eventually have his forces bolstered by a squadron of three ships from England, and by troops from Ulster that had been securing that province since the flights of Tyrone and Tyrconnell, and a last, unsuccessful, native uprising, led by Sir Cahir O'Doherty.[21]

Given that coercing the chiefs into a more consistent level of allegiance to the crown was the major thrust of this effort, Ochiltree succeeded reasonably well. In August, 1608, he enticed a number of the leading chieftains aboard his ship the *Moon*, anchored in the Sound of Mull, ostensibly to join him for dinner and to hear a sermon preached by his adjutant, Andrew Knox, bishop of the Isles. To the dismay of his guests, however, dinner ended with Ochiltree's announcement that they were his prisoners, and that henceforth they would be warded in castles nearer to Edinburgh until their loyalty to the government and its policies could be assured.[22] Several months of imprisonment followed, during which time the government received the assurances that it wanted from the chieftains and released them back to their lands. In terms of greater assertions of central authority into the region, this could be counted as a step forward. But what of the man who had commanded the effort?

Service on behalf of the king and Privy Council certainly increased Lord Ochiltree's prestige, but it had quite the opposite effect on his personal finances. The Privy Council had failed to gain subsidies from the Scottish parliament to finance the 1608 mission, and Ochiltree had engaged ships, men, and supplies out of his personal resources. He had floated many disbursements on behalf of the government in advance of the operation, and – even worse – had managed his accounts badly. His situation became so serious that in 1613 he was forced to appeal to the Privy Council for the moneys owed to him.[23]

It was probably because of these dire financial straits that Ochiltree next turned to Ulster and the escheated lands of the earl of Tyrone for a new financial opportunity. In 1609 he received the grant of a 3,000-acre estate in the precinct of Mountjoy. Thereafter, the Scottish government used him as a consultant on port facilities for improving travel and trade between Scotland and Ireland, and, unlike some of his fellow under-takers (those licensed to plant Anglo-Scottish settlers in Ireland), he seems to have tried to live up to the terms of his grants.[24] The demands of meeting his obligations as an undertaker were heavy, however, and they left Ochiltree with little time, and fewer resources, to devote to his interests in Scotland.

In addition, he was still in debt owing to the expenses he had incurred while leading the expedition to the Isles, and he was forced to continue borrowing in order to maintain some level of liquidity.[25] It was for these reasons that in June 1615 he transferred his Scottish title to his cousin, James Stewart of Killeith, himself an active agent of the king's centraliz-ing initiatives in Orkney, who thereby became the fourth lord Ochiltree.[26] (We need to remember this transfer, and the man who now became Lord Ochiltree, as he will loom large in our consideration of the emerging North Atlantic story (chapter 7.) The former lord Ochiltree did not remain without a title for long. In 1619 James VI/I elevated him to the Irish peerage as Baron Castle Stuart.[27]

What is noteworthy about this case is that it demonstrates how serv-ice to the crown in remote regions of the British Isles carried personal and financial risks, not unlike the risks one might incur by investing in a char-tered trading company, or agreeing to invest in the planting of a new colony overseas. Outlays of cash and material were accepted components of such efforts, and actual repayment for these services might take years to be realized, or might never take place. Rewards were more likely to take the form of elevated titles, governmental or parallel promotions to positions that could yield access to money, eased terms for acquiring lands, and most important, greater access to future favours from the king.

In short, everything operated in a climate of speculation, where the metaphorical currency of the future outstripped the hard coinage of the here and now. Two other figures from the Hebridean theatre further serve to illustrate this situation: Bishop Andrew Knox, the third lord Ochiltree's former adjutant, and Captain John Mason, whom we have encountered briefly in connection with England's first colony in Newfoundland.

In 1609 efforts were made to follow up the success Lord Ochiltree had orchestrated the previous year. This time, Bishop Knox, returned to the Isles as part of a commission charged with ascertaining the value of crown lands and with ensuring local ascription to the king's laws and authority. On Iona Knox convened a meeting with the major local chieftains, many of whom had recently returned from their imprisonment in Edinburgh, and obtained their signatures to the statutes of Icolmkill. Key among the provisions of the statutes were promises that the chiefs would help spread Protestantism, clamp down on bards or others who might encourage feuding, observe the king's laws, and send the heirs of local elites to the Lowlands for their educations.[28] This apparent victory for the policy of attempting to calm the region by gaining the adherence of as many local chiefs as possible did not last, however. Within the year the crown had resumed its former practice of achieving a form of pacification through the patronage of selected, favoured clients, most notably the seventh earl of Argyll in the southwest, and Kenneth Mackenzie of Kintail in the northwestern Isles. Knox had proven his worth in the theatre, however, and it was decided that his talents could be used elsewhere. Accordingly, in 1610 he was appointed to the Irish bishopric of Raphoe, where he supplemented his episcopal duties by assisting with Scottish plantation schemes in his dioceses.[29]

As a component of this new charge, Knox undertook extensive reforms within his diocese and was particularly effective in providing preachers from Scotland who could speak the Irish language, or at the very least, readers who could teach the catechism to the natives. It is estimated that through Knox's efforts, by 1622 every second parish in Raphoe had some form preaching minister, compared to a national average of one minister for every six parishes.[30] Knox was also active in recruiting new settlers for his diocese, and by 1632 claimed that he had settled some three hundred families.[31] This influx in turn benefited the financial health of the established church. When Knox assumed the see in 1610, Raphoe carried an annual income of £30. By 1616, this sum had grown to £200 and in 1629 to £650.[32] Of the clergy who were brought over to Raphoe, in 1622, fifteen were either Masters or Bachelors of Divinity.[33] The Lord Deputy of Ireland, Sir Arthur Chichester claimed in 1611 that Knox, through his dedicated and diligent service, had accomplished more for his diocese in two years than other undertakers had managed in five.[34] This was exactly sort of transformation James VI/I desired within the remote regions of his kingdoms, but to achieve it, new forms of co-operation were often needed.

The reader will recall that the third lord Ochiltree's 1608 expedition to the Hebrides had featured ships and personnel from England, as well as a contingent of troops from Ireland. The inter-kingdom component of efforts in this theatre had not ended there. In 1610 it was an English skipper who provided the government with an element of naval muscle in these waters.

The man in question was Captain John Mason, a native of the port of King's Lynn in Norfolk. Although almost nothing is known about his early life, it is likely that his family were fairly wealthy merchants, with access to both cash and ships. This surmise stems from the fact that Mason first appears in the public record through the provision of four ships to patrol in the waters around the Hebrides in 1610, an expenditure that exceeded £2,000.[35] Mason purportedly paid for the vessels under his command from his private resources, and when the government was unable to provide reimbursement in cash, he agreed instead to accept a license to police Scotland's herring fishery against (mainly Dutch) interlopers.

As bad luck would have it, however, the king acceded to complaints from the Dutch ambassador in London and overturned the fines Mason had imposed, thereby undercutting his authority.[36] He encountered further difficulties from Scottish fishermen who challenged the validity of his commission and then had him thrown into prison. In 1615, he tried again, and once more found himself at the mercy of incredulous fishermen who turned him over to the authorities in Edinburgh.[37] The potential benefits of serving his king in an inter-kingdom context were about to reveal themselves for the Englishman Mason, however. It was probably

while he was being extricated from this most recent difficulty with his
licenses that he met the head of the court of chancery for Scotland, Sir
John Scot of Scotstarvet. That Mason felt gratitude to Scot for his assistance in freeing him from prison and from further indignities can be
inferred from the fact that he dedicated his eventual pamphlet on Newfoundland to Scot. (Significantly, Mason also appears to have known
someone else at this point who will be of major importance to this story:
Sir William Alexander, the future founder of Nova Scotia.[38])

Mason's fortunes soon improved. After cashiering his ship to the
deputy treasurer for Scotland, he returned to England. It was at this point
that the Newfoundland Company, impressed by his record in the king's
service, named him governor of the Cuper's Cove settlement, succeeding
John Guy. It has been reasonably speculated that this appointment may
have constituted an effort to recompense Mason for his recent difficulties in royal service.[39] What is important to recognize is that, in accepting the governorship in Newfoundland, Mason became a link in a chain
uniting men who served the crown in remote parts of the British Isles
and then became figures of importance in early ventures in the New
World and, ultimately, with the royal court itself. They compared and
communicated their common experiences with each other, with government officials at home, and with wider audiences.

In 1620 Mason published his 1617 description of Newfoundland in a
pamphlet, entitled *A briefe discouse of the New-found-land*, dedicated to
Scot of Scotstarvet. He hoped that its contents would apprise his patron,
and his intended audience, of the ultimate benefits of colonization in
Newfoundland. The document was concise, highly descriptive, and significantly, it did not sugar-coat the climate or topography of the island,
particularly in comparison with Virginia. Nonetheless, Mason argued
that, owing to its proximity to the British Isles, the wealth to be gained
from its fisheries, its position as a way station for shipments to Virginia,
New England, and Bermuda, and the ease with which it could be defended, Newfoundland could be "a thing of great consequence to our
Nation not only at present, but like to bee much more beneficiall when
the plantation there shall increase which God grant to his owne glorie
and the good of our Common-Wealth."[40]

Like the third lord Ochiltree's experiences, Mason's story up to 1620 featured direct outlays of personal resources in support of crown initiatives (with corresponding – and often unfulfilled – expectations of greater rewards to follow), quasi-military service to the crown in exercises that had become *British* in scope in the wake of the union of the crowns, the ongoing use of patronage networks either to maximize opportunities for greater gain or to alleviate debt, and eventual recourse to a colonial periphery (Ireland or Newfoundland) to try and rescue his fortunes.[41]

Mason's pamphlet was not the only publication in 1620 extolling Newfoundland's virtues. The English Privy Council approved that same year Richard Whitbourne's "A Discourse and Discovery of New-Foundland" for release. Whitbourne had been venturing to Newfoundland since 1579 and probably knew the island better than any of James VI/I's other subjects. He had survived hostile raids and capture in 1612 by the pirate Peter Easton; he had operated a special Admiralty Court there on behalf of the government in 1615; and had been appointed by William Vaughan to serve as governor of his colony in 1618.[42] By the time his pamphlet was released, Whitbourne's governorship had unexpectedly come to an end, but that did not preclude efforts on his part to encourage further colonization. In particular, he built upon allusions Mason made to the strategic importance of Newfoundland, especially as a potential linchpin in communicating with more southerly colonies.[43] Two years later, then in the employ of Sir Henry Cary, lord Falkland, Whitbourne published a revised edition, and offered detailed advice on incremental measures that would ensure a successful colony.[44]

The examples of these men, and their writings, suggest important patterns of royal service, patronage, and kinship ties, which, when coupled with the waxing and waning of personal wealth, might lead a man to seek his fortune in Ireland, or in the New World, in order to gain or retain crown favour. These were men of action who had been proven in either official or private service, and they could make compelling cases for supporting new efforts. It is against this backdrop that we now turn to the man who in 1621 gained crown approval for the founding of Nova Scotia, Sir William Alexander.

Sir William Alexander, Earl
of Stirling (c. 1567–1640).

Alexander was born in the village of Menstrie, near Stirling in central
Scotland, during the uneasy years of James VI's minority.[45] His ances-
tors and family were relatively wealthy property holders of the Mac-
Donald line, erstwhile lords of the Isles. By the time of his birth, however,
his family enjoyed the patronage of the earls of Argyll.[46] Alexander
received his early education from Thomas Buchanan, the nephew of the
king's celebrated former tutor, as well as more formal training from
the universities of Glasgow and Leyden, in Holland. Most important,
Alexander became a companion to Archibald Campbell, the seventh earl
of Argyll, whom he accompanied on a grand tour through Europe, and
through whom he received his entrée at court.[47]

    It was also through this connection that Alexander saw first hand the
halting development of plantation policies as initiatives to extend the
king's sovereignty in the more remote corners of Scotland. His patron,
the earl of Argyll, did not initially welcome these policies because they

would have entailed the extension of Lowland influences – and the powers of the crown – into southern parts of the Highlands that he coveted for himself and his clan. As we have seen, however, the Scottish crown ultimately abandoned plantations in the Highlands in return for proxy assistance from Argyll and others, a development that correspondingly strengthened the earl's influence in the Highlands, and at court.[48] It can reasonably be assumed that Alexander was aware of the ramifications of these shifting approaches to the perceived Highland problem inasmuch as they directly affected the power and prestige of his patron, Argyll.

It is not entirely certain what first sparked Alexander's interest in colonization, but most of his biographers have suggested that, because he knew many individuals in England who were involved in commercial and colonial schemes, he became interested too.[49] Such a scenario is entirely likely, but its implications require reconsideration. It has been suggested, for example, that Alexander's nascent plantation schemes were inspired by the new spirit of Anglo-Scottish co-operation that James had tried to create in the wake of the union of the crowns, and that this made him someone, "who tried to extend the incipient Jacobean pattern of a 'three kingdoms' pattern of overseas colonisation to his native Scotland."[50]

In fact, one of the remarkable things about Alexander's first years at court is that in the face of the king's desire to foster a British identity amongst his peoples, Alexander continued to write at least some poetry that glorified an image of his native kingdom, and he never wavered in asserting a separate Scottish identity. As can be seen from his 1604 poem "The monarchick tragedies," Alexander harboured a strong sense of pride in his native land and its people; a pride that belies the likelihood of using unionism to curry favour with the king:

> No doubt our warlike Caledonian coast
> (Still kept unconquered by the heau'ns decree)
> Expelled the Pictes, repelld the Danes, did boast
> In spite of all the Romane legions free,
> As that which was ordain'd (though long time crost
> In this Herculean Birth) to bring forth thee.
> Whom many a famous Sceptred Parent brings
> From an undaunted Race to do great things.[51]

The metamorphosis of what became Alexander's Nova Scotia scheme indicates that although he appreciated and was able to capitalize on participation in ventures that featured components of the three kingdoms, he initially intended the plantation to be an exclusively Scottish one.

Alexander's first investment was in lands obtained from the Newfoundland Company on the island's south coast, part of an effort on the company's part to diversify settlement on the island, and one that featured the previously mentioned plantation efforts of William Vaughan, Sir Henry Cary, and Sir George Calvert between 1617 and 1621 (chapter 2).[52] As Alexander later recorded, however, his ambitions soon turned to the founding of a mainland colony, and his lands in Newfoundland never again received extensive attention. In 1621, James VI/I granted him a charter covering lands in the New World that covered nearly all of the present-day Maritime provinces of Canada and the State of Maine.[53] That this new endeavour was envisioned to be distinctly Scottish was later made clear and explicit: "My Countrimen would neuer aduenture in such an Enterprize, unlesse it were as there was a *New France*, a *New Spaine*, and a *New England*, that they might likewise haue a *New Scotland*, and that for that effect they might haue bounds with a correspondencie in proportion (as others had) with the Coutnrey whereof it should beare the name, which might hold of their owne Crowne, and where they might bee gouerned by their owne Lawes.[54]

By all appearances, Alexander had no personal experiences in the New World, and knew little about how make his new colony a reality. Neither could he point to active service in the remoter regions of the British Isles that had marked the careers of men like the third and fourth lords Ochiltree, Bishop Knox, Captain John Mason, Lord Falkland, or Lord Baltimore. However, he was not entirely unaware of the difficulty of the task he had set for himself. He had discussed the general points relating to plantation schemes with no less an authority than John Mason, who in 1620 had returned from Newfoundland, and had penned his observations on that country. Alexander was further encouraged in his efforts by Sir Ferdinando Gorges, an officer of the newly formed New England Company and someone involved with parallel efforts to plant settlements to the south of Alexander's mainland patent.[55]

What was perhaps most telling was that Sir William Alexander understood that there was scant desire among his countrymen to abandon their native lands for the wilds of an unknown New World. As he wrote: "The sendong forth of Colonies (seeming a nouelty) is esteemed now to bee a strange thing, as not onely being aboue the courage of common men, but altogether alienated from their knowledge, which is no wonder."[56] This insight suggests that he had developed a reasonably clear sense of the challenges facing a would-be colonial planter within a few years of receiving his charter. He knew, or learned very quickly, that if he was going to found a colony, it would be a long-term enterprise.

Experience was a hard teacher. Alexander's first practical efforts to initiate his colony were far from promising. In 1622 he engaged a ship in London to go to the port of Kirkcudbright, on the Solway Firth, in southwestern Scotland. While agents provisioned the ship, Alexander went about recruiting potential settlers. Although the identities of the eventual party are unknown, the expedition finally departed in August, making first for Cape Breton Island; but after being buffeted by storms, they were forced to sail for Newfoundland. Once safely landed at St John's, the company fell apart, some of its members signing on for fishing duties, and others eventually making their way back to Britain.[57]

Alexander tried again. He sent a second ship across the Atlantic, this time from London in 1623. That venture similarly failed to further the planting of a colony, even though the party did explore the coastline of some of Alexander's mainland tract, and proclaimed it favourable for settlement. Nevertheless, Nova Scotia remained but a dream and its benefactor was no closer to realizing his overseas ambitions than he had been when the grant of lands was first tenured three years earlier. Clearly, fresh inducements for colonists and new rationales for colonizing were required.

As 1624 dawned, Sir William Alexander returned to his two most formidable allies to try and save his dream. The first and most significant was the king, whose trust and favour he had earned through his many years of service to the Stuart dynasty. The second was his pen. What separated Sir William Alexander from other, arguably more famous and celebrated figures who had earlier written in support of overseas ventures, however, was that he truly enjoyed the support of his king, and knew how to play the political games of early Stuart Britain with almost unparalleled skill. This was an advantage that requires deeper analysis. Therefore, we must take a step back into Alexander's earlier life and career, and re-examine some of the factors that had shaped his vision and would play a role if he were to make his dream a reality.

4

THE POET COURTIER:
SIR WILLIAM ALEXANDER
AND HIS CHARTER

No gain is easier or more safe than what is made by planting
new colonies in foreign and uncultivated regions.
ORIGINAL CHARTER FOR NOVA SCOTIA (1621)

In the summer of 1618, Sir Walter Raleigh hurried to finish a pamphlet, the contents of which he hoped would stave off his execution for treason or, at the very least, defend his reputation for posterity. Two years earlier, he had won release from prison courtesy of a begrudging James VI/I, to undertake a voyage of exploration in search of the fabled golden kingdom of El Dorado. Unsuccessful, his expedition had sparked conflict and bloodshed with the Spaniards in their sphere of influence in South America. The king of England feared war as a result, and the new Spanish ambassador, Count Gondomar, was only too happy to suggest that Raleigh's execution would serve as a gesture of goodwill to mollify his sovereign. As his tempestuous career reached its climax, Raleigh turned to his pen, the one instrument that might save him.

In August, while on a visit to Salisbury, he wrote his *Apology for the Voyage to Guiana*, in which he not only sought to explain his actions on the recent expedition but tried one last time to make the king of England realize his imperial potential. He was reaching back to the halcyon days of the Elizabethan sea dogs when English mariners made their reputations by "singeing the King of Spain's beard."[1] Those days had passed, however, and Raleigh's efforts were to prove in vain. Raleigh understood the precariousness of his position. As he stated in a letter appended to the *Apology*: "I returned into England with manifest perill of my life, with a purpose not to hold my life, with any other then his Majesties grace, and from which no man, nor any perill could disswade mee; To that grace, and goodnesse, and Kinglynesse I referre my self, which if it shall find that I have not yet suffered enough, it yet may please to adde more affliction to the remainder of a wretched life."[2]

James never received his copy of the apology, and within weeks its author was re-arrested. He was executed in October 1618. The downfall of this Elizabethan icon epitomized an important distinction between late Tudor and early Stuart policies toward overseas ventures. Rather than engaging directly the Spanish where his subjects found them in the New World, James was content to pursue trans-Atlantic exercises – when he pursued them at all – in an *ad hoc* fashion, taking as few financial and military risks as possible. Furthermore, whereas Raleigh had continually tried to press the case for intensive colonization efforts in the Americas, James had resisted most ventures that called for the planting of his subjects on the other side of the Atlantic. At the time of Raleigh's death, only the fledgling settlement at the mouth of the James River in Virginia and the more tenuous plantations in Newfoundland could be considered "colonies."

It has been suggested that Raleigh and those like him who called for a more aggressive and systematic approach to colonization were problematic for James VI/I because their projections of English might were bellicose and dangerous.[3] They were imperialists in the sense that we now understand the term – men looking for overseas aggrandizement. The early Stuart monarchs were largely uninterested in such far-flung schemes. And yet, the period coinciding with Raleigh's death, and with the passing of the last of the Elizabethan generation of notable seamen, also witnessed the beginnings of British plantation efforts in the New World that were more pragmatic in nature, and as a result, received greater official attention and support than had ever been given to boisterous imperialists like Raleigh. As a potential leader of overseas ventures, Raleigh strikes an interesting contrast with Sir William Alexander, the original factor of Nova Scotia.

While Raleigh was impetuous and has always been regarded as a man of action, Alexander, a man of letters as well as a statesman, was and is seen in softer terms. At times, contemporary descriptions border on condescension.[4] Fellow Scots poet Sir Thomas Urquhart was actually quite venomous in characterizing Alexander, but for other reasons: "The purity of this gentleman's [poetic] vein was quite spoiled by the corruptness of his courtiership; and so much the greater pity; for by all appearance, [if] he had been contented with the mediocrity of fortune he was born unto, and not aspired to those grandeurs of the court, which could not without pride be prosecuted, nor maintained without covetousness, he might have made a far better account of himself."[5]

Urquhart's scathing assessment of Alexander has generally been dismissed as overly harsh, and in truth its strident quality constitutes something of a mystery. Both men were staunch supporters of the Stuart monarchy during quite tempestuous periods in the dynasty's history, so they shared a key, common loyalty on a subject that created very bitter divisions for the men of the age. We could choose to ignore the remarks altogether, and accept, as most modern historians have, that they paint an exaggerated, unfair portrait of Alexander, who, in terms of his colonizing efforts, is widely judged to have simply been out of his depth.

Even those who have tried to give him his due as a prominent figure in the history of early British overseas ventures end up noting that, being a poet, Alexander was less than prepared to oversee a successful colonial enterprise. For many, his downfall lay in the fact that he seemed to be a dreamer, rather than a doer. D.C. Harvey, in his entry for Alexander in the *Dictionary of Canadian Biography*, wrote of his apparent lack of success as a colonial leader: "This is perhaps not a matter of surprise when one considers his previous lack of experience with *practical affairs* [my italics], the difficulty of combining the roles of dreamer and a man of action, and the magnitude of the task which he had undertaken singlehanded; for he alone had to remould the Scottish national outlook and create favourable public opinion, whereas the promoters of Virginia, New England, and Newfoundland were numerous, and had the English nation behind them."[6]

This portrayal requires revision for several reasons, beginning with the mistaken notion that Alexander lacked experience in practical affairs. If we look again at the substance of Urquhart's criticism, we can see that it was political and based on his disdain for the mode of Alexander's rise to prominence. He castigates the poet from Menstrie for being what we would call a social climber, and for aggressively playing the game of court patronage and politics. Herein lies the story that is at the heart of understanding this man, his reasons for pursuing a colonial project in the first place, and the ways in which he tried to make it succeed. In the end, we will see that he was much less the dreamer, and far more the accomplished courtier-politician than has been allowed, and that in trying to make Nova Scotia a reality, he acted in a fashion that was wholly consistent with a remarkably successful political career.

We can assert this partly because Alexander achieved something that almost none of his contemporaries was able to. He enjoyed sustained and growing favour from both James VI/I and Charles I, right up until his death in 1640. Apart from George Villiers, the eventual duke of Buckingham and favourite of both kings, Alexander may have been the only courtier to so successfully bridge the two reigns of the early Stuart period and see his powers rise exponentially. Indeed, this success is more impressive than Buckingham's because it was much more long-lasting. That fact alone marks Alexander as a person who cannot be easily dismissed. How, then, ought we to understand this man, his career, and the ways in which his background shaped his colonial ambitions?

———————

Sir William Alexander must first be placed within the context of his times and his class – the early seventeenth-century Scottish nobility, and particularly, those who came of age between the union of the crowns, and the Covenanting crisis of the late 1630s. This was a generation of Scots acutely aware of the relative poverty of their native kingdom, and of the heavy debts that hampered the liquidity of their families. Crown patronage was often the key to maintaining or increasing one's power, and after the king moved his court to London in 1603, a whole new set of dynamics and rivalries were added to what was already a highly competitive situation. As Keith Brown has observed in his seminal work on the topic:

Noble society [in Scotland] was in a constant state of flux, houses rising while their neighbours were in decline, and this threat of decay was appreciated by contemporaries whose thought patterns encouraged them to believe that decomposition was an inevitable state of nature. Hence, the constant striving for advantage. No one believed that wealth and status lasted forever, and it was a commonplace idea that the lineage was under perennial threat from decay or from the chance of fortune. This suggests that for all the trumpeting of ancient blood ties, nobles faced with the inconstancies of succession, economic vagaries and political fortunes, were acutely aware of the sand on which they built their houses.[7]

It is within this historical reality that Alexander's rise to positions of power under the early Stuarts, and the ways in which he applied his advantages in the pursuit of his colony and his future prosperity must be assessed.

We have already seen that Alexander owed his first experiences with power and patronage to his relationship with Archibald Campbell, seventh earl of Argyll, who, Brown reminds us, at the height of his powers, controlled the largest private army in the British Isles.[8] Certainly these ties to the House of Argyll and the wider fortunes of Clan Campbell introduced Alexander to the vagaries of crown policies toward the Scottish Highlands and Isles, and Ireland. He witnessed early, unsuccessful, efforts to pacify the former regions via colonial enterprises from the Lowlands, and he took note of later, more successful, Anglo-Scottish plantation efforts in Ireland, particularly in Ulster. He also saw the power and authority of his first patron grow apace because the crown determined to use Argyll as its proxy in the southwestern Highlands and Islands, rather than trying to curb him as part of an overall effort at pacification.[9] Alexander took these lessons on the importance of crown patronage into his own career, but it was his pen that put him on the first rung of the ladder to success.

His rise to prominence as a literary figure came with the publication of *The Tragedy of Darius* in Edinburgh in 1603. This poem was dedicated to King James VI but seems to have been particularly favoured by his eldest son and heir, Prince Henry, who may have arranged a royal introduction for Alexander. By this time, James had learned of his ascension to the English throne, and plans were underway for the removal of the royal family and the Scottish court to London. It was some time during that transitional period that Alexander was appointed tutor to the new Prince of Wales and invited to move to the English capital. The following year Alexander added to his canon with the London publications of another tragedy, *Croesus*, and the sycophantic *A Paraenesis to the Prince* (dedicated to Henry). In 1605, his *Alexandrean Tragedy* appeared, to be followed shortly by *Julius Caesar*. By 1607 Alexander's literary talents and court connections had earned him a promotion to the position of Gentleman of the Prince's Privy Chamber.[10] In the wake of these publications, tangible social and political perquisites also began to accrue, and they helped transform him into a political figure of increasing note.

In 1608 Alexander and a relative were granted rights to collect debts that were outstanding to the crown for the years between 1547 and 1588, a monopoly that allowed the partners to keep 50 percent of their returns.[11] The following year Alexander was knighted, and his connections with the royal family, and the king and Prince of Wales, deepened. When Henry died suddenly in 1612, Alexander captured the dynasty and the kingdoms' sense of grief in a poem entitled "An Elegie on the Death of Prince Henrie." Significantly, the verses reminded the peoples of England and Scotland that though their king had not achieved his political union, union was still manifested in their collective grief:

> What wit could not perswade, authoritie not force,
> An union now at last is made [ah made by a divorce!]
> Both once did noe thing with, and both one want do waile,
> Thus miserie hath match'd us now, when all things else did faile.
> We might as all the rest, so this exception misse,
> I rather we had jarr'd in all, or we had joyn'd in this.
> This the first tempest is, which all this Ile did tosse,
> His cradle *Scotland*, *England*, tombe, both shar'd his life and losse.[12]

Alexander's position at court remained secure after Henry's death, and right away, his role as gentleman usher and tutor shifted to the new heir to the throne, Prince Charles. Even more valuable evidence of James's ongoing favour to the poet was soon forthcoming, for in 1614, Alexander was appointed Master of Requests for Scotland, a position that made him the conduit for any Scottish subject petitioning the king, and thus someone for whom supplicants were willing to do favours of their own. In 1615 he was appointed to the Scottish Privy Council, thereby becoming a member of the most important policy-making body for his native kingdom; and in a separate appointment was placed at the head of a commission charged with apprehending Scottish vagrants who passed into England.[13] When James VI/I returned to his native kingdom for his first and only post-union visit in 1617, Alexander accompanied him and was soon appointed to yet another important commission, this time to oversee the king's desired changes to religious worship and observance for the Scottish Kirk, as expressed in the Five Articles of Perth.[14]

Although we cannot here completely describe and analyse Alexander's growing list of official responsibilities and interests *prior* to his receiving the charter for Nova Scotia in 1621, the following aspects of his experiences are clear, particularly for the years between 1614 and 1621. He travelled regularly between Scotland and England and was on intimate terms with the highest-ranking members of both governments. As a member of the Scottish Privy Council, he had a say in nearly all aspects of the operation of that state, and dealt with issues touching on everything from trade and commerce, to security, to religious policy. He knew that for his generation, credit (especially with the king) was often more important than cash, and he was steadily accumulating offices and honours that should have been increasing his access to both. As a servant, Alexander tried to implement the king's wishes, but he also worked to explain political realities to the king. He steered through ever-changing preferences among royal favourites at court, and he thrived throughout. He helped facilitate the movement of Scots to the new plantations in Ulster. He raised money to assist James's son-in-law, Frederick of the Palatinate and erstwhile King of Bohemia, as the Thirty Years' War in Europe opened and progressed. Finally, he was acquainted with British overseas ventures during these years and, while he may have been more sanguine about potential successes than wary of failures, he was clearly much more than a dreamy poet as his plans for a Scottish overseas colony began to crystallize.[15]

It is often suggested that Alexander's real interest in colonization accelerated after conversations in London in 1620, first with Sir Ferdinando Gorges, the leading partner in the New England Company, and even more with John Mason, who had recently returned from Newfoundland. There is a chicken-and-egg element to these anecdotes. Alexander had already known Gorges for years and it is almost certain that he had known – or known of – Mason for some time as well, owing mostly to the Englishman's services to the Scottish government in 1610 and later, when he had patrolled the Hebrides with Bishop Knox and tried to enforce Scottish fishing laws.

This acquaintance was strongly suggested by Mason in one of his letters. Alexander was a good friend of Sir John Scot of Scotstarvet, the Chancery judge who had helped clear Mason of erroneous piracy charges in 1615, and to whom Mason dedicated his pamphlet on Newfoundland. In a 1617 letter to Scot, Mason acknowledges Alexander as one of his "heartiest wellwillers, to whome with my hartiest acknowledgement with chiefest duty I rest."[16]

If Alexander and Mason had not known each other previously, it is quite likely that they would have met in either Edinburgh or London in 1615, just when Mason was appointed to replace John Guy as governor of Newfoundland. What is most important for our purposes is that when they had their documented conversation about Alexander's desire to found a "New Scotland" in 1620, the "poet" was already, through his government service, more than acquainted with such basic issues as the procurement of ships, raising money and credit for campaigns, enforcing monopoly rights, and even arbitrating among competing trading interests – specifically when they involved competing English and Scottish parties.[17]

These experiences thus formed the background both to Alexander's desires to form a Scottish colony and to his eventual application to James for a charter that would make it a reality. We need to remember, however, that neither Jamestown nor the settlements on Newfoundland were particularly successful precedents at this point, and that neither endeavour had captured the public's imagination.[18] To that extent, Alexander was proposing to embark on a project that contemporary examples had already shown to be risky. So why did the king endorse a new colonial plan?

Although some contemporaries castigated James for his liberality when it came to issuing grants, the king's decision to back Alexander's scheme must not have seemed especially inordinate, at least initially. Alexander had already proven himself on a number of official levels, and in principle, the idea of planting a "New Scotland" in 1621 was no more a pipe dream than was the founding of a "New England." It is noteworthy that a king who had tried to encourage political union between England and Scotland, and who tried to portray his reign as a period of inter-kingdom co-operation would now back a venture that smacked of old national identities, rather than of a new British future. However, James was already aware of several instances in which his subjects had joined forces overseas. Perhaps Alexander's scheme appealed to him for a different reason.

By 1621 the king was aging noticeably and becoming increasingly world-weary. He was vexed by divisions within his court and within his governments. The generation of men with whom he had grown up was passing, and it seemed less and less as if he ruled his native kingdom with his pen.[19] His proposed changes to the Scottish Kirk contained in the Five Articles of Perth were meeting with strident opposition from several quarters. And yet, on his only post-1603 visit home, James had become overwhelmed with nostalgia for the land of his birth and confessed his regret at not having returned home more often.[20] There is at least some possibility that Alexander's proposal struck James as a way of injecting pride back into his native kingdom, and of ensuring that whatever the future held for the separate kingdoms of the British Isles, the name of Scotland would endure overseas. As the king's charter giving Alexander the rights to Nova Scotia stated: "Know ye, that we have always been eager to embrace every opportunity to promote the honour and wealth of our Kingdom of Scotland, and think that no gain is easier or more safe than what is made by planting new colonies in foreign and uncultivated regions."[21]

Alexander moved with alacrity to make Nova Scotia a reality. Knowing he would need both financial subscribers and willing colonists, in November 1621 he conveyed Cape Breton Island to Sir Robert Gordon of Lochinvar, a former soldier who was a fellow landholder in southwestern Scotland and a figure who enjoyed his own network of connections at court and in the Scottish government. Lochinvar intended to call his territory "New Galloway" and made swift efforts to fit out ships in the Welsh port of Angelsey.[22] He was unsuccessful in making a departure for his holdings that year, but this did not dissuade Alexander from trying to organize a separate voyage. In March 1622 he engaged a ship in London to go to the port of Kirkcudbright, on the Solway Firth, relying on his own network of contacts and clients to assist both in provisioning the ship and in raising manpower for the expedition. Unfortunately, two difficulties prevented these expectations from being realized. First, with war now raging in Europe, many potential adventurers who might have signed on for a period of service in the New World had opted to fight as mercenaries in continental armies. These included several unnamed gentlemen whom Alexander obviously hoped to entice to his colony as well. [23]

The second problem was that crop failures in Scotland the previous year had made foodstuffs harder to come by and much more expensive, so that preparations for the voyage were slowed.[24] Alexander was also disheartened by the lack of enthusiasm that the scheme engendered, especially among trained artisans and others whose talents might be useful in a new colony.[25] As we saw in the previous chapter, the hopes for this first venture were unrealized, and it can at best be judged a qualified failure.

Alexander kept trying. In the interim, he had received additional powers and prestige from the Scottish government, and was now styled Lieutenant of Justice and Admiralty in New Scotland. His correspondence also suggests that he remained optimistic about the colony's prospects.[26] The plans for a 1623 expedition called for a supply ship to be sent back across the Atlantic, this time from London, but the eventual voyage of the St Luke produced similarly mixed results. Although its exploration of coastline of Alexander's holdings in Nova Scotia led to the production of the first map of his territory, its return also confirmed the failure of the 1622 expedition.

So, in spite of royal favour, government support, and the mounting of two voyages to the New World, New Scotland seemed no closer to becoming a reality. Alexander had personally invested an estimated £6,000 by this point, with nothing to show for it. Equally ominous was that the French ambassador in London began making formal complaints about British activities in the claimed territories for Nova Scotia and New England. A 1624 letter from the count de Tillières, the French ambassador in London, to Sir Edward Conway, the English secretary of state, gave evidence of this attitude. In the letter, Tillières accused the English of fostering hostilities in the New World and warned that such provocations might irreparably damage relations between the France and England. Even more illustrative of the potential for tensions was the ambassador's assertion that England's territories (as the French recognized them) stretched only from Virginia to the Gulf of Mexico, and that the king should prohibit his subjects from disturbing French settlements in Canada.[27]

A person who depended upon a nascent colonial scheme to help secure his fortune would have been discouraged by all these setbacks, but in Sir William Alexander's case, Nova Scotia was at best a secondary concern in the later part of 1623 and early 1624. During this period, his priority was yet more service to his king, including journeying to the continent on a very delicate diplomatic mission.

James VI/I always saw himself as a peaceful ruler who had brought harmony to his peoples through the union of the crowns, and who could foster the same spirit on the European continent by bridging divisions between its Protestant and Catholic peoples. Dynastic marriages were one of the vehicles for furthering such a goal, and following the wedding of his daughter, Elizabeth, to the Lutheran prince Frederick of the Palatinate, James favoured a marriage for the Prince of Wales to the daughter of a Catholic ruler.[28] Among all the possibilities, James believed that a Spanish match offered the best prospect for securing peace in Europe and for benefitting his own kingdoms in a new alliance. Negotiations moved painfully slowly, however, and the onset of hostilities in Europe following the Bohemian crisis of 1618 only deepened antipathies against Catholics in Britain. By 1621 Spain had invaded and seized the Palatinate, in support of Austrian Habsburg Holy Roman Emperor. In the face of all this, Count Gondomar related demands for concessions to British Catholics and requirements for the practice of Catholicism within the royal household that would have been practically impossible for James to accept.[29] Meanwhile, a majority in the English parliament began demanding that James increase his support for Frederick from mere financial assistance, to an open declaration of war against Spain and the Holy Roman Empire.[30]

These conflicting pressures were difficult enough for the old king to endure; but in early 1623, Prince Charles and the royal favourite, the earl of Buckingham, made the situation infinitely worse by venturing *incognito* to the Spanish court, to press for a betrothal to Maria, the Spanish infanta, themselves. The results of this escapade are well known. The Spanish government refused to countenance the match without papal dispensation, public declarations of toleration for British Catholics, and freedom of worship and religious conversation for Maria and her court. Instead of successfully negotiating a marriage, the British visitors were diverted for weeks by hunting parties, tournaments, and other entertainments; and as the time passed, a few fleeting glances at his prospective bride dampened Charles's desire for the infanta.[31]

The result left the heir to the throne and Buckingham, the most important confidant to both the king and the prince of Wales, both thirsting for revenge over the perceived ill-treatment and bad faith negotiations they had been subjected to in Spain. The only immediate beneficiary was Buckingham, who had been raised to duke *in absentia*. The travellers now returned to London in October 1623, determined to support the parliamentary bloc calling for war against Spain.

Forced to seek marriage alternatives for Charles and to broker an alliance against Spain, James now turned his attentions to the Habsburgs' old rival, France. Princess Henrietta Maria, the sister of King Louis XIII, became the prospective bride, but as she too was Catholic, the French likewise demanded a papal dispensation. In an effort to obtain this concession, James entrusted Sir William Alexander with a secret mission to Rome. The details surrounding the mission are very sketchy, but it is known that an unnamed Scottish Catholic nobleman was dispatched from London in June 1624 to make a personal appeal for the pope's dispensation.[32] Evidently it was hoped that James's use of an openly Catholic courtier as his messenger would show the pope that his flock could prosper in the British kingdoms, and thereby ensure the dispensation.

Clearly, this figure was not Alexander himself. However, Thomas McGrail, Alexander's most thorough biographer, has demonstrated that Alexander accompanied the unnamed agent, probably to oversee and supervise his activities.[33] Because a Catholic match of any kind was bound to be unpopular in the British kingdoms, almost nobody knew about the delegation for Rome. The evidence that confirms it is a set of letters from a Brussels-based priest, Friar Giacinto da Casale, to Cardinal Francesco Barberini, describing the progress toward Rome of the Scottish nobleman that summer, and, after this person's illness in Florence, letters from that city's bishop and papal nuncio giving updates and confirming that the envoy had recovered sufficiently to leave for Rome in November.[34] Alexander's presence in this party is substantiated by requests he made to England's secretary, Sir Edward Conway, in January 1624 for moneys needed for the "King's special service," and by a February request for a picture of James, garnished with stones, which was to be a gift for the cardinal.[35]

That this evidence meant Alexander went to Rome, rather than just helping with preparations for the mission was triply confirmed by Alexander himself: in a letter to Cardinal del Bagno of Brussels in 1633, in which he alluded to their former acquaintance in connection to the dispensation business; in a second 1633 letter from the Catholic marquis of Douglas to del Bagno, who again recalled Alexander's dealings with the Cardinal;[36] and by Alexander's 1639 account to the Earl of Rutland that he had been in Rome during Pope Urban VIII's Great Jubilee in the early spring of 1625.[37]

The timing of this entire episode surrounding the embassy to Rome has been underplayed as it relates to Alexander's colonial interests, because the one is almost never mentioned in connection with the other. Scholars of Nova Scotia have so divorced Alexander's secondary interest (at this point at least) in his overseas venture from his political life in Britain, that it is rarely mentioned, and even McGrail treats the two subjects in separate chapters, as if Alexander could balkanize his roles. Clearly that was impossible for Alexander, and with the future of the dynasty at stake, and delicate negotiations on sensitive religious issues taking place, thoughts about Nova Scotia must have been at most a secondary consideration for him in late 1623 and early 1624. That he was sent to Rome, by contrast, confirms again that he occupied a position of utmost trust with the king and Prince of Wales.

It was perhaps as a diversion from these more pressing duties that Alexander turned to his pen as a means for raising interest in his overseas venture among his countrymen. Using the Anglo-Scots plantations in Ulster as his inspiration, Alexander tried to stir national enthusiasm for his colonial venture in a pamphlet entitled *An Encouragement to Colonies*. It was first printed in London in 1624, although it was nothing less than a call to his fellow Scots to extend their kingdom's boundaries into the New World.

Alexander's *Encouragement to Colonies* included the map of the territory that had been coursed the previous year, and showed the subdivision of "Nova Scotia" into plantation sites, named for shires and other identifiable areas in Scotland. Alexander made the following arguments. He first asserted that colonization was a natural extension of a nation's authority and talents, and he used examples from classical antiquity to buttress his case – a comparison contrived to appeal to the literary elites of his own day. He also cited contemporary Spanish, French, and English colonial efforts in order to stir the Scots to action.

Alexander then opined that colonial efforts could be of immediate benefit to the homeland because of the security they offered. Plantations in Ulster had brought peace to the British Isles because: "Our King hath onely diuided the most seditious families of the *Irish* by dispersing them in sundry parts within the Countrey, not to extinguish, but to disipate their power [and] hath incorporated some of his best *Britaines* with the *Irish*, planted in sundry places without power to oppresse, but onely to ciuilize them by their example."[38]

Third, Alexander recounted the history of French efforts in the region, and described the engagement that had taken place between Samuel Argall's squadron from Jamestown and the French at Port Royal in 1613 (see chapter 2). If planted, Nova Scotia would assure the sovereignty of James VI/I in the region once and for all, and forestall further French ambitions.

Alexander went on to describe the natural resources of the region in detail, defend colonization as a better use of surplus Scottish manpower than mercenary service in Europe, and project pseudo-mercantilist ben-

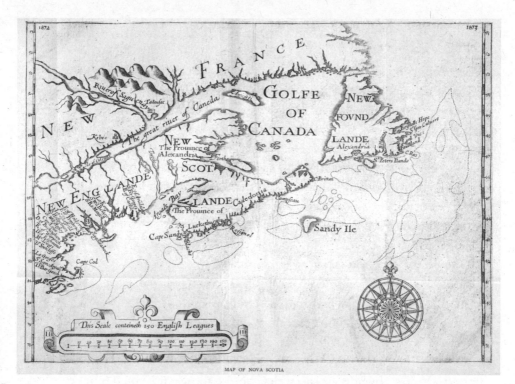

MAP OF NOVA SCOTIA

New Scotlande. This map was published in Sir William Alexander's promotional book, *An Encouragement to Colonies*, in 1624.

efits for domestic merchants and shipping. He was not indiscriminate in projecting how profits could be made in the colony, however, and he specifically castigated the Spaniards for transporting African slaves to the Caribbean.[39] Finally, he cited a religious imperative to colonial efforts, noting: "The greatest incouragement of all for any true Christian is this, that heere is a large way for aduancing the Gospel of Iesus Christ, to whome Churches may bee builded in places where his Name was neuer knowne."[40]

Encouragement to Colonies was likely written before Alexander's departure for Rome, and we can reasonably surmise that its first imprints were released while he was still away acting as the king's emissary. It is frequently noted that the *Encouragement* had at best a minimal impact on any potential colonists, but Alexander's service was certainly noted where it mattered most – with James VI/I. Just six months before he died, and with his trusted servant still away in Italy, James ratified his support for Alexander and his colonial scheme by ordering the creation of a new

social distinction, the Order of Knights Baronet of Nova Scotia. The Privy
Council responded to the king by emphasizing the need for colonists
most especially, and on 30 November 1624 a proclamation was read at
the Mercat Cross in Edinburgh, announcing the new styling for any man
willing to invest 1,000 merks Scots in the venture.[41] For a further 2,000
merks a prospective baronet would have the option of sending six "sufficient men, artificeris or labourers" to the colony. Along with the title,
the investor would also receive 30,000 acres of land, of which 16,000
acres would be reserved for his own plantation, and 14,000 set aside for
public uses.[42]

The use of social inducements as a means of garnering support in
plantation ventures had been an established crown policy in Ulster since
1611, and Alexander had hinted in *Encouragement to Colonies* that such
rewards might benefit Nova Scotia.[43] We have no way of knowing
whether James read Alexander's pamphlet, or if the two of them had ever
discussed this contingency, let alone before Alexander's departure for
Italy. Regardless, by offering social elevation to those who would support
the colony, James was using a customary means of crown patronage in
a society that knew better than to expect timely payments in cash from
the king. Just as important, however, James was providing his loyal servant Sir William Alexander with the best support he could offer for the
nascent colony.

We do not know how or when in Rome Alexander learned of James's
death in March 1625. We do know that he was back in London for the
royal funeral in May.[44] The old king had done what he could for Alexander and Nova Scotia. More important, he had kept the British kingdoms
at peace. As the new reign dawned it became clear that peace was not at
first the new king, Charles I's, primary objective.

5

THE PAPER COLONY:
CHARLES'S PRIVATEERS
AND THE PROXY WAR

It is considerable that the grant of all patents for sole trade and plantation
is laid upon conquest or discovery.
"The State of Business of Canada or New France" (1628)

John Williams, Lord Keeper of the Great Seal of England, Dean of Westminster Cathedral, and Bishop of Lincoln, had been a great favourite of the late king. In the unfolding confessional struggle that would so divide early Stuart Britain, James saw Williams as a theological moderate in the Church of England's growing rift between its Calvinist and Arminian wings.[1] He had loved to discuss theology with the Welshman, made him his court chaplain, and as the end approached had sent for Williams to administer communion on his deathbed on 24 March 1625. A witty and amiable man, Williams was a tremendous comfort to James in his last hours and did not leave the royal bedside until the king expired on 27 March.[2] A few weeks later Williams performed one final duty for his late master by preaching the oration at James's funeral.

On 7 May, before a large assembly of mourners at Westminster Abbey, Williams began his sermon with words that for students of the early Stuart period have echoed down through the centuries. One reference in particular has continued to frame the debate over how James's reign(s) should be judged.[3] It was Williams who, in recalling an age marked by peace and unity among James's peoples, first referred to the dead king as "Great Britain's Solomon."[4]

Among those assembled for the funeral that day was Sir William Alexander, recently returned to London from his diplomatic mission in Rome.[5] Although Alexander probably agreed with many of the bishop's accolades, he would have found one aspect of the eulogy slightly jarring. In recounting how Britain had prospered since 1603, Williams noted that one could now find "manufactures at home daily invented, trading abroad exceedingly multiplied[,] the navy royall magnificently furnished [it wasn't]; Virginia, New-found-land, and New England peopled."[6] That Nova Scotia merited no mention from Williams could only have served to underscore that Alexander's colony still existed on paper only. The allusion to England's overseas colonies also projected an image of greater success than had been achieved to that point, as Alexander's friends Mason, Calvert, Falkland, and Gorges could all attest. The situation in Virginia was actually so dire that the crown had revoked the license of the Virginia Company in 1624 and had been forced to assume the colony as a crown responsibility.[7]

The ensuing first years of the reign of Charles I would nevertheless see Alexander rise even higher in terms of his political powers under his former pupil and new ruler; and they would also see the near birth of Nova Scotia as part of a yet larger possible enterprise – a truly British, co-operative enterprise across the Atlantic. However, the years 1625–29 especially would be fraught with external warfare and highly divisive internal conflicts within the British kingdoms. To see how this narrative unfolded, let us turn our attention to national and international developments during these years.

For King Charles I, and the duke of Buckingham, the 1624 pursuit of a French marriage seemed to have paid off. Within a few days of burying his father, Charles met his new wife, Queen Henrietta Maria, at Dover.[8] The match was not initially a happy one, but marital bliss was less relevant in the larger scheme of things than gaining a French alliance for the war that Charles and Buckingham wished to prosecute against Spain. To the chagrin of the kingdoms' political classes, this policy of confrontation was fraught with miscalculation from the start.

Since 1621 the English parliament had been providing subsidies for assistance to James's son-in-law Frederick of the Palatinate, but James VI/I had always stopped short of declaring war, hoping to the end that his diplomacy could broker a general European peace. Even though Charles and Buckingham had become clearly identified with the war party in the English Parliament, they now faced a growing willingness, among members of the House of Commons especially, to extend further monies without a clear military agenda.

When Charles met the first parliament of his reign in June 1625, moods were further soured by the poor performance of a mostly impressed English force that had been fighting alongside Dutch, Danish, and Protestant German allies under the command of the mercenary leader count Ernst von Mansfeld.[9] Relations were strained once more when parliament assigned the customs revenues known as tonnage and poundage to Charles for only two years, instead of for life, as was traditional when a new monarch ascended the throne. Thus began a long and unseemly quarrel over English finances that would ultimately lead to Charles's decision to rule without his parliament in 1629.[10]

In an effort to regain the military initiative, Buckingham prepared a naval expedition to attack the Spanish treasure fleet and strangle Spanish shipping by seizing key ports. With disputes surfacing over the actual aims of the war, and no consensus emerging on the financing – or the execution – of campaigns, things got off to an inauspicious start. In the war's first belligerent act that October, England's viscount Wimbledon led a poorly organized force to disaster in an attempted raid on the Spanish port of Cadiz.

By early 1626 Charles's military debts had risen to over £1 million, and enraged members of parliament were starting impeachment proceedings against Buckingham, who was not only the king's leading advisor but was also England's Lord Admiral. He was failing as a military leader and it was also becoming clear that he had failed as a diplomat. The French government, instead of joining the British kingdoms in the war against Spain as Buckingham had projected, was employing ships that had been borrowed from Charles's Royal Navy against the Huguenot stronghold of La Rochelle. For ardent Protestants in England and Scotland this was all the proof that was needed of Catholic treachery.[11]

The next two years would be as tumultuous as any England had experienced since the Armada crisis of 1588. Charles tried to take the heat off Buckingham in parliament by making the duke's known enemies ineligible to sit in the House of Commons, but calls for the duke's impeachment became so loud that the 1626 Parliament was dissolved. Critically, it had not voted funds to support Britain's Protestant allies in Europe. To supply Charles's allies and continue the war effort, the English government initiated a program of forced loans from property holders. In spite of the collection of £240,000 in the first ten months, this was a public relations disaster for the crown. The City of London refused a request for £20,000, while in the celebrated "Five Knights Case" of November 1627 royal prerogative was used as a justification for imprisoning defaulters without trial. Finally, the escalating cold war with France, which had featured cargo seizures and growing recriminations, turned hot. France's unwillingness to fulfill the dowry obligations of the marriage treaty, and Cardinal Richelieu's increased persecution of the Huguenots in violation of the Edict of Nantes, led the British kingdoms to declare war.[12]

Now clearly facing Spain and France, Charles and Buckingham tried to revive support for their flagging war effort by harnessing anti-Catholic sentiments in Britain,and concentrating on the relief of La Rochelle. Unsuccessful amphibious operations by English troops on the approach to La Rochelle on the Ile de Ré in July 1627, and failed relief expeditions to La Rochelle itself in May and September 1628 only added to the growing list of disgraces. In October, the Protestants of La Rochelle surrendered to Louis XIII's army. For Charles I, even this was not the greatest cause for regret, however. He found himself dealing with a personal tragedy worse than all these military setbacks, and was starting down a road toward alienation from many of his subjects, and eventually, to civil war.

In August 1628, John Felton, an embittered officer who blamed the duke for the slow pace of his career advancement, assassinated Buckingham.[13] Instead of sharing in their king's grief, however, many people in England greeted the act with joy. Significantly, when Buckingham's murderer was transported to prison, the assembled crowds hailed him as a "little David," clearly casting Buckingham as the evil Goliath.[14] And yet, popular gloating over the demise of the hated royal favourite only masked a deep sense of humiliation stemming from the war with Spain and France. It is in the unfolding context of those events that Sir William

Alexander and the challenges and compromises he had to face to plant his colony of Nova Scotia must now be assessed.

If the duke of Buckingham was at the eye of a growing storm over the conduct of national affairs in these years, the rising tide of controversies that marked Charles's early rule served to lift the fortunes of Sir William Alexander even higher, in ways that benefitted both his political career, and potentially, Nova Scotia as well.

For Alexander, the transition from James's reign to Charles's had been seamless. In fact, his former pupil increased his powers as they related to Scottish politics, and provided even greater support and encouragement for the Nova Scotia colony. An appointment in June 1625 to be a burgess of the burgh of Aberdeen, and thus to enjoy trading privileges from one of Scotland's key ports, was quickly followed by the award of an annual pension to Alexander of £2,400 (Scots).[15] These rewards brought new responsibilities, because Charles was eager not only to gain the greatest range of financing for the war effort from Scotland as possible but also to reform the collection of revenues he received from each of his kingdoms.

In the case of Scotland, rumours had been swirling among the Scots at court, and the members of the Privy Council in Edinburgh, that Charles intended to issue an *Act of Revocation*. This was a customary method whereby a Scottish king could, prior to his twenty-fifth birthday, recover grants of lands that had been made during his minority. By the autumn of 1625 it emerged that Charles intended something much more sweeping – the revocation of all lands granted by the crown dating back to 1540, regardless of whether these grants had been made during a period of royal minority. The majority of landholders in Scotland felt threatened by this scheme, as it seemed to attack rights of property, and contract. Overall, critics feared that the plan would adversely affect the privileges of the landed classes and alter the existing social order in Scotland.[16] Concerns were so widespread that in January 1626 the leading members of the Scottish Privy Council were called to London for a conference on Scottish affairs. It would be the first time that they would see something as central to their government as the actual text of the planned revocation.

In anticipation of the reception the proposal was likely to receive, in late January 1626 Charles elevated Sir William Alexander to the position of Secretary for Scotland, thereby making him the virtual agent of contacts between the crown and his government in that kingdom. When Charles shuffled the Privy Council in March, Alexander remained a member of that body, and was tendered further responsibilities on Scotland's Council of War and the new Revocation Commission. It is quite likely that Alexander had been one of a small circle of Scottish advisors who had helped to formulate the Revocation plan in the first place.[17] Unquestionably, he had become one of Scotland's most important political figures, with unparalleled access to the king.[18]

Linked to the expanded range of duties Alexander was expected to perform for his ruler were renewed instances of royal support for his colony. Shortly after ascending the throne, Charles sent letters to the Privy Council reaffirming the creation of Knights Baronet of Nova Scotia and instructing that a commission be created to start conferring the honour on willing subscribers who would pay the sum of 2,000 merks to Alexander.[19] What irked the Scottish aristocracy, however, was that Charles intimated that the newly created Knights Baronet would gain social precedence over existing lesser nobles. Serious resistance arose when the Scottish Parliament met that November. Wrangling over protocol continued in an exchange of correspondence between London and Edinburgh until Charles trumped his critics in a February 1626 letter warning them that opposition to the new order and its privileges constituted an attack on his royal prerogative. That was something, real or imagined, he proved time and again he would not tolerate.[20]

Problems related to the colony continued, however, and the summer of 1626 featured efforts by the Scottish College of Heralds to exact fees from Nova Scotia baronets for registering coats of arms, whereas Alexander and the king believed exemptions should be permitted to defray costs for potential leaders in the new colony. Although such distinctions and privileges were of importance, in actuality, the niggling over precedence and heraldic fees was really like shadow boxing. By the summer of 1627 only thirty-five patents for Nova Scotia had been granted, a far cry from the 150 subscribers Alexander believed his colony needed to become profitable.[21] There had, however, been one very significant addition to the enterprise. Alexander's eldest son and namesake was granted a knighthood on 22 March 1627, and he now began to take a most active role in establishing his father's colony.[22]

With the war ongoing, and Charles and Buckingham determined to brook no opposition to their prosecution of the conflict, it was unsurprising that moneys for speculative overseas ventures were slow to materialize. The resources of the royal navy and the king's other military resources were already stretched to the limit; a situation that in England had necessitated such unpopular actions as the levying of forced loans, the quartering of troops in private households, and the expropriation of rations and goods for Britain's forces.

The need to defend the coasts of the British kingdoms spawned three high-level proposals to deploy civilian shipping and material from the three British kingdoms to provide for maritime defences. In September 1626, Buckingham, in his capacity as lord admiral of the royal navy, had issued directives calling on all English and Irish skippers to license themselves for the purposes of assisting in the patrol and defence of home waters.[23] Similar orders were also issued under the king's signature for Scotland, so that: "all this dominions may be provided and fournished with sufficient strength both for the defense of themselves and the mutuall assistance each of other against attempts of any enemie."[24] Then, in early 1627, English secretary of state Sir John Coke sent a memorandum to Charles I, urging a strict co ordination of all English, Scottish, and Irish military material and personnel, including shipping, for the duration of the war.[25] As secretary for Scotland, Alexander was not only involved in formulating these sorts of policies but was also travelling between England and Scotland and playing a role in their implementation.[26] He further knew from direct experience that these calls to use all maritime resources of the three kingdoms for the war effort offered correspondingly unique opportunities for overseas ventures.

In the summer of 1626, Sir Robert Gordon of Lochinvar purchased a ship on credit that was intended to transport himself and his household, three other baronets who had subscribed to the Nova Scotia colony, and their attendants, to settle his lands on Cape Breton Island. Under the terms of his agreement with the government, there would be an equal division of "anie prise or prises that shall happen to be taken by the said shipp, commander, souldiers, and marineris therein."[27] As we have seen previously, recourse to privateering had been an established practice since Elizabethan times, and it was possible that Lochinvar's ship might come into contact with enemy vessels from Spain or Portugal.[28] Given his destination, however, encounters with the French were more likely; in light of the deteriorating relations between France and the British kingdoms, hostile actions were not unknown against potential enemies, when tensions were high. As it happened, Lochinvar died before the expedition could depart, and Cape Breton Island would not see the arrival of any British settlers until 1629, but this setback did not prevent efforts to people Nova Scotia from moving forward.[29]

In early 1627 Sir William Alexander had requisitioned a 300-tonne ship (its name does not appear in any records) and ordnance to be prepared at the Scottish port of Dumbarton, while two other armed vessels, the *Eagle* of London, and the *Morning Star*, owned by a Scotsman named Andrew Baxter, were dispatched from the Thames for Dumbarton for the purposes of transporting settlers to Nova Scotia. The small armada was diminished almost immediately because Baxter's English creditors seized his ship in the Dover roads, and prevented it from sailing northward.[30] In spite of this, Alexander continued to pull political strings and under a warrant from the king he learned that the Scottish Treasurer of Marine had been instructed to reimburse him the £6,000 he had lost on his 1622 and 1623 ventures.[31]

While the *Eagle* was being outfitted, the younger Sir William Alexander was engaging in a bit of privateering of his own. In June he appeared in the Firth of Forth with a captured salt freighter called the *St Lawrence* from the Hanseatic port of Lübeck. He had taken this prize taken under Admiralty authority that his father had recently received in connection with Nova Scotia, to attack Spanish and other enemy shipping.[32] Privateering was obviously an effective way for the crown to prosecute war by proxy, and for the parties under license to earn profits for themselves. Such profits might, in fact, even be expected to eclipse potential earnings from normal commerce.

Unfortunately, the additional monies gained from this particular privateering venture did not provide immediate benefits to the Alexanders, or advance the settlement expedition to Nova Scotia in 1627. After the younger Alexander's return voyage to Dumbarton in June, his ship and the *Eagle* remained at anchor in the Clyde, while fundraising and provisioning efforts continued. This was a very uncertain time, and as the ships' crews awaited departure for what must have seemed an interminable period, they became bored, restless, and insubordinate. In late August a sailor named William Somerville was imprisoned for "his insolencie and trubill offerit to utheris of his cumpanie ... and raising factionis and seditionis amangis his cumpanie and sailers." Upon his release, Somerville got drunk and "vpoune the Sabboth day, in tyme of preiching, he abusit the Sabboth day, being drinking all nyt." What seems to have particularly scandalized Dumbarton parishioners that Sunday was that Somerville was trying to peddle goods of some kind, as the worshippers were leaving their service.[33]

This incident highlights not only the uncertainty about the expedition's departure date but also the difficulty the Alexanders were experiencing in paying their crews. On 24 January 1628, the baillies of Dumbarton were again forced to intercede in an altercation involving the Alexanders' sailors. On this occasion, one James Powar committed a series of assaults while drunk, including upon Captain Barclay, master of the *Eagle*. Powar's complaint was that Barclay had been withholding wages. He told the authorities who imprisoned him that he "wissit the first cumpanie that sayllit w[ith] Sir William sank all to the sea grund."[34] It is not known whether Somerville or Powar were still with the younger Alexander when the long-awaited voyage to Nova Scotia began in March 1628.

The delays, and problems with money, provisions, and personnel, had unquestionably created grave difficulties for the party, and many individuals who had agreed to subscribe to the colony, sail with Alexander, or undertake settlements, had deserted and absconded with Nova Scotia assets prior to departure.[35] But, if the pitfalls associated with the embarkation of this fleet are reasonably clear, what happened next remains confusing.

Young Alexander's small fleet did indeed sail from Dumbarton in March 1628 but it likely never reached Nova Scotia. There are only two documents that provide any real clues about what happened on this voyage, and they need to be assessed carefully. On 18 November 1628

the elder Alexander wrote to his friend the earl of Menteith, president of
the Scottish Privy Council, to tell him: "My sone, praised be God, is returned safe, haveing left a colonie neare Canada behind him, *and I am
dealeing for a new setteing forth from Loundoun* [my italics]."[36] The
only other snippet of information about the fate of this party comes in a
letter from a William Maxwell of Edinburgh, who on 23 November
informed his kinsman John Maxwell of Pollok: "It is for certaine that Sir
William Alexander is come home againe from Nova Scotia, and heathe
left behind him 70 men and tua weemen, with provision to serve them
be the space of one yeir, being placet in a pairt of the countrie quhilk is
a natural strenhe." And then, more tellingly he added: "*The Englische
men ar suiten of his Majestie a patent to plant and possesse quahat-
sumever lands thairof quhil they please* and these to be halden of the
Crowne of England [my italics]."[37]

It is in relation to these developments that the Kirke brothers, whom
we initially met in relation to their attempt to force the surrender of
Samuel de Champlain and his party of French colonists at Quebec in the
summer of 1628, become a central part of this story. Before that can be
conveyed, however, we need to take a chronological detour to explain
who the Kirkes were, why they had obtained letters of marque to act
as privateers, and what their service to Charles I suggested about the
broader European conflict and its impact across the Atlantic. Finally, we
will see how the Kirke brothers came to be connected with Sir William
Alexander, and the still chimerical colony of Nova Scotia.

The story of the Kirke brothers begins with their father, Gervase
(sometimes called Gervais, or Jarvis) Kirke, who was born in Norton,
Derbyshire, in 1568.[38] The Kirkes were apparently reasonably prosperous landholders, but some sort of dispute caused Gervase to be
disinherited by his father. Although he was the eldest of the family's
nine children, he was barred from pursuing his legal destiny and inheriting the family estate and moved to London to work his way into the
mercantile trading community.

Such a career decision was not something to be taken lightly. Merchant trade was a guild-regulated profession and Gervase Kirke would

have had to serve an apprenticeship of as long as ten years with an established merchant before striking off on his own. By then he would have learned to handle accounts and inventories, as well as undertaking trading missions on behalf of his employer.[39] Ultimately, he was successful. By the early 1590s he had set himself up in business and was conducting merchant shipping between the English capital and ports in Flanders and France. As a feature of this, Gervase Kirke sailed on these trading routes himself, and eventually he settled in the French port of Dieppe. There, in 1596, he married Elizabeth Goudon, the daughter of a local merchant. Within a year, she gave birth to their first son, David, who was followed by brothers Lewis (b. 1599), and Thomas (b. 1603). In all, the Kirkes would have five sons and two daughters.[40]

There has always been some question about the Kirke brothers' early lives, and whether they should be seen as English or French. Indeed, their biographer in the *Dictionary of Canadian Biography* even suggests that their mother might have been the daughter of an English merchant, who, like Gervase Kirke, was merely residing in Dieppe in the 1590s.[41] If that was the case, then perhaps notions of the Kirkes' English and French duality are overly romantic. There is very little manuscript evidence that tells the story of the their early lives and training, or that verifies any hints about their early family life. However, a piece of documentation exists that suggests the Kirke children were considered subjects of the king of France until March 1621, when the English House of Lords passed an act naturalizing "David Kirke, Lewis Kirke, Thomas Kirke, John Kirke, James Kirke, Peter Kirke, Catherine Kirke, and Marie Kirke, Children of Gervis Kirke, Englishman, and Citizen and Mercer of London."[42]

Samuel de Champlain, who was to get to know the Kirkes much better than he would have wished in 1628 and 1629, made some interesting observations on their cultural backgrounds. He noted, for example, that Lewis Kirke, to whom he was forced to surrender Quebec in July 1629, was "French in disposition and always had a liking for the French nation [and that he found] intercourse and conversation with them more agreeable than with the English, to whom his nature seemed to be adverse."[43] It is also clear that they had been raised as Protestants, and that if they grew up thinking of themselves as subjects of the king of

France, the anti-Huguenot policies pursued by Louis XIII and Cardinal Richelieu from the mid-1620s may have strengthened their sense of identification with their father's homeland.[44]

What can be discerned from the few extant records of the family's activities prior to 1628 is that their mercantile and shipping interests had focused on the wine trade between England and France, but that the threat, followed by the outbreak of hostilities between the two kingdoms in 1627, forced them to find alternatives.[45] By now the ships of Gervase Kirke and his London-based partners were barred from French ports, but if they gained licenses to operate as privateers, they would likely obtain more lucrative booty.[46] It is possible that this syndicate, now called the Company of Merchant Adventurers to Canada, dispatched a ship to reconnoitre the Gulf of St. Lawrence sometime in 1627.[47] At the end of 1627, however, the Kirke brothers themselves had applied for and received, letters of marque to operate against French shipping in North American waters.[48] These developments thus bring us to two questions related to the eventual partnership formed between the Kirke group and Sir William Alexander senior. When was it formed, and under what circumstances?

A number of historians have suggested that when the Alexander and Kirke expeditions sailed in 1628, they departed together from London and perhaps sailed as a squadron until their different destinations, Nova Scotia for the former, and the St Lawrence for the latter, caused them to separate.[49] Subsequent disagreements arose, they say, when the Kirkes' near success in taking Quebec caused Sir William Alexander to fear that they might ultimately violate his charter. A close reading of the evidence offers a somewhat different scenario, however, and shows that the Alexanders were ignorant of the Kirkes' designs on Quebec and New France until at least August 1628.[50] As we shall see, it would take the personal intervention of the king and others to formally bring the two parties together.

We know that the younger Alexander's party sailed from Dumbarton in the spring of 1628, having already procured the *Eagle* from London the previous year. Under the circumstances, it seems highly unlikely that a party undertaking a voyage across the Atlantic from a port in south-western Scotland would risk a hazardous preliminary voyage to the

Thames. Furthermore, there is no evidence in any of the documents relating to the younger Alexander's preparations for the 1628 voyage that either he or his father knew about the Kirkes prior to his departure for the New World. How, then, did they find out about each other, and what led to their eventual partnership?

The answer seems to be found in the convergence of Alexander's voyage of 1628 with that of the Kirke brothers, and in hurried efforts that took place at Charles I's court to prevent an internal conflict. That story can be extrapolated from several clearer pieces of written evidence. As we have noted, it is not known definitively what happened to the "70 men and tua weemen" that Alexander left behind "neare Canada" when he returned to Britain in the autumn of 1628. It has been speculated elsewhere that he left his party at Tadoussac, in the company of the Kirkes' men who wintered there in 1628–29.[51] We do know that his father told the earl of Menteith, in the letter quoted previously from November: "I am dealeing for a [colony] now setteing forth from Loundoun."[52] This statement suggests that the elder Alexander was surprised to learn about the presence of a new colonial venture, in lands he believed belonged to him. The earlier quoted letter, between William Maxwell of Edinburgh, and John Maxwell of Pollok, also indicates surprise in Scotland over the presence of Englishmen in Canada.

Given his surprise and the fact that he challenged the validity of the Kirkes' claims in Canada to the king in the autumn of 1628, it is apparent that in "dealeing" with this development, the elder Alexander at that point saw the Englishmen not as partners or allies but rather as interlopers. Had his son, upon discovering English privateers operating on the St Lawrence, and thereby encroaching on his father's charter, seen things the same way?

Once more, the absence of a full account of the young Alexander's 1628 voyage makes a definitive answer impossible. However, given his cryptic references to having left his colonists "neare Canada," rather than in Nova Scotia, it can be speculated that he saw the need to assert his father's supposed claim on the St Lawrence. Perhaps when he learned of the Kirkes' exploits there, Alexander decided not to make for Nova

Scotia, but opted instead to assert his father's authority over the Kirkes and their party. If this inference were correct it would explain why he left his settlers at Tadoussac (if that is indeed where they were left) – to watch the Kirke party – rather than as part of a co-operative effort. It may be that the senior Alexander had been informed of some of this prior to his son's return voyage.

On 9 August 1628, a nobleman named Edward, lord Newburgh, petitioned the king on behalf of himself, and his partners, the Merchant Adventurers to Canada. The petition stated that they were prepared to accept a compromise over Canada with Sir William Alexander that had been proposed by the Lord Keeper (Bishop Williams) and the lord chancellor of Scotland, Viscount Dupplin.[53] Specifically, the petition asserted that the Kirkes had no in way encroached on Sir William Alexander's "patent of New Scotland yet are willing to part with the greatest part of the territory within their own discovery, and to limitation of their trade for a term of years, and in their patent to yield a portionable acknowledgement of interest to Sir Wm. Alexander." And then, tellingly, given the ongoing hostilities with France: "The time is pressing for sending out their fleet to reduce those countries which petitioners are ready to undertake with a charge of 30,000; a week's delay may hazard the voyage."[54]

This is the earliest mention in any of the documentary evidence of word of the Kirkes' exploits on the St Lawrence reaching Britain. Given the scale of maritime traffic to the New World fisheries, it is not unreasonable to assume that a third party transmitted rumours of an English success against French shipping or installations in Canada before any of the actual participants returned home.[55] It is less clear how the elder Alexander learned about this, and whether others such as Newburgh knew the Kirkes had achieved something tangible and were trying to ward off his complaints or offer an *a priori* compromise. The efforts of Williams and Dupplin, however, seem to suggest that the latter was taking place within the context of Charles I's own court.

Subsequent negotiations in London in the autumn of 1628 buttress the view that a partnership was not a foregone conclusion and was certainly not in place when the two expeditions left the British Isles the previous spring. It can also be discerned that high-level figures at Charles I's court had backed the Kirkes and were prepared to mount a domestic challenge to Alexander's definition of his charter for Nova Scotia for the first time. The entire situation carried the risk for Charles that an Anglo-Scottish rift might develop, thereby jeopardizing the unity of his court, hazarding the project of a long-standing and loyal counsellor, and – perhaps most critically – undermining the war effort against France.

A second, and crucial, piece of evidence related to these events is entitled "The state of business of Canada, or New France, 1628," contained in the papers of Sir John Coke, who was then one of England's two secretaries of state. In a subsection of the document entitled "1628. Propositions of accommodation for the settling of the trade and plantation in Canada or New France" we read: "Upon advertisement of the success of Captain Kerck's ship in Canada, Earl Newburgh, for himself and his partners, repaired unto His Majesty to acquaint him with it, and to demand a patent for the sole trade and plantation of those countries, and which he was graciously pleased to promise." The document goes on to describe Alexander's challenge to these claims, explain that a compromise was reached, and eventually state: "That the whole [territories along the St Lawrence River] being divided into 16 parts, Sir W. Alexander shall have two parts and Earl Newburgh two parts, and the rest to be shared."[56] Thomas McGrail, in his biography of Alexander, asserts that Newburgh[57] was already in partnership with the Kirkes (which the aforementioned petition from 9 August would seem to confirm), and that in the late of autumn of 1628, his efforts on their behalf elicited a letter to Charles from the Scottish Privy Council expressing concern over any violation or dilution of Sir William Alexander's patent.[58]

The Scottish Privy Council did indeed take up the issue of Alexander's charter and its integrity. Their letter stated: "There are some making sute to your Majestie for a new patent of the said lands of Canada and of the trade thairof ... which in our opinioun will prove so derogatorie to this your ancient kingdome, under the greate seale whereof your Majestie hes alreadie granted a right to the saids bounds."[59] This statement of national will was odd, given the lukewarm reception that Nova Scotia and the Knights Baronet scheme had received in Scotland so far. Nevertheless, the intent of the letter was unmistakable.

It is in the novel reference to Newburgh that both the nature of Alexander's problem and the solution to the dilemma of conflicting

British claims in this part of the New World seem to lie. Newburgh was, in fact, an Englishman named Sir Edward Barrett. In 1625 and 1626 he had served as ambassador to France, on the latter occasion travelling with the duke of Buckingham.[60] For this service he was elevated to the Scots peerage by Charles I as Lord Barrett of Newburgh, County Fife. In 1626 he was appointed Chancellor of the Exchequer for England, and Chancellor of the Duchy of Lancaster. In 1628 he was admitted to the English Privy Council.[61] It is quite likely that his brother-in-law (and Alexander's friend) Lord Falkland, and his ventures in Ireland and Newfoundland, had piqued Newburgh's interest in colonial ventures. It is also possible that his time in France had given him some knowledge of the profits to be made from the Canadian fur trade, and the contemporary expectations that surrounded the new Company of One Hundred Associates.[62]

Although Newburgh and his partners – and perhaps other more neutral parties who simply wished to avoid further divisions at court – had been prepared to be felicitous where Alexander was concerned, they did have an advantage over him in terms of delivering an actual success against the French, which he had not yet been able to accomplish. As the supplication stated: "In opposition to the obtaining of this [the exclusive right to trade in Canada that the Kirke-Newburgh syndicate was claiming] His Majesty's gracious promise Sir William Alexander, Knight, Secretary of Scotland, pretends a sole right to the trade and plantation of those countries upon a grant from His Majesty under the great seal of the kingdom of Scotland procured *since the rupture between England and France* but hath not yet effected anything towards the displanting of the French, which patent is not yet produced [my italics]."[63]

What is most significant here is that the memorandum emphasizes Alexander's checkered past in his ventures, particularly since the war with France began, and notes that the displacement of the French from the St Lawrence was a regal priority. Given his role as secretary for Scotland, and the duties relative to the overall war effort that he was constantly performing, Alexander was scarcely in a position to disagree with any of this. Once more, the documents paint a somewhat different picture of this event than has generally been envisioned. Furthermore,

Alexander's son had already benefited from privateering activities in 1627, and he himself was often involved in similar issues, notably clarifying letters of marque issued under the authority of the government of Scotland. He could not gainsay a policy that had already worked to his favour, was a clear element of British military strategy, and touched upon his king's honour.

The Kirkes and their backers had a tangible success and the prospect of greater prizes on their side, whereas Sir William Alexander could point to nothing save the presence of some potential settlers, probably at Tadoussac. Indeed, a prevailing view that the exigencies of war would predominate was contained in the memorandum's third point, which asserted: "It is considerable that the grant of all patents for sole trade and plantation is laid upon conquest or discovery."[64] Surely a compromise could be reached, however. The memorandum answered that too:

> Supposing that Sir W. Alexander's patent doth invest him in a right
> of title to the trade and plantation in New France, yet Earl New-
> burgh and his partners having destroyed so much of the French
> plantation, taken so many of their ships, possessed themselves of
> their best pilots, pledges, and interpreters for the trade, and of all
> materials and instructions wherewith the French fleet was furnished,
> and discovered all the Gulf Islands, and River unto Kebeck, may
> well be admitted solely to the merit of having begun this conquest,
> so as to unite both kingdoms in a work that is large enough to
> spread the glory of it over both.[65]

It is highly significant that at this moment when Sir William Alexander's dream for a "New Scotland" was undergoing its greatest challenge, third parties should invoke the old principle of unity between England and Scotland that had animated King James VI/I. Ironically, the fluidity that multiple rule sometimes offered to the early Stuart monarchy had also laid some of the groundwork for a solution to this problem. Edward, lord Newburgh, was already a Scottish peer. On 2 October 1628 a major step toward a compromise between his faction and Alexander was taken, when Newburgh was enrolled as a Knight Baronet of Nova Scotia.[66]

Although this formal enlistment to Alexander's colonial enterprise did not remove every barrier to eventual co-operation (as Alexander's afore-mentioned November letter to Menteith demonstrates), third parties were clearly drawing the contestants closer together. Before completing that narrative, however, we need to take a closer look at the story of the Kirke brothers and their voyage to Canada in 1628. An understanding of the impact of those events will give us a better appreciation of the emerging partnership in London. After all, a war was on.

6

The Demands of Honour
and Charles I's
Unfolding Strategy

Wherefore now consider what you wish to do: whether you are willing
to surrender the settlement or not; for sooner or later, with God's help,
I must have it, and I should desire for your sake that it might be rather
with a good grace than on compulsion.

DAVID KIRKE (1628)

For a small and isolated outpost, home to fewer than seventy people in
the autumn of 1627, the murders of two members of the community
came as a great shock and stoked fears for the future. That October the
bodies of two young herdsmen who had been attending Quebec's
small stable of cattle on Cap Tourmente were found floating in the St
Lawrence. They had been stabbed, and their heads had been bashed in,
probably by repeated club blows. Samuel de Champlain was in a
quandary. His fellow Frenchmen at Quebec were certain that the guilty
party or parties must belong to a band of Montagnais who had been
encamped nearby. They wanted justice, as it was understood in Europe –
prosecution of the guilty and, following a trial, capital punishment. They
wanted an eye for an eye.[1]

This was not the first time Champlain had been forced to deal with the
stain of murder in the colony. Previous experience had shown him, however, that even if an admission of guilt was obtained, he would have to
accept the native definition of justice. He had learned this first in 1618
when a Montagnais killed a French locksmith and sailor while they were

fishing. The identity of the perpetrator was discovered when the two bodies, which had been weighted with stones and sunk in the river, floated
to the surface, and an accomplice gave him away. It was native custom
in such circumstances to punish the crime, rather than the criminal; the
family of the guilty man would give gifts to the victim's family in compensation for the life that had been taken.[2] Champlain had only agreed
to the observance of this custom after lengthy councils with the natives,
the Recollets, and his companions at Quebec. He even had to forestall an
attempted rescue of the murderer, in an incident that nearly led to further
bloodshed. Finally, with an eye to the future, he had agreed to accept the
native definition of justice and freed his prisoner in return for compensatory gifts from the Montagnais.[3]

In 1625 another shocking incident had taken place. That year Father
Nicholas Viel, one of the most ardent Recollet missionaries to the Huron,
failed to return to Quebec as arranged with the spring fur flotilla. The
Hurons with whom he had been travelling were elusive when the French
questioned them about the whereabouts of the priest, and only after
much badgering did they finally admit that Father Viel and a young Huron
convert had drowned in a canoe accident near the Island of Montreal.[4]
Champlain was away in France, but the French who remained at Quebec
deemed it safest to accept the story and make no further inquiries, even
though there were rumours of foul play among the Hurons, and despite
their belief that Viel had been drowned deliberately.

The death of the two herdsmen in 1627 was a different case again,
because even though they had clearly been killed with malice and fore-
thought, the identity of the guilty party had yet to be discovered. The
Montagnais promised to look for the perpetrator, and Champlain took
several hostages while the search proceeded. By January no trace of the
killer had been turned up. Then a party of starving Montagnais appeared
at Quebec offering to exchange three more hostages for food. Even though
winter provisions were already being rationed, Champlain agreed, and
thus became the guardian of three Montagnais girls who were baptised
"Faith, Hope, and Charity." Brother Gabriel Sagard recorded that
Champlain "took care of them as his own daughters."[5]

These dramatic events were only harbingers of greater troubles for
Champlain and the residents of Quebec in 1628. By June, rations were

so low that the company was reduced to eating mouldy hardtack and dried peas, and disaster was feared if a supply ship from France did not arrive soon. In desperation, Champlain fitted out a shallop to journey downriver to Tadoussac in hopes that supplies or news from France might be forthcoming. Before the excursion could set out, however, an Indian appeared at Quebec to report the sighting of six strange vessels in the St Lawrence.[6] Champlain was about to have his first encounter the Kirke brothers.

The partners in the Kirkes' syndicate, known as the Merchant Adventurers to Canada, had indeed been busy since receiving their letters of marque from Charles I at the end of 1627. They had used their connections with the Huguenot merchant community and, in assembling the crews for their ships, had enlisted a number of Protestant sailors from ports like La Rochelle and Dieppe. One of the vessels that departed for the New World that summer was skippered by a Huguenot named Jacques Michel, who had lost his right to trade in Canada when the Company of One Hundred Associates was formed.[7] Clearly, the Kirke-led expedition that was about to be launched cannot be seen simply in terms of state loyalties in time of war. In the coming conflict, allegiances would at times be maddeningly difficult to determine.

Arriving in the St Lawrence in early July, the Kirkes' squadron first encountered and captured a Basque fishing vessel, and used its crew to help pilot them up the river. Meanwhile, Champlain, desperate for information about the approaching flotilla, sent what he described as a "Greek" interpreter who was among the company at Quebec, on a secret scouting mission downriver, disguised as an Indian. The scout returned with terrible news. The squadron was English but it included several French Protestants, including Captain Michel. The Greek was accompanied by another man, Foucher, the overseer of the farm at Cap Tourmente.

Foucher reported that the Kirkes had taken Tadoussac and from that base had sent a raiding party of Huguenots upriver to Cap Tourmente. This party gained entry by claiming to have been sent by the Company of One Hundred Associates.[8] They soon dropped this pretense. Foucher's assistant, Nicholas Pivert, Pivert's wife and niece, and two servants were taken prisoner. Foucher had only escaped with the help of some Indians and he had been injured when the English fired after him. The destruction at Cap Tourmente was wholesale. The raiding party killed and butchered fifty cattle, and then burned the remainder of the herd in one of the stables. Two farmhouses and other buildings on the farm were also destroyed.[9] Champlain had no doubt that Quebec would be the next objective. He did not have to wait for long.

On 10 July a small boat crewed by some of the Basque fishermen and containing the former hostages, the Piverts and their niece, came ashore at Quebec. They carried a letter for Champlain that gave him the clearest indication of the situation the French now faced. It read:

Sirs, I give you notice that I have obtained a Commission from the King of Great Britain, my most honoured Lord and Master, to take possession of these countries, to wit: Canada and Acadia; and for that purpose we have set out eighteen sail strong, each vessel of which has taken its course as ordered by his Majesty. For my part, I have already seized the establishment at Miscou, and all the small craft and boats along that coast, as also those here at Tadoussac, where I am at present at anchor. You will also take notice that among the vessels that I have taken is one belonging to the New Company, which was on its way to you with provisions, and refreshments, as well as goods for trading purposes, and which was under the command of a man named Norot: the Sieur de La Tour was also on board and was coming to you; which ship I have boarded for my own vessel. I had made preparations for going to see you myself, but I have thought it better only to send an advice-boat and two shallops to destroy and seize the cattle at Cape Tourmente; for I know when you are distressed for want of food, I shall more easily obtain what I desire – which is, to take your settlement. And in order to prevent any ship arriving, I am determined to remain here until the season of navigation has closed, so that no ship may come to revictual you. Wherefore now consider what you wish to do: whether you are willing to surrender the settlement or not; for sooner or later, with God's help, I must have it, and I should desire for your sake that it might be rather with a good grace than on compulsion, so as to avoid the bloodshed that might occur upon

"Farm at Cap Tourmente, 1627," by Francis Back. The cattle kept at this farm provided meat and dairy products for the residents of Quebec. It was destroyed by the Kirke Brothers on their first incursion against Quebec in 1628.

both sides. If you surrender the place with courtesy, you may rest assured of receiving good treatment in every respect, both as regards your persons and your goods, which latter, on my faith and on my hope of paradise, I shall preserve as carefully as if they were my own, without diminishing them by the smallest possible portion. These Basques that I send you are men from the ships I have taken; and they will be able to tell you how the affairs of France and England are going on, and even the course affairs are taking in France touching the New Company created for this country. Send me word what you wish to do; and if you desire to treat with me in this matter, send me a man for that purpose, whom I promise to treat as well as myself, giving him every kind of satisfaction, and to grant any reasonable requests you may make on your resolving to give over

to me the settlement. Awaiting your reply, and your decision to do
as above expressed, I shall remain, Sirs, your affectionate servant,
David Kirke.[10]

The Kirkes had now played their card, and it remained for Champlain
to respond. Following consultations with his closest confidants he decided not to surrender Quebec. Perhaps the Englishmen would abandon
plans to take Quebec, or perhaps relief from France would save them. In
any event, he was resolved not to surrender to an enemy who had yet to
show himself. Champlain replied as follows:

Sir, We entertain no doubt as to the commissions which you have
obtained from the King of Great Britain. Great Princes always
choose men of brave and generous disposition, amongst the number
of whom he has selected you to fulfil the duty he has assigned to you
for the purpose of carrying out his commands; while, on your side,
you do us the favour of particularizing them, amongst others, the
capture of Norot and La Tour, who was bringing out our supplies.
It is true that the better a fortified place is provisioned, the better
it holds out against the storms of time; nevertheless the place can
make good its defence upon slender supplies when good order is
maintained in it. That is the reason why, having still grain, Indian
corn, peas, and beans, not to mention what this country produces,
a diet that the soldiers of this place can content themselves with as
well as they could with the finest kinds of flour in the world; and
knowing well that, were we to surrender a fort and a settlement
conditioned as we now are, we should not be worthy of the name of
men in the in the presence of our King, but rather be reprehensible
and merit chastisement in the sight of God and men, honour demands that we fight to the death. For these reasons I know that you
will think more highly of our courage if we firmly await the arrival
of yourself and your forces than if, in a cowardly fashion, we abandoned something that is so dear to us without first making proof of
your cannon, your approaches, entrenchments, and battery against
a place which I am confident, when you see and reconnoiter it, you
will not judge to be so easy of access as perhaps you have been led

to believe, nor its defenders to be persons destitute of courage to defend it, seeing they are men who have tried the hazards of fortune in many different places. Then if the issue is favourable to you, you will have more cause, having vanquished us, to bestow your offers of kind treatment, than if [without a struggle] we placed you in possession of a place the preservation of which is enjoined upon us by the strongest considerations of duty that can be imagined. So far as the destruction at Cape Tourmente and the burning of our cattle is concerned, this was only a little thatched building with four or five men in charge, who were taken unawares by the help of the savages. It is a matter of a few beasts dead which in no way diminish what we depend upon for our living; and had you come a day later, there would have been nothing for you to do [at that place]. We are now waiting from hour to hour to receive you, and resist, if we can, the claims you are making to these places, exempt from which I shall remain, sir, Your affectionate servant, Champlain.[11]

Champlain had called David Kirke's bluff and now awaited the attack on Quebec he was certain could come at any time. He soon discovered from the messengers who had conveyed his letter to Tadoussac how agonizingly close to being relieved they had actually been. Shortly after sending his initial letter to Champlain, David Kirke had learned of the arrival in the Gulf of St Lawrence of a fleet from France, sent by the Company of One Hundred Associates, and commanded by Claude Roquemont, de Brison. The convoy, authorized by Cardinal Richelieu himself, consisted of four ships, carrying around four hundred new settlers. They had departed from La Rochelle, and by July, were at Gaspé, fully aware of the presence of the English squadron at Tadoussac.[12]

Roquemont had dispatched a messenger alerting Champlain to his arrival. But, instead of trying to evade the English, and sneak upriver to Quebec, Roquemont decided to attack them. On July 18 the St Lawrence witnessed its first great battle between French and English forces. In fifteen hours of close naval engagement some twelve hundred salvoes were fired. Then, with several of his sailors dead, a wounded leg of his own, and knowing that he was running short of ammunition, Roquemont signalled his willingness to surrender.[13] The Kirkes' victory was complete.

Only one small ship in the French squadron managed to escape, but Roquemont, three of his captains, the crews and passengers, and the cargoes of the remaining ships were now in their possession.

With August approaching, and with it, the onset of autumn, the Kirkes now decided to abandon their plans to take Quebec until the following spring.[14] They doubtless knew that Champlain's situation was more precarious than he had admitted and that by leaving behind a garrison and ships at Tadoussac to watch the entrance to the St Lawrence, they could block approaches to Quebec and mount a siege at their convenience. [15] As suggested in the previous chapter, circumstantial evidence suggests that Sir William Alexander junior had also become aware of their encroachment on his father's charter, and may have opted to leave his party at Tadoussac as well.

Champlain was bitterly angry at the foolhardy risk that Roquemont had taken by engaging the Kirkes' squadron. Now, bereft of the much needed supplies from France, and with their ranks swollen by the addition of eleven refugees from Cap Tourmente and Tadoussac, the party at Quebec set about the grim work of provisioning themselves for the winter. Before the spring came they would, as in the previous winter, be on rations of just seven ounces of peas meal per day, much of which went into a broth containing acorns, roots, bran, straw, and, if they were lucky, fish.[16]

For their part, the Kirke brothers returned to England and to new celebrity. Most of their prisoners had been allowed to return to France, and it was members of this party who spread the word of what had taken place across the Atlantic. They also related that the agents of New France's peril were sons of Dieppe. When the news reached Paris, Louis XIII is reported to have declared the brothers public enemies, while investors in the Company of One Hundred Associates performed a ceremony in the Place de Grève, in which David, Lewis, and Thomas Kirke were burned in effigy.[17] France's Calvinists, a contemporary observed, were on the other hand joyful, and quietly boasted that they now controlled Canada.[18]

In London, where news about the war had been uniformly bad since the Cadiz campaign two years earlier, reports of the Kirkes' exploits on the St Lawrence were a fortuitous bolt from the blue. That autumn, a well-known London balladeer named Martin Parker captured some of the heartened public spirit in a new patriotic song, "England's Honour Revived." Sung to the tune of an earlier ballad, "King Henries going to Bulloyne," Parker's lyrics constituted both a triumphal expression of patriotism and a massive sigh of relief. As its first stanza enjoined:

> Attention give unto this gallant newes:
> Which commeth to revive our hearts
> Lately dul'd; to feele the smarts,
> Of those true Christians whom our foes misuse.

In the course of no fewer than twenty-two verses of sometimes very tortured metre, Parker retold the story of what had taken place on the St Lawrence, and made David Kirke the hero of late events:

> Thus our valient Captaine Kirk,
> Did the French men soundly jerk,
> And pur[ch]ast honour unto h' native land
> Oh had we many like to him,
> Then England would in credit swim,
> And France nor Spaine could not against us stand.

And finally:

> Our gracious King and Queene God save,
> With all the Privy Counsell grave,
> And send reliefe to Rochel in distresse,
> Oh now when earthly meanes doth faile,
> Let Heavenly power at last prevaile,
> Amen, cry all that doe true Faith professe.[19]

Parker had no way of knowing, of course, that distress was about to be caused for the "Privy Counsell grave," and the king for that matter, from two rather significant figures who did not entirely share London's joy over the Kirkes' exploits.

Once the sirs William Alexander, elder and younger, were aware of what had taken place along the St Lawrence the previous summer, they argued that if the Kirke-led company maintained and extended the territories it now claimed in Canada, they would infringe on lands promised to the elder Alexander as part of the original charter for Nova Scotia. That others in Scotland were aware that this potential encroachment created a novel situation and problem is evidenced by the previously cited letters exchanged between William Maxwell of Edinburgh and John Maxwell of Pollok, and by the letter the Scottish Privy Council sent to Charles I on 18 November 1628.[20]

The Alexanders certainly felt anxiety about the future integrity of their North American holdings. But, their unfolding challenge to the Kirke syndicate's claims need to be seen in the context of two other factors – Sir William Alexander senior's key roles within the government of Scotland, and the king's ongoing priorities for the war itself.

A brief survey of Alexander's duties over the course of the previous year finds him, not surprisingly, at the centre of a number of Charles I's key (and controversial) initiatives for his northern kingdom. He had also continued to accrue rewards from the king, and this strengthened his position when the crisis with the Merchant Adventurers to Canada came. In November 1627, for example, Charles had appointed Alexander Keeper of the Signet for Scotland, which basically meant that he collected a fee for every legal transaction that took place in the kingdom requiring crown sanction.[21] Charles's trust in his former tutor was implicit.

Naturally, the king expected dutiful service in return for such a handsome sinecure, and Alexander seems to have been providing that. The Revocation Scheme for recovering funds (technically) withheld from the crown during recent royal minorities had now expanded its inquiries into a very touchy subject for many Scottish landholders, monies they had received from former church lands, which the king now sought to recover. As a leading figure on the commission established to investigate these funds, Alexander found himself the object of increasing dislike and suspicion in Scotland, especially from those landholders who saw him as the lackey of a distant and arbitrary king. Charles pressed on, however, and continued to add to Alexander's responsibilities. In July 1628, when the Kirkes were conducting their naval operations on the St Lawrence, Alexander was commencing service on yet another controversial commission, this time, to undertake a full inventory of printed and unprinted laws in Scotland, with the objective of publishing a definitive compendium of Scottish law.[22]

Then, amid these other priorities, Charles made it known that he wished to visit Scotland for a coronation ceremony, within the next year if possible. A royal visit, with all of the accompanying pageantry of a coronation was bound to be expensive and Charles expected this to be funded by the Scottish Treasury. However, Alexander's kinsman by marriage, the lord treasurer of Scotland, the earl Mar, was convinced that the kingdom could not afford the king's presence unless a general tax was levied. As Mar wrote to the king on 18 July: "For munie, thaer is non in your coffers; your housssis ar in so evill caes as I feir, ye, nottonly I bott the Master of Wor and all your best and most skillfull servantts heir thinks itt onpossible that agaenst the tym prefixtt in your Majesties letters thay can be reddie to receive you according to that majestie that doth becom you."[23]

Just one month after Mar sent his letter, the duke of Buckingham was assassinated at Portsmouth, and the royal court was thrown into a frenzy, with individuals for and against the late favourite jockeying for position around the distraught king. Despite his grief, however, Charles seems to have been determined to press ahead with plans for a Scottish coronation. What followed was an unseemly round of political manoeuvring involving Mar, who opposed the king's plans, and his deputy treasurer, lord Napier, who had assured the king that Scotland's government could fund the visit.[24] Sir William Alexander was drawn into the dispute several times that autumn in his role as secretary for Scotland, and he seems to have tried to broker a compromise.[25] Regardless, this was a highly sensitive time for those in the king's employ, and in the wake of Buckingham's murder, Charles became even more discriminating over those he felt he could trust, and those he could not. Alexander had proven himself time and again, so when he approached the king with his concerns over the Kirkes' claims vis-à-vis Nova Scotia's charter, he did so discreetly, but from a position of long-held strength. The king did not wish to alienate his faithful servant.

The conduct of the war was another matter. In the late autumn and early winter of 1628–29, it remained an unmitigated disaster everywhere, with the lone exception of the Kirkes' exploits the previous summer. Now, pressed by both the Kirke-Newburgh and Alexander factions for clarification regarding distant and abstruse colonial boundaries, and realizing that victory over the French in Europe was unlikely to come any time soon, Charles and his advisors appear to have recognized a new reason for prosecuting the war. If the Kirkes' gains could be solidified, and a successful plantation was made in Nova Scotia, the French might be swept from North America and its waters, the lucrative fishery and fur trade would belong to British interests, while a British empire, stretching from Newfoundland to Virginia would be in the offing.

That a pressing need for some coordinated strategy in the North Atlantic existed was already apparent from reports the Privy Council had received earlier that autumn. Newburgh had reiterated the need for additional ships to shield the St Lawrence in his petition of 9 August (although at that point his consortium was offering to pay for this protection themselves), while in late August, Lord Baltimore, now resident in Newfoundland at his colony of Ferryland, had written letters to both Charles and Buckingham, describing naval actions he had undertaken against the French. To the king, he related that England's fishing fleet had been greatly disturbed by French raids, but that he had engaged them with his own ships, captured seven French vessels, and returned them to England. In his letter to Buckingham (he had no way of knowing that the duke was now dead), Baltimore added that he had been responsible for sixty-seven French prisoners of war for most of the summer, a burden that had taxed his and the colony's resources. In both letters he emphasized the need for naval support from home, and to the king, he requested that "two men-of-war at least may be appointed to guard that coast for his own safety and that of many thousands of British subjects."[26]

Charles and his advisors evidently believed that Baltimore was giving a reasonable assessment of Newfoundland's security needs. In December Secretary of State Francis Cottington wrote to Lord Treasurer Weston informing him that Baltimore's request for a ship had been granted. The ship initially to be discharged was the *St Claude*, one of the French vessels Baltimore had captured the previous summer. It was described as "good and warlike," but Will Peasley, Baltimore's agent in London, subsequently asked that a different ship, the *Espérance*, be provided instead.

By the end of the month it was recorded that Baltimore's son, Leonard Calvert, had taken delivery of the *St Claude*, and also that Baltimore and his merchant investors were having difficulty dividing the prizes that he had seized under the terms of his letter of marque.[27]

Lord Baltimore's actions off Newfoundland, the Kirke brothers' operations on the St Lawrence River, and the young Sir William Alexander capture of the *St Lawrence* of Lübeck in June 1627 were just three examples, close to this story, of how Charles I was using proxy naval forces in the North Atlantic, operating under letters of marque, to prosecute his war. We can only speculate about how far desires for profit may have eclipsed patriotism for those who were involved in these operations, but it is reasonable to assume that they represent a mixture of motives.

It is evident that such operations did not yet constitute any sort of overall strategy for continuing to engage the enemy, or consolidating territorial gains that had been made in Canada. To this point, all operations had taken place independently and on an *ad hoc* basis. It seems, however, that in the early winter of 1629, Charles, his advisors, and the private individuals who would have to carry out future actions against the French in the North Atlantic, were devising something much more comprehensive.

Charles I rarely received plaudits for his diplomacy or his ability to create a coalition of interests. In the case of the competing parties for Canada and Nova Scotia, however, he was successful in bringing the Kirke-Newburgh syndicate and the Alexanders together. As we discussed in the previous chapter, efforts had been made throughout the autumn of 1628 to stave off further quarrels between these factions. Charles doubtless wished to avoid having to choose between a loyal advisor who had known him since boyhood, and had proffered long service to his father and himself, and a syndicate that had delivered his only real success in the war with France.

Indeed, Charles seems to have taken an active role in bringing the factions together and in February 1629, a new incarnation of the Company of Adventurers to Canada was formed.[28] This success stands as an important, though underrated effort on Charles I's behalf, to provide crown leadership in directing an overseas ventures, with particular reference to reconciling the desire to found colonies, with commercial interests, and the prosecution of the war. Furthermore, given the nationalities of the principal figures involved, the formation of a new company that featured both English and Scottish interests demonstrated that this king remained eager to see subjects from both of his sovereign kingdoms co-operate in specific colonial and commercial efforts.

The result of this intervention was that when the Kirkes made their successful return to the St Lawrence, and Sir William Alexander the younger led a renewed colonial expedition to Nova Scotia in the spring of 1629, they now did so as part of an effort that was "British" in scope, and that had, as one of its goals at least, carrying the war with France to the North American theatre.[29]

Once more, the context of the European war, and the geography of the North Atlantic world, must be presented as supporting evidence for this hypothesis. As Charles I and his advisors worked to bring the Kirke-Newburgh and Alexander interests together in the winter of 1628–29, they must have realized what such a partnership could accomplish. There was every reason to believe that the Kirkes would complete their operations against Quebec when they returned to the New World that summer, and the French would thereby be eliminated from the St Lawrence.

For his part, Sir William Alexander had capitalized on one opportunity opened up by the new partnership. Over the winter he had gained the allegiance of Claude de La Tour, the French licensee in Acadia and one of the prisoners the Kirkes had captured on the St Lawrence the previous summer. Alexander, therefore, had good reason to expect that the coming summer would finally witness the planting of a successful colony in his chartered territories.[30] But, separated by hundreds of nautical miles, the English and Scottish partners in the Merchant Adventurers to Canada would be unable to coordinate their defences, and were unlikely to be able to share intelligence regarding any French activities in their respective areas. Lord Baltimore's situation at Ferryland had already demonstrated the vulnerability of existing colonies. Finally, it was essential to consider the defensive capabilities of these existing and prospective holdings in the late winter of 1628 and early spring of 1629, because British intelligence sources in France confirmed that the Company of One Hundred Associates was outfitting a fleet of its own in Dieppe, to be deployed for the relief of Quebec, and to sweep British shipping from the St Lawrence. Defensive needs were recognized as well, and specific mention was made of the need to reinforce the naval resources of Lord Baltimore in Newfoundland.[31]

The pieces were almost all in place to secure what amounted to British or allied possession of the North American coastline from Newfoundland, all the way south to Virginia, with one exception.[32] Sir Robert Gordon of Lochinvar had never managed to plant his colony on Cape Breton Island. In the eighteenth century, the French would come to recognize the strategic importance of this position, and affirm its priority by making the fortress of Louisbourg their pivotal defence position for guarding the St Lawrence River. The British interests who in early 1629 were planning for the defence of Newfoundland, the conquest of Quebec, the planting of Nova Scotia, and the co-ordination of operations against the French in the North Atlantic seem to have recognized the need to secure Cape Breton Island and its adjacent waterways as well, because in the spring of 1629, hasty plans were laid to plant a British colony there.

To better understand the strategic imperatives attached to the Cape Breton installation we must next turn to the story of the man who was tapped to lead it. As will be seen, his life intersects with many figures we have met so far, and his decision to go to the New World when he did, and for the reasons he did, offers a useful case study of the workings of contemporary politics, patronage, and colonial ventures. That man was James Stewart of Killeith, fourth lord Ochiltree.

7

A MAN OF CONTROVERSY: JAMES STEWART OF KILLEITH, FOURTH LORD OCHILTREE

> Ochiltree insisted still vith his accustumed bauldness. His arguments
> var far mor vittie nor having any ground of treu vidsom
> or judgementt founded upon reson.
>
> THE EARL OF MAR (c. 1626)

On 3 September 1651, Oliver Cromwell's English New Model Army defeated a Scottish force of fifteen thousand men at the Battle of Worcester. For most Scots, this was a dolorous event. It meant that their kingdom, which had been ardently defending its independence since the union of the crowns in 1603, was about to be absorbed into an expanded English republic. But one who must have welcomed the new order was an otherwise frustrated old man, who within a few weeks, obtained release from his prison near Linlithgow, at Blackness Castle. For James Stewart of Killeith, fourth lord Ochiltree, the freedom granted him by the new regime marked the end of a twenty-year ordeal, and perhaps, a chance to be reinvented yet again. Much was now changing in the British Isles on the heels of more than a decade of civil war and revolution, and most people were having to adapt to altered political and religious realities. For them, the need to change was obvious. Ochiltree, by contrast, was fighting with ghosts from a generation that had now passed.

What had happened to cause a former advisor to the king, a leading figure in Britain's early colonial efforts, and a scion of one of Scotland's most remarkable families, to be sentenced to perpetual imprisonment, only to emerge twenty years later to a world he barely knew? The answers lie in the dynamics of the early Stuarts' kingdoms and courts, and the vagaries of colonial and military activities on both sides of the Atlantic in the early seventeenth century. Together, they created a potent mixture, which, when added to Ochiltree's ingrained foibles, set him up for a remarkable rise ... and a terrible fall.

Lord Ochiltree's personal trajectory is important in our story for three reasons. The first is that he illustrates perfectly the blend of service to the crown and expectation of patronage that was so central to personal advancement in early modern Britain. In his case, service to the crown in remote parts of the British Isles, the Orkney Islands and Ireland gave him the desired resumé to lead a new colony when that opportunity arose. In this context Ochiltree presents a useful case study, showing some of the reasons why an individual, and in this instance a member of the Scottish nobility with significant political connections, would opt to go to the New World. The second element of importance is the nature of Ochiltree's colony. Its origins lay in strategic concerns that were particular to the spring of 1629 and the British kingdoms' war with France. In that sense it stands out from other contemporary colonial initiatives. Finally, Lord Ochiltree's fall from grace in the eyes of his king, Charles I, is a hitherto under-appreciated component of the story of Sir William Alexander's efforts to create a "New Scotland" in North America. Had Ochiltree's life not taken the fateful turn that it did in 1631, his presence might have helped Alexander hold onto his disputed lands in North America, and Britain's colonial profile in North America might have been very different. In order to understand these interconnections, we must, therefore divert our attentions to Ochiltree's life and times, and bring them into the context of British initiatives in the North Atlantic world in the late 1620s.

Controversy was part of the fourth lord Ochiltree's birthright. His father, James Stewart of Bothwellmuir, had been a solider of fortune in the army of the United Netherlands in the late 1570s. When he returned to Scotland, his guile and family connections brought him to court, where he made an immediate impact on the young James VI. In December 1580 he helped strengthen the position of the royal favourite of the time, James's cousin, the duke of Lennox, by accusing the former regent, the fourth earl of Morton, of complicity in the 1567 murder of the king's father, Lord Darnley. As a reward, Stewart was admitted to the Privy Council, and was granted the earldom of Arran in Bute in April 1581.[1] The importance of crown patronage for this family was clear almost from the outset.

As earl of Arran, James Stewart fell out with Lennox shortly after Morton's execution, however. During the Ruthven conspiracy, when the king was kidnapped by a coterie of ultra-Protestant nobles who feared the Catholic Lennox's influence, Arran was in turn imprisoned. Crucially, during this tumultuous period Arran managed to retain James's confidence. When the king escaped from the Ruthven Raiders in 1583, Arran emerged as his leading counsellor, and eventually became his chancellor. He fell from power, however, because he could not overcome the triple threats to his position that came concurrently from the opposition of Queen Elizabeth's counsellors to his role in James's government, the animosity of ardent Presbyterians in the Kirk, and the deep resentment he had fostered among prominent members of the Scottish nobility.

In the summer of 1585, when Arran was implicated by Elizabeth's council in the death of an English courtier in a border skirmish, James was forced to make him a ward in St Andrews Castle. Further intrigues followed, and by April 1586 Arran had been sent into exile.[2] When he returned to Scotland, he found his efforts to re-establish himself at court and to reconcile himself with the kirk were not to be realized, and his diminished position was affirmed by the fact that he thereafter resided on his estate in Ayrshire under the name Captain James Stewart. The story of the rise and fall of Captain Stewart, Ochiltree's father, came to a conclusion in 1595, when was ambushed and murdered by Sir James Douglas of Parkhead, the nephew of Regent Morton.[3]

The impact of all these events on the future lord Ochiltree can only be surmised, but it is more than evident that he was the subject of a different sort of controversy even before his birth. His mother, Lady Elizabeth Stewart, was the eldest daughter of the fourth earl of Atholl. Prior to marrying Arran she had been the wife of Hugh, sixth lord Lovat, and following his death she had married the bishop of Caithness,

Robert Stewart. As the bishop was already in his sixties when he wed Lady Elizabeth, and perhaps because his early training in the pre-Reformation church had dampened his desire for marital relations, the union was not a happy one. Soon, Elizabeth was seduced and became pregnant by Arran. Even though a divorce was granted and Arran married her in July 1581, their son James was born three months in advance of the wedding. This meant that baptism could not immediately be performed and that Elizabeth had to endure the discipline of the Kirk.[4] Young James thus carried the aspersion of being born out of wedlock, and his earliest memories must have been affected by his father's political fall and exile. It should also be recalled that he was just thirteen when his father was murdered.

Controversy and decline, therefore, were central elements of young James Stewart's life. This notwithstanding, the fortunes of his branch of the family did not prevent his relatives from maintaining prominence in Scottish affairs and their position would eventually permit James Stewart to try and recover his and his family's fortunes. In the years after his father's fall, it was James Stewart of Killeith's cousin, Andrew Stewart, third lord Ochiltree, who retained the closest family connections with the crown. This was the same lord Ochiltree whom we met in connection with the Scottish government's efforts to pacify the Borders region, and the Highlands and Islands in the early years of James VI/I's reign (see chapter 3). We recall that he had played a prominent role in both initiatives, but that his outlay of funds for the crown in the 1608 expedition to the Isles had especially damaged his financial situation, and that as one remedy, he had transferred the Ochiltree lordship to his cousin, James Stewart of Killeith in 1615.[5]

James Stewart of Killeith, the newly minted fourth lord Ochiltree, had not merely waited for his cousin to open doors for him. Prior to receiving the title, he had tried, albeit unsuccessfully, to regain the lost earldom of Arran. Although he was frustrated in this endeavour, he still managed to obtain a potentially lucrative sinecure from the king, and to draw attention to himself while in royal service.[6] When the government in Edinburgh began to assert greater crown control over the earldom of Orkney in 1613, James Stewart of Killeith was named lord chamberlain and sheriff, and obtained a nine-year tack on crown lands in the Orkney and Shetland islands.[7] This meant that he was given the lease on these crown lands and was able to assume the rents of the tenants on those lands.

The new lord's assumption of these positions came during a turbulent period in the northern islands that saw the kinsmen and supporters of earl Patrick Stewart rise in rebellion against the central government. Until late in 1614, when the earl of Caithness assumed command, James Stewart of Killeith was entrusted with the task of suppressing the rebellion, and in this role, he managed to earn praise from the king and the Privy Council.[8] In performing these services he was essentially assuming roles for the crown in a remote sector of the kingdom that was analogous to the contemporary services provided by the likes of his cousin Andrew Stewart (the third lord Ochiltree) and Captain John Mason in the Hebrides, and the Protestant planters who were establishing settlements in Ulster.

Along with these achievements, and his elevation to the peerage in 1615, the new lord Ochiltree's political future seemed to brighten. He was appointed to be among the forty men to comprise the Lords of the Articles (the committee that prepared business for full meetings of the Scottish parliament) for James VI/I's visit to Scotland in 1617.[9] In 1618 he was selected to be a member of the General Assembly of Perth, which addressed James's desires for sacramental changes in the Scottish kirk.[10] If Ochiltree had not known Sir William Alexander previously (and it seems most likely that they were already acquainted), he would certainly have met and begun to work with him in these years. Circumstances would soon align them closely.

In 1619 Ochiltree was made one of the new commissioners of the peace for Ayrshire, and in February 1620 he was named to the commission considering voluntary contributions from Scotland for the relief of the Palatinate.[11] Again, he would have worked with Alexander in this capacity. Overall, as Ochiltree approached his forties, it would have been reasonable to suggest that he had risen above the problems associated with his father's past and had become a fairly significant actor in his native kingdom. However, Scottish affairs were not that simple. Beneath the appearance of progress, Ochiltree was in fact a highly vulnerable figure, owing to his kingdom's political factionalism, and his own heavy debts. As we shall see, although his career had already touched Sir William Alexander's in some fairly significant ways, they differed in one important respect. Unlike Alexander, Ochiltree did not enjoy open-ended credit in the form of ongoing royal patronage and escalating favours from the king. How did his financial liabilities affect his future decisions?

––––––––––

Money was a considerable problem for the fourth lord Ochiltree, despite his apparent successes in the political arena. In particular, his anticipation of profiting from the collection of crown rents in the northern isles had proven to be a false hope. The funds he expected to obtain from his Orkadian tenants were insufficient to cover his tack from the crown, and records suggest that during the years in which he held it, he made himself infamous among his tenants through his methods of rent collection.[12] That he owed money to the crown, and that the king may have come to regret the commission he had made to Ochiltree, is evident in related state correspondence.

In July 1620 James VI and the Privy Council exchanged letters on the subject of overdue rents from Orkney, and these imply that Ochiltree's superiors were strongly considering transference of the tack. In one instance the members of the council promised to: "acquent youre maiestie quhat, in oure opionionis, we holde fittest to be done bothe for youre maiesteis proffeit and weel of the subiectis. We haif beene spairing to be too hastie or to precipitat this bussynes, becaus thair is tua yeiris of the said Lord Vchiltrie his tak as yitt to rinne, bot we sall vse such conuenient diligence thairin, as sall giff vnto youre maiestie satisfactioun."[16] A year later, Ochiltree's financial problems were again mentioned in a letter to court, this time by the earl of Melrose, secretary of state for Scotland. Melrose intimated that Ochiltree had fled from Edinburgh rather than attend a meeting with his creditors that had been organized by the second marquis of Hamilton.[14]

Ochiltree's situation did not improve and in 1622 he was one of a number of men cited in a list by Melrose for being delinquent in their taxes. In Ochiltree's case, he owed £20 for that year alone, which represented half the yearly rents for the Kirk in Orkney.[15] Not surprisingly, a combination of debts to the crown and others, coupled with numerous protests over his behaviour from his Orkadian tenants to the Privy Council, caused him to be deprived of his tack when it expired in 1622.[16]

These incidents represented just one facet of the new lord Ochiltree's financial difficulties. Like his cousin Andrew Stewart, Ochiltree had gained property in Ireland, and by 1623, it can be inferred from the Privy Council records that he was spending much of his time there, presumably as a way of avoiding his creditors at home. His negative balance was serious enough that a lien was put on his Scottish property to prevent him from selling without first paying his debts. A petition to the Privy Council on 20 August 1623 by no fewer than nineteen of his creditors (including several merchants, an advocate, two burgesses of Edinburgh, a minister's son, and an apothecary) demonstrates the situation he was in. "Lord Stewart owes them large sums of money under various obligations and for satisfaction thereof, he has come from Ireland to Scotland at the petitioners' request, intending to sell his estate for their benefit, which he cannot conveniently do in the face of an execution raised against him by the petitioners, which prevents him from freely negotiating with buyers. The petitioners, therefore crave the Lords to grant a protection to Lord Stewart, that he may be free from arrest for a certain time."[17]

From these developments, it can fairly be stated that by the closing years of James VI's reign, the fourth lord Ochiltree was walking a tightrope between political advancement and financial ruin. As we have seen, he was not alone among the Scottish nobility in having debt problems. Two things about Ochiltree need to be emphasized, however. First, references to him in various letters and state papers give the impression of a man who inspired scant confidence among those with whom he had business dealings.[18] Second, he did not enjoy the advantage of easy access to crown patronage, or the confidence of the king, that benefited others of his class like his colleague Sir William Alexander.

Finally, Ochiltree's political career to date had not been free of damaging personal controversies. With the king residing in London after the union of the crowns, competition for royal favour among his subjects who remained in Scotland was always intense. But, the relatively smooth lines of communication that had existed between the court and Scotland during the first years of James's reign were coming to an end. After the king's only return visit to Scotland in 1617, it became ever clearer that to succeed in Scotland, one needed to have friendly advocates present at the court in England.[19] James was always short of money himself, and he was concerned over reports, of whatever veracity, that suggested financial irregularities in Scotland. It is in this context that another significant incident from Ochiltree's political career must be viewed.

We have seen that a combination of factors ultimately led to the revocation of Ochiltree's tack on crown lands in Orkney and Shetland in 1622. In the years preceding this, one of his most dogged critics had been Sir Gideon Murray of Elibank, Deputy Treasurer for Scotland. In early 1621 Ochiltree became incensed with what he perceived to be harassment from the deputy treasurer, and "the strictness which he [Murray] had used in calling him [Ochiltree] to an account for the duties of Orkney." His response was to accuse Murray of embezzlement and the abuse of his office. When these accusations reached the court, James ordered an investigation of the deputy treasurer's conduct.

Murray was humiliated. Most historians, and many contemporaries, have credited him with being a sincere and effective official, and the fact that the king would launch an investigation into his conduct seems to have driven him to the breaking point. On 28 June 1621 he was found dead, and speculation soon arose that he had either taken his own life or had died of melancholy brought on by his loss of the king's trust. Whatever the case, Murray's supporters were certain that Ochiltree's accusations made him culpable in the deputy treasurer's death, and they were not reserved in their condemnations. As Archbishop John Spottiswood of St Andrews remarked· "By his death the King did lose a good servant as ever he had in that charge, and did sore forethink that he should have given ear to such detractions. But of that pestilant sort some will never be wanting in the Courts of Princes, and happy is the King that can rid himself of lyers in that kind."[20]

On its own, the story of Ochiltree's accusations against Murray, and the latter's untimely death, might be passed off as an unfortunate incident of personal rivalry. It was more than that, however. The investigation of Murray's conduct in 1621 took place in the context of court-centred anxieties over revenue shortfalls from Scotland, and a desire at court to finance relief for the Elector Palatinate, which was at that time James's major foreign policy priority. While Ochiltree had come close to prospering from his political involvement in these issues, he had consistently been stained by controversy. Certainly there was little evidence from his career to this point that he could, or would, rise any higher in political circles. But, the accession of Charles I in March 1625, and the new king's desire to obtain new revenues in Scotland, soon offered Ochiltree the chance to wield some real influence.

In early October 1625, when Thomas Erskine, the earl of Kellie, wrote one of his regular letters from the royal court to his cousin in Scotland, John Erskine, the 19th earl of Mar, political tension was in the air. In the course of the letter Kellie shared the impressions he had gleaned in England about the new ruler of the British kingdoms and his advisors' handling of affairs for Scotland. He noted: "The pairtye that first motioned the seperatione of the Consell from the Cessione hes bein and is now berrye bissye upone that subject ... Their hes bein mutche discourss bothe in Court and Consell of the managin of the Kings steate their, and as I heir all proceids from one waye, and as I heir the Lord Ochilltrye is a great doeare."[21]

Kellie was referring to a proposed restructuring of the political and legal systems in their native Scotland – a scheme favoured by the king, and one that would have prevented members of the nobility or the Privy Council from serving on the Court of Session. Given the fourth lord Ochiltree's checkered career up to that point, it was surprising that Kellie would identify him with such a major initiative. In the weeks to come, Kellie and Mar would have further cause to be concerned about his activities. They would eventually come to see Ochiltree as a menace who was using new-found influence with the king and over certain Scottish affairs in what they believed was a most harmful fashion.

This correspondence took place at the time when Charles and his closest advisors on Scottish affairs were formulating the controversial Revocation scheme, with its unprecedented aim of seeking revenues that may have been owed to the crown dating back for almost a century.[22] We have already recounted that concerns about this scheme were widespread enough that in January 1626 the leading members of the Scottish Privy Council were called to London for a conference on Scottish affairs. It was at this gathering that they saw for the first time the actual text of the planned revocation. It was also here that Ochiltree showed how far he had risen politically in just a few months, and how superbly capable he was of alienating those around him.

The earl of Mar, who attended the meetings in his capacity as lord treasurer of Scotland, kept a journal of what occurred during the sessions at the palace of Whitehall. From Mar's account, we learn that Ochiltree had become part of a faction of younger (and generally dissolute) lesser Scottish nobles and lairds who, through their connections with Charles's entourage, had begun to assert an increasing degree of influence with the new king. Charles's antipathy toward many of his father's former advisors, especially older members of the Scots nobility, was already the subject of court gossip. At the January 1626 meeting, James's principal advisors from Scotland – Mar, Melrose (who was then president of the Privy Council but was soon replaced by Sir William Alexander), and the lord chancellor, Viscount Dupplin – confronted this newly ascendant group for the first time. Prominent among them were several courtiers of note: Robert Maxwell, the earl of Nithsdale (who, despite heavy debts and the fact that he was Catholic, was connected by marriage to the royal favourite, the duke of Buckingham); Patrick Lindsay, the bishop of Ross; Sir Alexander Strachan of Thornton; and Lord Ochiltree. Sir William Alexander and Sir John Scot of Scotstarvet, who were veterans of Scottish politics by this point, were also included in this circle. To the amazement of the privy counsellors who had made the journey south, this block had increased its function to that of a sounding board for Charles on both the Revocation scheme and the proposed alterations to Scotland's government, specifically the new provisions for membership on the Court of Session.[23]

The antipathy that Mar and his colleagues felt for their compatriots was never far from the surface during the conference. At one meeting, in the presence of the king, Melrose described Nithsdale and Ochiltree as men who: "hes maed shipwrak of thaer aun esteitts, and vald now fish in drumlie vatters by shakkin all things louss that thay may gett sum partt to thaem selfs; sum of thame having no vitt att all, sum of thaem bot half vitted, and nether of thaem grett honestie."[24] For the likes of formerly trusted Scottish councillors like Mar, Melrose, and Dupplin, such pointed criticisms can only have been made out of supreme frustration and disillusionment.

Ochiltree's part in these proceedings seems most incongruous. Surprisingly, he was chosen to act as the king's spokesman on the Revocation during a session held on 19 January, despite the fact that he had virtually no experience in this level of government. In this role he signally failed to impress the senior privy counsellors with his grasp of the Revocation's conventions and potential liabilities. Mar's view was that Ochiltree had encouraged the king's mistaken belief that there was no difference between his proposed revocation and those of his predecessors. Armed with a clear knowledge of the relevant statutes and precedents, Mar must have had Ochiltree (and Charles) on the defensive throughout the meeting. Nonetheless, ignorance does not appear to have restrained Ochiltree in his enthusiastic support for the king's sketchy program. As Mar later recorded: "Ochiltree insisted still vith his accustumed bauldness. His arguments var [were] far mor vittie nor having any ground of treu vidsom or judgementt founded upon reson."[25]

This was not the only time during the sessions that Ochiltree earned the lord treasurer's criticism. At the meeting on 13 January they had disagreed over the king's assertion that privy counsellors should be shielded from prosecution for their debts, while on 18 January, Mar accused Ochiltree of spreading gossip about possible Catholic leanings among the Scottish entourage.[26] Overall, one gets the sense that Ochiltree was operating far beyond his own capacities, in the presence of men who had good grounds to disdain him.

In trying to step back from the very real political issues that swirled around the Revocation issue and assess how much Ochiltree's participation in the 1626 meetings indicated a rise in his political fortunes, we encounter a frustrating lack of evidence. Why was he attending meetings of this sort? Had he done something, or did he know someone who helped to ingratiate him with the new regime? Should Ochiltree now have been seen, for example, as an "Anglicized courtier" of the sort who represented Charles I's emerging disinclination to seek counsel from his senior advisors in Scotland, as some historians have suggested?[27]

Altogether, this explanation seems unlikely. What we have seen of Ochiltree's career up to this point stands against this characterization and shows rather that his activities prior to 1625 were confined to Scotland, and perhaps Ulster. There is no indication before the beginning of the new reign that he had been in England at all, let alone that he had been there long enough to become *Anglicized* (my italics). How he managed to gain influence at court upon Charles's accession is, therefore, very much in question.

Circumstantially, it seems most likely that a more powerful patron – the senior Sir Alexander perhaps, or more likely, the earl of Nithsdale – had recommended him for inclusion in the circle. All three had worked together previously, and Nithsdale and Ochiltree were both from the southwest of Scotland. Mar's journal entries portray them as allies. And yet, there is very little concrete evidence from which to speculate further. Ultimately, what seems most significant is that after the meetings of January 1626, Ochiltree's name is absent from the records relating to the implementation of the Revocation, as well as Charles's other alterations to Scotland's government and legal system. Even modern scholars who have commented on his participation in the early stages of these schemes have been (not unjustifiably) content to forgo further consideration of his role in Scottish affairs.[28] Lord Ochiltree seems to have disappeared.

The most likely explanation for the lack of further information about Ochiltree is that in the wake of the difficult meetings at Whitehall, where he had not performed particularly well, the king and his inner circle saw no further need for his services. Thereafter, he may simply have retreated to his position of relative obscurity, from which he may have kept in touch with court events through friendly contacts like Alexander, whose star was clearly on the rise among the Scots at court. Alexander would later demonstrate his own confidence in Ochiltree where his proposed colony was concerned.

In the meantime, this inference may be supported by considering Nithsdale's immediate fate as a mirror for Ochiltree's. Nithsdale had been one of Charles's most enthusiastic proponents of Revocation, and although the scheme's actual origins have never been proven, he probably helped in its conception. Charles had made him collector-general for taxation in Scotland in 1625, protected him from his creditors, and in the spring of 1626 made him a member of the newly created Scottish Council for War, where he served with the likes of Alexander. In early 1627 Charles named him to the Scottish Privy Council and sent him to Edinburgh, where his personal unpopularity had grown so great that it was rumoured he might be assassinated. With a reputation among his enemies as a rather dim-witted, Catholic rumour monger, and as someone whose

personal debts exceeded £126,000, Nithsdale faced bleak prospects if
he chose to tarry in his native kingdom.[29] It is not surprising, then, that
by the spring of 1627, he had embraced his king's military ambitions in
the Thirty Years' War as a way to retain favour and influence.[30] Did
Ochiltree wish to do the same sort of thing? If so, what options were
open to him?

It seems that Ochiltree, like Nithsdale, was also forced to look elsewhere for new opportunities because his avenues in England and Scotland had closed. Unlike Nithsdale, however, Ochiltree was no longer so
well connected. Where could he turn? The senior nobility of his native
kingdom reviled him. His debts were considerable, and fear of his creditors likely dissuaded him from trying to live in Scotland any longer. He
had once enjoyed access to the king and the opportunity to influence
policy making, but his poor performance in connection with the Revocation scheme had ended this option and made him an outcast. What he
did possess, however, was quasi-military and administrative experience   .
in a maritime theatre (the Orkney Islands), plantation experience in
Ulster, and a long-standing working relationship with Sir William
Alexander. In the spring of 1629 these factors combined to offer Ochiltree yet another opportunity to serve his king, and to attempt a personal
reclamation in the process.[31]

We can now return to the plans that had been unfolding in London for
operations in North America in the spring and summer of 1629, and fit
Lord Ochiltree into that story. The reader will recall that during the early
winter of 1629 the elder Sir William Alexander had agreed to unite his
endeavours in planting Nova Scotia with the Kirke-Newburgh syndicate's aspirations to control the St Lawrence, in a new incarnation of the
Merchant Adventurers to Canada. We have also mentioned that this
partnership represented more than a simple harmonization of commercial interests. If successful, these two initiatives would see agents loyal to
the king of France swept from Canada and Acadia. In the process, another blow could be delivered against the French as part of the ongoing
war; British interests in Newfoundland, New England, and Virginia
would be buttressed; and defensive resources could be shared. Such co-

ordination was wholly in keeping with home defence measures that the British governments had employed in the current war since 1625 and indeed with security needs for British installations in North America that had been speculated upon in writings dating back to the first Elizabethan interests in Newfoundland.[32] Now, the convergence of wartime priorities, in combination with the right personnel, created the potential for a new and coherent British strategy across the Atlantic.

The decision reached sometime in the spring of 1629 to place a colonial installation on Cape Breton Island under the command of James Stewart of Killeith, fourth lord Ochiltree, has its place within this wider context. As we have discussed, overall plans for the year called for the Kirkes to renew their assault on Quebec, while the young Sir William Alexander proceeded to finally plant his colony at Port Royal in Acadia.[33] Ochiltree journeyed to London sometime during the winter of 1628–29, and even though his name had never appeared in any document connected with Nova Scotia, or any other overseas venture, prior to this point, he obtained a grant of £500 from the king for the purpose of planting a new colony on Cape Breton Island.[34] While no correspondence survives to indicate the origins of Ochiltree's interest in overseas ventures, the timing of the financial grant, along with the composition of his party, suggests several possibilities.

It may be that Charles's grant to Ochiltree was a reward for his efforts on the king's behalf in relation to the Revocation scheme in 1625–26. Or, as Ochiltree's debts at home and his failure as an advocate for the king's controversial Revocation program cannot have given him many opportunities for success in his native kingdom, he may have viewed emigration as a chance for a fresh start. It is also possible that Charles saw the grant as a way of ridding himself of an underling who was no longer useful as an advisor and may have been a lightning rod for dissent, but who could be of service in establishing firm colonies. Finally, it has been suggested that Alexander solicited Ochiltree's assistance because he was experienced with colonial ventures, dating from his efforts in Ulster.[35]

One thing does seem certain. Ochiltree did not have a complete knowledge of the colonists who were to settle with him on Cape Breton Island, and many of them do not appear to have fit the profile of "Best Britainnes" that Alexander had defined, years earlier, in *An Encourage-*

ment to Colonies.[36] According to one contemporary observer, Ochiltree's party contained eight families of English Brownists who were leaving their homeland because they could no longer countenance membership in the Church of England. Richard Guthry, who had sailed with Ochiltree as part of the young Alexander's contingent, noted that: "Eight households of his company hiding fire under ashes for a time, at last it burst forth shewing there ingratitude to my Lord, having been at great charge with them and the rottenewss of there hearts, a thing verry common among all factionists and schismaticks for in plain terms they refused to joyne stocks with my Lord, and did separate themselves from their company they will admitt none to their society without publick confession ... they glory in the name of Brownists."[37]

Whatever his other characteristics, Ochiltree never seems to have been associated with sectarian controversies, and it is most likely that he either played no role in enlisting these settlers, or that they were engaged so quickly that incompatibilities were never gauged.[38] Again, this rush to place a colony on that island intimates strongly that strategic, military imperatives were of primary concern in the spring of 1629; otherwise, Ochiltree's party might have been better employed settling with Alexander's group in Acadia. The Alexanders probably thought they were on the verge of entrenching Nova Scotia once and for all that spring, thanks to the presence in their company of another significant individual.

Claude de Saint-Étienne de La Tour had been involved with the fur trade and French colonial initiatives in Acadia since first joining the installation of sieur de Poutrincourt at Port Royal in 1609. He had survived Samuel Argall's 1613 raid on Acadia, had constructed a fortified residence called Fort Pentagouet near the mouth of the Penobscot River, and had managed to make handsome profits over the years by selling furs and fish. Just as was the case with Quebec and related trading issues along the St Lawrence, La Tour had, over the years, been forced to navigate through a number of licenses and monopolies. Poutrincourt's son Charles de Biencourt had remained close to La Tour and his family, and when Biencourt died in 1623 his will designated La Tour's son Charles as his heir in Acadia. The family's interests were soon undermined, however, by renewed threats from England.

The establishment of the Pilgrims' colony at Plymouth in 1620 had already occasioned some conflicts, and an increased English presence in the region had forced the La Tours to abandon Fort Pentagouet in 1626. The news that France and the British kingdoms were at war in 1627 thus caused the elder La Tour to return to France, hoping to gain military support in Acadia. It was there that he learned of the formation of the Company of One Hundred Associates and the cancellation of existing fur trade monopolies in the New World. Although this threat to his son's inheritance from Biencourt and to the family's interests in Acadia may have caused concern, Claude de La Tour accepted an assignment from the new syndicate, and the spring of 1628 found him aboard ship for Quebec as part of the sieur de Roquemont's squadron.[39] It was as a member of one of these ships' companies that La Tour participated in the naval battle with the Kirke brothers' fleet that had caused Champlain's supplies to be cut off that July. La Tour's ship had been captured, and La Tour taken prisoner.

La Tour's story in the ensuing year illustrates how fluid loyalties could be where overseas ventures were concerned. Evidently La Tour was treated very well by the Kirkes, and upon their return to England, he gained an introduction at Charles I's court in London. His extensive knowledge of Acadia and his personal charms meant that he had no difficulty meeting important people and gaining their trust. La Tour was now a widower and soon began a romance with one of Queen Henrietta Maria's ladies-in-waiting. They were married in the early spring of 1629.[40] More important for our purposes, he became fast friends with Sir William Alexander, and agreed to accompany his son on his expedition to settle Acadia/Nova Scotia.

The Alexanders unquestionably saw the advantages of having a seasoned colonial hand, with extensive knowledge of the country they wished to plant, as part of their operation. For his part, La Tour's actions speak of pragmatism rather than disloyalty. The French government had provided little support in the past, and now the Company of One Hundred Associates had trampled on his family's rights. Altogether, he had seen plenty of first-hand evidence of the French government's inability to protect its claimed territories in the New World. Enlistment by the Alexanders probably seemed to be the best way to get back to his son, and to shield their interests. As we shall see when our story shifts back to Quebec, he was not the only individual who faced this sort of stark choice in the face of the current war.

By the spring of 1629 everything seemed to be in place for comprehensive British actions on the North American Atlantic seaboard. A well-armed ship had been sent to Lord Baltimore to help defend Newfoundland. The Kirkes had assembled a new flotilla to renew the assault on Quebec. Sir William Alexander the younger not only had reassembled a colonial party to take to Nova Scotia but he also had the advantage of Claude de La Tour's expertise and assistance to ensure that this time the plantation efforts would be successful. Finally, they had the recent inclusion of Lord Ochiltree and his colonial party, who could be expected to provide a screen for Nova Scotia on its Atlantic approaches.

They had to make haste that spring, however, because British intelligence sources in France confirmed that the Company of One Hundred Associates was outfitting a flotilla of its own in Dieppe, to be deployed for the relief of Quebec and to sweep British shipping from the St Lawrence.[41] The renewal of hostilities was imminent, and the British partners would have to move with alacrity if they were to succeed – for themselves and for the honour of their king.

8

MIXED MOTIVES AND THE
COMPANY OF MERCHANT
ADVENTURERS TO CANADA

But whatsoever shall haue beene taken by them, shall be restituted on the
first asking, if so be that present restitution and relaxation hath not beene
made thereof, as soone as they cam into the Port or Hauen.

THE PEACE AGREEMENT OF SUSA (1629)

The syndicate that now styled itself the Company of Merchant Adventurers to Canada represented an obvious compromise. It also promised
opportunities for everyone involved, including its proprietors, investors,
prospective settlers, and King Charles I and his governments. Altogether,
success for the Kirke brothers in taking Quebec and controlling shipping
in the St Lawrence, if coupled with the planting of secure installations
under Lord Ochitree on Cape Breton Island and the young Sir William
Alexander in Acadia, could spell profits, new colonies, and military
victories against the French. There were good reasons for co-operation.
But a niggling mystery surrounds the extent to which the various expeditions being mounted by the Merchant Adventurers in the spring of
1629 operated in concert with each other.

As with the 1628 voyages, some historians have suggested that
Alexander's fleet, which was destined for Cape Breton and Acadia, joined
the Kirke brothers' flotilla, bound eventually for Quebec.[1] Given the
recent origins of their partnership and the advantages that would be
gained from sailing as a convoy, there are good circumstantial reasons
for assuming this sort of co-operation. The scant documentary evidence

relating to these operations in the spring of 1629, however, argues against a joint sailing.

In November 1629, David Kirke made a deposition before England's High Court of Admiralty in which he stated that his fleet, consisting of six ships and two pinnaces, set sail from Gravesend on 26 March 1629 and arrived on 15 June at Gaspé at the mouth of the St Lawrence, where they traded with the local natives. From there the party made for Tadoussac to plan the assault on Quebec.[2] By contrast, in the only surviving description that refers to the departure and voyage of the Alexander parties, we are told that they weighed anchor at the Downs off the coast of Kent on 24 May 1629. The author of this account was the aforementioned Reverend Richard Guthry, who was part of Alexander's party bound for Acadia.[3]

The difference in these dates may only indicate that the Kirkes' flotilla lingered in the Downs for several weeks, taking on provisions, or waiting for Alexander and Ochiltree to get their ships ready. Only four names of the six ships that comprised the squadron of David Kirke are known, so the other two may have been conveying the Alexander and Ochiltree parties.[4] What is intriguing, however, is that Guthry's account, in addition to telling the story of a near engagement on the high seas with a Dutch fleet, which Kirke omits, states that their contingent arrived at Newfoundland in mid-June and then made for Cape Breton Island.[5] Kirke's deposition makes no mention of landing in Newfoundland, and neither account mentions the other party.

In light of the ways in which things unfolded in the spring and summer of 1629, the discrepancies between these accounts may only be minor curiosities … except for one thing. Owing to events that were taking place simultaneously in France and Italy, it would prove absolutely crucial to determine who departed from where, and when, and what the individuals concerned knew when they sailed for North America. First let us explore the French component of this dynamic.

We have already noted the reaction in France to the Kirke brothers' near success in taking Quebec in 1628. Not surprisingly, governmental, corporate, and public outrage led to immediate steps to try and save Quebec, defend the monopoly rights of the Company of One Hundred Associates, and avenge the King of France's honour.[6] Cardinal Richelieu solicited a wide range of opinions before appointing a veteran naval officer, Isaac de Razilly, to outfit and command a relief flotilla for Quebec. Razilly in turn recruited Captain Charles Daniel, who had previously served in New France in the Compagnie de Caën, and had led fishing expeditions in the waters off Cape Breton where he had engaged in conflicts with Basque fishermen. Daniel was to provide two ships to the expedition, but it was as a combat officer that he would make his greatest mark.[7]

English agents in France were aware of the plans being mounted for the spring of 1629 and, as early as February of that year, reported to the Privy Council that the French were organizing some twenty ships for "Canada, Terra Nova [Newfoundland], and St Christopher."[8] This intelligence had played an important role in causing the new formation of the Merchant Adventurers to Canada in the first place. Captain Daniel's report of his actions that spring states that he prepared his two ships at Dieppe, and left there on 29 April for Chef de Baie to await Razilly, who was outfitting nearby at either La Rochelle or Brouage. The entire operation was thrown into confusion on 19 May, however, when a proclamation was posted in Chef de Baie.[9] France and the British Kingdoms had reached a peace agreement. The importance of that development emerged from the northern Italian city of Susa.

Louis XIII's and Charles I's representatives had actually been engaged in quiet negotiations for several months. The death of Buckingham in August 1628, and the capitulation of the Protestants of La Rochelle that October had removed both Charles's most hawkish advisor and the primary justification for a continued war. With Buckingham gone, a significant factor in Charles's household turmoil had also vanished. Furthermore, in January it was announced that Queen Henrietta Maria was pregnant; the French and British royal families would therefore be drawn even closer together by blood ties. Meanwhile, on the part of the French, rising tensions with Spain over their traditional rivalries in Italy had caused Cardinal Richelieu to rethink the potential value of a British alliance. Although there were delays, and mediation from the Venetian ambassador proved crucial, by 14 April 1629 the peace agreement was reached at Susa.[10] Its publication one month later (the proclamation that forestalled Captain Daniel) included the following stipulations:

And whereas many Commissions on both parts haue beene
graunted to make warre vpon the sea; and forasmuch as vpon the
day prefixed in the Treaty, nor vpon the day of publication thereof,
the Captaines that are at sea cannot haue knowledge thereof, there
is granted vnto them the space of two moneths from the day of the
signature of the said Articles, to returne home; during which time
what may be done by them, shall not be taken for a rupture or con-
trauention to this present peace: But whatsoever shall haue beene
taken by them, shall be restituted on the first asking, if so be that
present restitution and relaxation hath not beene made thereof,
as soone as they cam into the Port or Hauen.[11]

The cessation of hostilities had an immediate impact on the proposed
French squadron. Razilly was ordered to remain in port and was eventually given new orders to sail for the Mediterranean to protect French
shipping from Moorish pirates.[12] Charles Daniel, on the other hand,
recorded that he waited until 26 June before departing for Canada with
a fleet of four ships and one barque belonging to the Company of One
Hundred Associates. He was fully aware of the changed circumstances
related to the late war, and that his task was to re-provision Quebec, not
to engage in naval warfare or plunder.[13] It is not at all clear whether the
Kirke brothers, or the Alexander-Ochiltree parties, were aware that peace
had been reached when they embarked, separately or together, however.
Nonetheless, May 1629 found both expeditions at sea, and because their
destinations and specific objectives were different, it will be clearer to
deal with their immediate fates separately. We begin with the Kirke
brothers and their designs on the St Lawrence.

As commander of the expedition, David Kirke had three immediate
objectives that spring. The first was to reconnoitre the Gulf of St
Lawrence and to gather information about the presence and strength of
any enemy vessels in the general vicinity. He accomplished this via trade
with the local Indian population at Gaspé in mid-June. Tadoussac, the
port of first call for any European ships heading upriver toward Quebec,
had been taken the previous summer and had been occupied by the
Kirkes' agents, and possibly by the aforementioned settlers deposited by
the young Sir Alexander. Once he had returned to Tadoussac (the second

objective) and confirmed that his force would not be threatened immediately by any hostile shipping in the area, David Kirke could take his time planning to capture Quebec. If the Kirke brothers had not already suspected it, intelligence gained at Tadoussac would have confirmed that Champlain and his company had emerged from the previous winter in very dire straits.[14]

Champlain was explicit in his memoirs in recording that the winter of 1628–29 had been even more difficult than was anticipated. Facing starvation, illness, and grave divisions within the population at Quebec, he adopted stern measures to ensure bare survival. Nevertheless, the grinding agonies the company faced had even caused discussion of such desperate contingencies as the complete abandonment of Quebec, if a friendly Indian village could be persuaded to act as hosts, or a raid of conquest into Iroquois territory, which would have seen them capture and occupy a provisioned village. Ultimately fears that the exertions involved in either venture might be too much for his party, and perhaps as important, that they risked the expenditure of precious shot and powder that were also in short supply, made Champlain decide to wait for relief from France, and hope that the crops they planted in the spring might provide them with enough food when they could begin harvesting in the late summer.[15]

By early June, however, the need to do something tangible had become overwhelming. A reconnaissance expedition was dispatched to Tadoussac to try and make contact with any French ships that might be in the area, but that party soon returned with word of the arrival of the Kirkes' squadron. Champlain's brother-in-law, Eustache Boullé, was placed in command of thirty men and the habitation's only pinnace, and instructed to sneak past Tadoussac and resume a search for French ships as far afield as Newfoundland. If none were discovered they were to undertake the dangerous trans-Atlantic crossing, and alert the authorities in France to Quebec's plight. The expedition departed on 26 June but was soon captured by the Kirkes' party at Tadoussac, where they became David Kirke's prisoners.[16]

Those remaining at Quebec were not left in anticipation over their own fates for very long. On 19 July three English ships commanded by Lewis and Thomas Kirke appeared in the St Lawrence below Quebec, and when low tide permitted it, a tender was dispatched containing an English officer, who under a flag of truce, delivered the following message to Champlain:

> Sir, In pursuance of what my brother wrote to you last year, that sooner or later he would take possession of Quebec, unless it were reinforced, he has instructed us to assure you of his friendship, as we assure you of ours, and knowing well the state of extreme destitution in which you are with respect to everything, he calls upon you to place the fort and habitation in our hands, assuring you of the best treatment for yourself and your people, and also of as honourable and reasonable a settlement as you could desire. Awaiting your reply we remain, Sir, Your very affectionate servants, Louis and Thomas Kirke. On board the Flyboat, this nineteenth of July, 1629.[17]

Champlain read the letter before his adjutants and sent this reply:

> Gentlemen, The truth is that negligence, or the hindrances caused by bad weather, or the perils of the sea have prevented the arrival of the relief that we were expecting in our suffering, and have put it out of our power to resist the carrying out of your design, as we did last year, without giving you an opportunity of making good your claims, which, if it please you, will only be realized now on condition of your carrying into effect the offers you made us of a composition, the terms of which we shall communicate to you very shortly, after we have decided on them; awaiting which, you will be good enough not to allow your vessels to come within cannon shot, nor attempt to set foot on land until everything shall have been settled between us, which will be for tomorrow. Meantime I shall remain, Gentlemen, your affectionate servant, Champlain. This nineteenth of July, 1629.[18]

The ensuing parleys, between Champlain and Lewis Kirke especially, revealed that the courteous tone of the exchange of letters was genuine. Champlain's request that the Kirkes produce warrants showing that they were acting under Charles I's authority in conjunction with the war could not be met immediately because David Kirke held these documents at Tadoussac. Champlain had asked for a provisioned ship to convey the members of the Quebec garrison back to France, but the Kirkes could only promise transport to England, with guarantees that from there, passage would be arranged to France. Champlain wanted Quebec residents to be able to purchase food for the voyage by trading beaver skins, and assurances that any surplus pelts would not be confiscated. Humane treatment was to be guaranteed to all persons, and special mention was made of good carriage for the Jesuit and Recollet missionaries. Most especially, Champlain demanded that Hope and Charity, two of the three native girls to whom he had acted as foster father, be allowed to go to France with him.[19]

The younger Kirkes would not give final consent to this last demand, and replied that their brother David would explain his reasoning personally. In the interim, Champlain seems to have impressed upon Lewis and Thomas that his relationship with the girls was paternal, and that they wished to accompany him wherever he might go. Beyond this, it was agreed that the residents would be permitted to take whatever pelts they owned personally, and the garrison's soldiers were guaranteed the possession of their arms, personal property, and one beaver skin. The priests could take away their clothes and books. A particularly bitter discovery for Champlain was that three men of long acquaintance, Étienne Brule (who had first come to Quebec in 1608, and in 1610 had been sent to live with the Hurons); Nicolas Marsolet (a veteran fur trader and interpreter of Montagnais), and Pierre Raye (whom Champlain describes as a "waggon-maker by trade, [and] one of the most perfidious traitors and scoundrels in the lot," were now in league with the Kirkes. Yet another Frenchman working for the Kirkes, a Huguenot named Le Baillif, from Amiens, was also in the contingent. Champlain recalled him as a sometime agent of the Compagnie de Caën, and it is significant that once he disembarked at Quebec, Le Baillif immediately seized the de Caëns' storehouse, which Champlain said contained between 3,500 and 4,000 pelts.[20]

Champlain on a number of issues attests that he and the two Kirke brothers overseeing the surrender of Quebec dealt amicably. He recalled

"Champlain Surrenders Quebec," by C.W. Jefferys.
This twentieth-century conception illustrates the
military honours that were observed when the Kirke
brothers took Quebec.

that Lewis Kirke refused Champlain's offer of his quarters, and that he
permitted the priests to celebrate Mass in their chapel one final time.
Lewis also acceded to Champlain's suggestion that an inventory be taken
of all goods and materials that were in the installation. In what must
have been a heart-rending moment, Lewis Kirke "had the English flag
hoisted on one of the bastions, ordered drums to beat to assemble the
soldiers, whom he had placed in order on the ramparts; he then had a
salute fired from the ships as well as with the five brass guns at the fort,
the two small falconets at the factory, and some iron mortar-pieces; after
which he made all his soldiers fire volleys of musketry – the whole in
sign of rejoicing."[21]

While such scenes must have carried an air of finality, Champlain
indicated that he maintained some optimism for the future. When the

widow and son-in-law of Louis Hébert asked his advice on whether to stay or leave, he told them there was no reason to believe the new masters at Quebec would violate their property or harm them if they stayed, and that the labours the whole family, including its late patriarch, had put in, justified protecting their assets. Besides, he told them, they could bide their time, make money selling produce to the garrison and trading, and await developments. Perhaps the French would return. If not, he suggested, their religious convictions should be their ultimate barometer, and if they were not permitted to practise as Catholics that this should be the major determinant for their return to France.[22] Nevertheless, Champlain also records that for him, remaining at Quebec to await final arrangements was painful. So, with Lewis Kirke's permission, he and the two native girls, and his belongings, were soon sent to Tadoussac with Thomas Kirke, to meet with David Kirke and await transportation for France.

The journey downriver was for Champlain both dramatic and sadly reminiscent of Roquemont's failed effort to relieve Quebec the previous year. On the second day of the voyage, when they were some twenty-five leagues from Quebec, a French ship was sighted. Émery de Caën, who had been dispatched by his cousin to collect their company's property and furs from their Quebec depot, was in command. Thomas Kirke sent Champlain and his companions below decks and then took aggressive action. In the ensuing battle, the two vessels first exchanged cannon fire at a distance and then moved in for close-quarters fighting. Kirke's crewmen flung stones and cannon balls onto the French ship's deck and soon the two vessels struck each other and were locked together. Three of Kirke's men had been killed, but when Kirke ordered the boarding of the French ship Caën surrendered. Champlain's last hope for delivery seemed to have passed.[23] In an ensuing interview, however, Caën related that he believed a peace agreement had been reached between France and the British kingdoms. Although Champlain does not say so, he may thereafter have speculated on the timing of this agreement, and whether it might cause Quebec to be transferred back into friendly hands.

To help understand this incident, we must emphasize that the nationalities and loyalties of those who had engaged in the recent battle on the St Lawrence should be viewed pragmatically. In his later discussions with

his brother-in-law (Boullé) at Tadoussac, Champlain heard more rumours
about the relief expeditions that were planned by the Company of One
Hundred Associates for the relief of Quebec, and about separate undertakings on the part of the Jesuits to send supplies and support to their
brethren. Boullé had met Émery de Caën on the river prior his capture by
David Kirke's men, and Émery had provided more information about the
composition of the proposed relief flotilla, the participation of Razilly and
Daniel, and the reduction of this fleet once peace had been declared.
Champlain was certain from these discussions that the Caëns' true
intention had been to remove as much of the fur stock as possible from
Quebec, and that the cousins feared the Company of One Hundred Associates every bit as much as they did the "English" privateers.[24]

On the surface, this would appear to indicate perfidious and self-
serving motives on the part of the Caëns. However, they may be excused
if a desire for profits outweighed an anachronistic sense of patriotism.
Guaillame Caën's Protestantism effectively barred him from participation in the Company of One Hundred Associates, and that royal consortium had supplanted the Caëns' monopoly rights, which had been
nominally guaranteed up to 1635.[25] Under the circumstances, they had
no more cause to expect the protection of their assets from their fellow
Frenchmen than they did from the new threat that appeared in the form
of the Kirke brothers.

France's religious divisions spilled over into the conflict on the St
Lawrence that summer in other ways that were quite personal. The
Huguenot captain, Jacques Michel, was described by Champlain as
David Kirke's "rear-admiral," and he appears to have thrown in his lot
with the Kirkes for both religious reasons and commercial reasons that
were similar to the motives of Émery de Caën.[26] Champlain castigated
him in their interviews for betraying both his king and his religion, thus
suggesting that Michel was a convert to Protestantism. Champlain also
cites these twin betrayals as the cause of Michel's demise, and the reasons why he soon died in raving, feverish state.

The evidence suggests that relations between Captain Michel and
David Kirke had deteriorated over the summer. Although they had acted
in accord up until the time Champlain was brought to Tadoussac, a joint
visit to Quebec sometime in August marked a turning point. Michel

claimed thereafter that the Kirkes had treated him with nothing but contempt and ingratitude, and that David Kirke had been an incompetent commander. Michel had evidently developed a disease of some sort, which caused paranoid ravings. He alluded to the brothers' French antecedents by calling David Kirke "formerly a mere wine merchant at Bordeaux and Cognac," and told Champlain bitterly: "I have left my country, as they left theirs, to serve a foreigner, and I shall never be happy again; everybody will abhor me, and I have no hope of returning to France."[27]

Michel reportedly said something else as well, however, which is significant toward our understanding of the North Atlantic seafaring community. His rant to Champlain reflected the frustrations of a dying man, who believed his partners had betrayed him. Nevertheless, he told Champlain that if he lived, and the Kirkes did not give him his just desserts, then he would have other options to explore: "They will have recourse to me again, I feel sure of that; they are not in as good a position as they think; and just as it was through my shrewdness that this business was set on foot, I know the way to turn them out of it, and to teach them and others that it is not prudent to provoke a man like me. There are plenty of Dutchmen and men of other nations; and if one thing fails me I can find something else."[28] Such, for some, was the mercenary nature of life on the high seas in the early decades of the seventeenth century. David Kirke, for his part, seems to have treated Michel's death throes as an anathema, and afterward ensured that his late colleague was buried with full military honours.[29]

A personal episode for Champlain, which also carried some religious undertones, concerned the fates of his "daughters," Hope and Charity. He had expected that Lewis and Thomas Kirke might be able to persuade their brother to allow the two native girls to accompany him to France, but David Kirke held firm in his opposition, citing correspondence from the aforementioned Nicolas Marsolet, Champlain's former protégé who had gone into the Kirkes' service along with Étienne Brûlé. It is unclear whether they had compounded this betrayal by rejecting Christian practice altogether or, as is more likely, they had commenced some Protestant practices that Champlain found abhorrent, such as eating meat on Fridays. Regardless, Marsolet related to David Kirke that natives from the vicinity of Trois-Rivières had threatened to attack Quebec and seize it themselves, if the girls were sent to France. In what must have been a most dramatic scene, Hope, the older of the two girls, accused Marsolet of lusting after her, and together with her sister, begged Kirke to ignore the letter and allow them to accompany Champlain, who had obviously earned their respect and affection.[30]

If Champlain's version of these events is true, then David Kirke emerges as cold-hearted and indifferent to the fates of two defenceless girls. Perhaps he truly feared that Quebec's safety required him to make concessions to native opinion. Marsolet might have duped him. It is also possible that the issue was seen as an irritant in his broader endeavour, which was to ensure that Quebec remained in British hands. Again, if Champlain is correct, then the brothers had quarrelled about other matters; he relates that David chastised Lewis Kirke for permitting the performance of a mass at Quebec after its surrender, and for accepting Champlain's written inventory of the goods that were at Quebec when he took possession. Overall, the sources that provide these anecdotes treat them in isolation, and relations between the Kirke brothers and their French prisoners seem to have been mostly cordial, and conducted according to the understood rules governing the treatment of prisoners of war. Champlain even says that he passed his time at Tadoussac hunting with David Kirke.[31] As will be seen, disputes over the contents of Quebec's warehouses would soon result in litigation, so it is possible that Champlain may have been altering certain facts to suit his later version of the story.

Of more importance is the fact that in these circumstances Champlain and his accomplices were treated leniently, and that the terms by which they had surrendered were essentially observed. In late September David Kirke embarked from Tadoussac with his prisoners. By 20 October they had reached Plymouth, where, according to Champlain, Kirke learned for the first time of the peace between France and the British kingdoms – news that apparently angered him greatly. In keeping with the surrender terms that Champlain and Lewis Kirke had reached at Quebec, the main body of the French party, including the Jesuit and Recollet missionaries, were deposited at Dover, where arrangements were made for their repatriation to France. Champlain decided to make straight for London and an interview with the French ambassador.[32] Although his encounters with the Kirkes would now shift to England's High Court of Admiralty, Champlain recognized that he had been properly treated as a prisoner of war up to that point, and had been granted his freedom as soon as it was determined that hostilities had ceased. These actions compared most favourably to the treatment given to the defeated parties in the other North Atlantic theatre that saw action in the summer of 1629 – Cape Breton Island.

Captain Charles Daniel, who already knew that the war between France and the British kingdoms was over, had departed from Chef de Baie, on his relief expedition for Quebec on 26 June. Somewhere on the Grand Banks he was separated from the other three ships of the flotilla in a heavy fog. Sailing on alone, he encountered and overtook an English vessel bound for Cape Cod. After inspecting its Captain's commission, and assuring him that the late war was over, Daniel let the ship go. He then anchored in an inlet known to the local natives as the Grand Cibou, close to modern day St Ann's on Cape Breton Island. It was here that he learned of the presence on the island of Lord Ochiltree and his installation, Fort Rosemar.[33]

Richard Guthry recorded that the Alexander and Ochiltree parties had reached Cape Breton Island from Newfoundland on 1 August. After trying to make contact with some fisherman who fled ashore, on 2 August they encountered three more fishing vessels at Port aux Baleines, located midway between the cape that gives the island its name and the present day village of Little Lorraine, some thirty miles from the site of the eighteenth-century French fortress of Louisbourg. As Guthry relates, the strategic possibilities of this general location were not lost upon the prospective settlers:

We drew toward the Shoare, and espied ane harbor called Port Ballance tuo leagues from Port Anglois where we found three Ships, fishermen, tuo of Rochell of the religion [presumably Protestant] the third a Bascaigne, we entered the harbour, and upon deliberat tryall found her prise to the General's use. My Lord Uchiltrie determined to plant there, and by ye advise of Capt. Ogilvy, built upon a small

rocke a fort with three small pieces of Ordinance, a place strong
enough, furnished with ordinance, to command the sea and land.
The fort was named by our Generale Rosemarine.

We have already indicated that Ochiltree's settlement should be viewed
as a hastily assembled military colony, one that owed its origins to the
exigencies of war, and the particular circumstances of the North Atlantic
theatre, and not one that falls into the more conventional classification
of a plantation, which would connote agricultural or other resource-
based activities that could sustain permanent settlement.[34] That was the
long-standing objective for Sir William Alexander junior's prospective
colony, but Ochiltree's primary responsibility that summer was to erect
a military post that could assert Charles I's claims, and by extension the
rights of the Merchant Adventurers to Canada, in a crucial theatre that
linked the St Lawrence with Nova Scotia. Again, if a successful planting
in Nova Scotia, which had proved so elusive in the past, had been the
Alexanders' sole objective, Ochiltree's party would have accompanied
them to their final destination on the Bay of Fundy.

The real value of placing a colony on Cape Breton Island was that it
could offer a communications and defence link between the existing and
projected British holdings in the North Atlantic. In addition, Ochiltree,
as leader of the settlement, fit the profile as a quasi-military leader for the
Cape Breton colony. As we have noted, just a few years earlier, while on
royal service in Orkney, he had administered and participated in such
activities as coastal patrols, the interdiction of pirates, and the establishment of fortifications.

Other members of the colony in addition to Ochiltree had a military
background. Along with the aforementioned Captain Ogilvy, who advised
him about the location of Fort Rosemar (and about whom nothing more
is said in any documents surrounding the venture),[35] his party featured
at least a third experienced military man, a Scottish mercenary officer
named Constance Ferrar, who was a veteran of the European wars.[36]
Equally telling was the fact that Ochiltree's party carried a hefty supply
of guns, ammunition, and heavy artillery, and were evidently prepared
to take an aggressive stance from the time they arrived on Cape Breton
Island.[37] While it is true that the make-up of the Ochiltree group con-

tained elements that were not conducive to the creation of a garrison settlement (the aforementioned Brownists), it can nonetheless be inferred that a good number of his party expected to play a combination of defensive and coercive roles in their new home.

Guthry's account gives a sense of the palpable frustration that arose when the dissenting faction of Ochiltree's contingent revealed that they were religious separatists who had no intention of living with the main body of the settlement.[38] Overall, however, that discovery seemed to be an inconvenient distraction, and religious differences would ultimately not prove crucial to the Cape Breton settlement's fate. As far as Ochiltree's colony was concerned, the assumption that the war was on, and that the king's rights must be asserted and defended, lay at the heart of all initial undertakings and caused the colonists to assume an aggressive stance from the start.

As Guthry relates, one of the party's first acts upon arriving in the waters off Cape Breton was to attack and capture a sixty-ton Portuguese barque (they mistakenly believed it was French) that they found at anchor near the site of their proposed settlement. The ship was dismantled and stripped of its cannon, which were then used as additional artillery to guard Fort Rosemar.[39] As well as building this defensive fortification, Ochiltree and his party showed further signs that their colony was meant to be something other than an agricultural plantation. Throughout July and August, Ochiltree supervised patrols of the fishing grounds around Cape Breton Island, and instituted a 10 percent duty on all catches made in the region. If the skippers of the fishing vessels, of whatever national-ity, were unable to produce a license from Charles I's government giving them permission to fish in those waters, Ochiltree confiscated their catches and, in some cases, their boats. That he and his party possessed sufficient arms and patrol boats of their own to carry out these operations is additional fodder for the notion that they were to be alert for ongoing hostilities.[40] These soon materialized.

Captain Charles Daniel, who already knew that the war was over, made up his own mind to take a hostile approach to the Anglo-Scottish party at Fort Rosemar. He had earlier in his expedition dealt peacefully with one English vessel at sea, but when he heard of the actions of the Kirke brothers against Quebec, and on the St Lawrence, and learned of the activities of the Ochiltree party from some local natives on Cape Breton Island, he determined to become an aggressor – and, perhaps, an avenger.

In reconnoitring the area, Daniel learned several intriguing and troubling things about the Anglo-Scottish settlement that had been planted near the place the French called Port aux Baleines. The party, he was told, was led by a Scottish lord, a certain "James Stuart," who had become the terror of French and other foreign fishermen in Cape Breton waters. According to one French captain whom Daniel met, the British interlopers had raided his ship and stolen his cannon. They were now using these as the principal guns for the fortified residence they called Fort Rosemar. Others had suffered as well. Since landing in early July, the British had been confiscating the catches of any fishermen who could not produce licenses issued by Charles I![41]

Daniel believed his course was clear. The region belonged to his king, by virtue of long-standing French claims, and because the Treaty of Susa precluded the taking of any new territories by the former combatants. While he might be unable to perform his duties to Champlain, he could certainly deal with the party at Fort Rosemar.

With his own command of fifty-three men and a cadre of friendly Indians, Daniel believed he stood a better than even chance of matching his adversaries. But, given the gunnery Ochiltree's party possessed, Fort Rosemar seemed unlikely to fall in a direct assault. So Daniel opted for a ruse. First, he captured two shallops manned by fishermen from Fort Rosemar, and imprisoned them on another part of the island. Next, on 10 September, he approached Rosemar and assured the British that his party was coming in peace. According to Ochiltree, Daniel cited the recent signing of the Treaty of Susa as proof of the new amity that existed between their sovereigns. Then, the accounts of the participants diverge. In a report on the incident that Captain Daniel prepared for Cardinal Richelieu in December 1629, he stated that Fort Rosemar fell in a direct assault, and that the party inside offered a stout defence.[42] This assertion was corroborated by André Malapart, another member of Daniel's force, whose own memoir of the event was published in Rouen in 1630. Malapart related that the French had bombarded Fort Rosemar from their ships, while a force of soldiers led by Daniel conducted the actual assault. Malapart also stated that he lost an eye and part of one hand in the action.[43]

Ochiltree's version of the taking of Fort Rosemar was different. He later stressed that the French had approached his installation under false pretenses, claiming that they came in peace owing to the suspension of hostilities between their kings.[44] Once inside the fort, however, they fell upon Ochiltree and his party, disarmed them, and took their clothes. Ochiltree's adjutant, Captain Ferrar, later testified that the French had tricked them.[45] Whichever version of the taking of Fort Rosemar one wishes to believe, the result was clear. Captain Daniel was now master of the installation and a party of British prisoners.

Hereafter, the sources are in basic agreement. Daniel proved to be a harsh captor. He ordered Ochiltree and his company to demolish their fort, after which he force-marched the prisoners from Port aux Baleines to Grand Cibou. There, he had them construct a new fortification, which Daniel christened Fort Sainte-Anne. Once the installation was completed, Daniel left a small party behind to act as a garrison, and set sail for France.[46]

Ochiltree later complained bitterly about the treatment his party received from their captors. In written testimony, he accused Daniel of treating his prisoners like slaves and depriving them of adequate food, water, and shelter.[47] On the return crossing, during which they were stowed in the hold of Daniel's ship, Ochiltree's party suffered deprivations and indignities. Ochiltree contracted pleurisy during the voyage, and he complained that several grief-stricken women had been forced to throw the bodies of their dead children into the sea. As a final humiliation, Daniel had refused to allow Ochiltree off the ship at Falmouth when he deposited the main body of the British party there, opting instead to take him and seventeen others to Dieppe as prisoners. Once they had landed at the French port, Ochiltree was thrown into jail, where he remained for at least a month. His extradition back to London did not come until the end of the year.[48] In the meantime, other events were at play that would play a key role in determining ownership over the disputed territories in North America.

9

Shifting Loyalties
and the Case of the
Embezzled Furs

There is no monie to be had here, which makes me as yet
dowtfull what I may do from thence.

SIR WILLIAM ALEXANDER (1630)

The clergyman Richard Guthry makes the site chosen by Sir William
Alexander junior for his settlement's new home on the Bay of Fundy
sound positively idyllic, blessed with enough wild game and seafood to de-
light the most discerning palates. He notes that it was: "fortifyed on both
sides with hills; and fruitfull vallies adorned and enriched with trees of all
sortes, as goodly oakes, high firres, tale beich, and birch of increadable
bignes, plaine trees, Elme, the woods are full of laurall store of ewe, and
great variety of fruit trees, chesnuts, pears, apples, cherries plumes, and
all other fruits ... We eat lobsters as bige as little children, plenty of salmons
salmon trouts, birds of strange and diverse kinds, haukes of all sorts,
doves, turtles, pheasants, partridges, blacke birds, a kind also of hens,
wild turkies, crannes, herones, infinit store of geese, and three or foure
kinds of ducks."[1] Surrounded by such bounty, the first British settlers of
Nova Scotia can only have approached their new lives with a sense of
optimism. The idyllic quality was not destined to last.

Alexander's new advisor, and likely the man who encouraged him to
choose this area, was well acquainted with the location. Claude Sainte-
Étienne de La Tour had already seen several French settlements rise and
fall on this site, beginning with de Monts's establishment of the French

community of Port Royal in 1605. Although that effort was eventually abandoned, La Tour had been there when the sieur de Poutrincourt had rebuilt it in 1610, and lived there until its destruction in the raid led by Samuel Argall from Jamestown in 1613. (In the negotiations over ownership of the site, the French would always call it Port Royal, and this styling was generally adopted by British agents too.) Claude's son Charles had subsequently transferred his trading operations to the region of the Penobscot River in what is now the state of Maine, while Claude ultimately moved to the southern part of what is now Nova Scotia.[2] As we have related, Claude, the elder La Tour, had agreed in early 1629, following his capture by the Kirkes in 1628, to co-operate with the Alexanders in their planting of Nova Scotia.

The new community was christened "Charlesfort," and under the direction of the Captain Ogilvie/Ogilvy,[3] whom we have mentioned in connection with Lord Ochiltree's ventures, its military readiness received first priority. As Guthry further narrates: "The platt of the fort wes drawn by Captaine Ogilvie in forme of a pentagonon, with many horne works good both for offence and defence befor the letter end of the moneth the fort with infinit pains and alacrity both of sea and land men was finished, eight pieces of ordinance plainted, foure demie culvering, and foure minion, oure magasene built and stored, the Generalls house formed."[4]

Within days of their arrival, the Charlesfort party had their first contacts with the local native population, who seem to have welcomed the new arrivals, exchanged gifts, and engaged in some minor trading. Significantly, however, Guthry's final lines recount that the settlers' major endeavour was planting corn and preparing for the agricultural needs of the community. This implies that the group that Alexander junior had assembled were serious about establishing a permanent colony, and that they did not initially foresee the fur trade, or other commercial enterprises such as fishing, to be their primary interest. Other British colonial efforts in North America, Jamestown most notably, had experienced early difficulties because the settlers were not prepared to provide for themselves.[5]

Apart from Guthry's account of the 1629 trans-Atlantic voyage and first days of Charlesfort, very little else is known about this colony. Sir William Alexander junior was committed to remaining in the new settle-

ment during its first winter. Accordingly, in the autumn of 1629 he sent
Claude de La Tour back to England to procure further supplies, to report
on the successful establishment of Charlesfort, and to furnish proof that
the local native population had given their allegiance to Charles I. This
took the form of a visit to England by a Micmac delegation. A local chief-
tain named Segipt, his wife, and his son were soon introduced at the
English court as a Canadian royal family, come to acknowledge Charles
I as their overlord and to request protection from the French. Several contemporaries noted that the emissaries were well feted, and genuinely
seemed to enjoy themselves during their winter in England.[6]

The future of the Nova Scotia colony was by no means certain, however. Although nobody at Charlesfort would have known it, a major
issue involving the conflicting French and Scottish claims in the region
remained to be settled. To what extent might Sir William Alexander's
charter become a bargaining chip in the pursuit of a lasting peace between France and the British kingdoms, now that the Treaty of Susa had
concluded the late war? That issue, which would obviously affect the St
Lawrence theatre as well, will be addressed shortly. Meanwhile, there
were at least some indications in Britain that Nova Scotia's prospects
might actually be brightening.

In the spring of 1629, the senior Sir William Alexander had received
a land grant at Largs on the Clyde estuary for the establishment of a port
to handle trans-Atlantic traffic.[7] Proposals were also floated for the
voluntary emigration of certain Highland families, a possibility that
would have addressed the problems of perceived over-crowding and
violence in the highlands, while adding to the numbers of settlers in Nova
Scotia. Ultimately neither scheme was carried through, but at this stage,
they represented hopeful signs.[8]

Many of the problems that had bedevilled Sir William Alexander since
the granting of the charter continued, however, and they spelled further
difficulties for the colony. In spite of ongoing and forceful support from
the king, the enlistment and recognition of Knights Baronet of Nova
Scotia proceeded at a maddeningly slow pace.[9] What is more, the younger
Sir Alexander had entrusted an agent, Sir George Home of Eckills, to
obtain supplies and enlist new settlers in Scotland for the colony, but
Eckills's own debts were so serious that he had to obtain a special license

from the Privy Council to carry out his duties without being seized by his creditors.[10] The somewhat dodgy financial straits of their subscribers had been a problem for both the Alexanders, dating back to the elder courtier's first efforts to outfit voyages. Now, however, with Charlesfort established, the strain of the colony's financial woes became even more apparent. In his correspondence over the winter of 1629–30, Alexander senior expressed grave concerns over his inability to better provide for the needs of his son and the colony. As he confided to the earl of Menteith in February 1630, "There is no monie to be had here, which makes me as yet dowtfull what I may do from thence."[11]

In the face of this uncertainty one development that seemed to offer better prospects was a more formal enlistment of Claude de La Tour to the ranks of Nova Scotia baronets, and to the wider cause of the Alexanders' colony. Before leaving Charlesfort in the autumn of 1629, La Tour had signed a bond of allegiance to Sir Alexander junior. Back in Britain that November, he had formally subscribed as a Knight Baronet of Nova Scotia and, more important, had convinced the senior Sir Alexander that he could win the allegiance of his son Charles and bring his settlement at Cape Sable into the British fold.[12] In the spring of 1630, the elder La Tour returned to Acadia in an attempt to complete these arrangements.

Things went wrong almost immediately after his return crossing to the New World. Charles de La Tour was evidently shocked by his father's defection and refused to join him or to accept Alexander's offer of a Nova Scotia baronetcy.[13] In fact, their respective determination to serve different sovereigns led to battle. Claude assembled a force of soldiers, and with two ships tried to storm Cape Sable. For two days the forces of the La Tours battled each other in what was effectively a civil war. Claude was forced to withdraw in humiliation to Port Royal. His wife, it will be remembered, had been a lady-in-waiting to Queen Henrietta Maria and had accompanied him to the New World that spring. Now, rebuffed by his son and defeated by him in the recent skirmish, Claude put his reputation on the line once again and offered his wife the opportunity to return to England. That she promised to stand by him was the only salve Claude de La Tour received that season.[14]

La Tour's failure to either win over or coerce his son's allegiance only damaged his relations with the younger Alexander. In spite of the optimistic note that Guthry had sounded at the settlement's birth, Alexander and his party had not enjoyed a snug winter at Charlesfort. Half the colonists had died, having succumbed to scurvy and the effects of privation during the frigid months. In the summer of 1630 Alexander's exasperation with La Tour grew to the point that the latter wrote to his son, begging forgiveness and a chance to return to the service of the king of France. Alexander may have been glad to let him go.

Reinforcements for Charlesfort had materialized that season in the form of Sir George Home (who had either paid or evaded his creditors) and a supply ship bearing additional settlers. Claude de La Tour evidently knew about these reinforcements, because, when his son agreed to accept him at Cape Sable (albeit under strict terms that limited his freedom), he warned the French settlement to await an imminent attack. It never came, but Claude was eventually able to restore his reputation under French service. For his part, Sir William Alexander junior decided to return to Britain to seek additional colonists and support for Nova Scotia. He would never see the colony again.[15]

Meanwhile, the party that had remained on the St Lawrence under the command of Lewis Kirke had been busy trying to make profits from the fur trade at Quebec. To this purpose, they wanted to use Tadoussac as an observation point to prevent interlopers from entering the river to engage in illegal trade. This task had also been a long-standing challenge for any French licensees and, not surprisingly, Kirke discovered that ships from a variety of kingdoms, including England, were quite prepared to voyage to Canada in search of trading opportunities without the slightest concern for his company's claims.[16] More pointedly, the French government and the Company of One Hundred Associates were eager to reassert their claims in North America as quickly as possible, and Isaac de Razilly began outfitting a squadron to sail for Quebec in the spring of 1630. Louis XIII's preoccupation with fighting the armies of Spain in northern Italy prevented the necessary royal orders from being issued, however and a smaller squadron of two ships under the command of the sieur de Tuffet was subsequently dispatched to supply the garrison that

Charles Daniel had left at St. Anne's Harbour on Cape Breton Island, and Charles de La Tour's settlement at Cape Sable.[17]

In October 1630 Thomas Kirke, who had led a supply squadron to Quebec in the spring of that year, returned to England with two ships, bearing a haul of furs that Champlain valued at 300 thousand livres. Of the ninety members of the English party that had remained at Quebec for the year 1629–1630, some fourteen had died, while many others suffered from scurvy and other illnesses. The fields that had been ploughed by the Jesuits and Recollets were sown, and the ramparts of Quebec had been strengthened in anticipation of French efforts to retake the installation. Champlain was informed that the major disputes that had taken place at Quebec were between French families like the Héberts, who had remained loyal to France, and individuals like Nicolas Marsolet, who had defected to the English. He retained his high opinion of the Kirke brothers, Lewis in particular. As he recorded retrospectively: "Captain Louis and the English ... did not annoy our people at all."[18]

As with accounts of life at Charlesfort in Nova Scotia, very little else is known about the period of English occupation at Quebec. There were probably some two hundred seasonal residents at most in the habitation, and in a report to the English government, David Kirke suggested that some of these men were engaged in exploring deep into the interior, to a distance of nearly four hundred leagues from Quebec.[19] Provisioning the settlement must have been a difficult matter for the new residents in spite of their efforts to grow crops in the gardens formerly cleared by the priests. At one point the Merchant Adventurers had to apply to the Privy Council for permission to send "one hundreth quarter of Pease ... and one hundreth hogsheads of Meale" to their agents in Quebec.[20]

The priority for the Kirkes and the Merchant Adventurers to Canada was to realize as much profit as possible from the fur trade, in the likely knowledge that the terms of peace between France and the British kingdoms would soon force them to surrender Quebec back to French interests. Champlain quoted Lewis Kirke as saying "they were fully expecting that [the French] King's ships would arrive this year with a commission from the King of England ordering the evacuation of the place by the English, which could otherwise only have been accomplished by force."[21]

Champlain gives some sense of the tension this may have created at Quebec in an allusion to a near mutiny that befell Lewis Kirke in the summer of 1631. He reported: "The thing was discovered, and Captain Louis inflicted punishment on some of them. The cause of this rebellion was the ill-treatment the captain was inflicting on his companions, by the advice of those two or three faithless Frenchmen [presumably Marsolet and Brûlé], in whom he had placed too much trust."[22]

Much of the documentary evidence on this interregnum between the English seizure and the return of Quebec to the French relates to the legal steps undertaken in London and Paris by the various parties who laid claim to property that had been at Quebec when it was surrendered in 1629, and who offered contesting views on who ought now to control the Canadian fur trade.[23] Seen on a larger scale, these actions mirrored even more important efforts at the governmental levels in France and Britain, to ratify and expand upon the Treaty of Susa. As we shall see, these negotiations did not take place quickly, and in the interim the status of Sir William Alexander's charter and his efforts in Nova Scotia became a major diplomatic consideration as well. Because these considerations constitute such an important part of the story, they merit separate consideration in the next chapter.

———————

For the moment, the tangle of competing claims that emerged from the phoney war of 1629 on the St Lawrence River can best be understood in the light of one salient fact. Whatever other arguments he might hear, Charles I had determined early on that the terms of the Treaty of Susa required the return of Quebec and the control of the St Lawrence River to the French. It was beyond dispute that the Kirkes had taken Quebec after the hostilities between France and the British kingdoms had ceased. Also foremost in Charles's mind was the anticipated payment of the outstanding balance of some 400,000 French crowns on Queen Henrietta Maria's dowry if this transfer were completed quickly.[24]

Charles clearly believed he was acting in good faith and in accordance with treaty obligations in this matter, and that his primary reward would come in the form of a much-needed infusion of cash. He was more guarded on the subject of Acadia, however, specifically regarding the

Champlain leaving Quebec as a prisoner-of-war aboard David
Kirke's ship, by C.W. Jefferys

French government's insistence that Port Royal/Charlesfort be surrendered or demolished.[25] Champlain recorded that in conversations with
the French ambassador in early 1630 Charles "made order that the fort
and habitation [Quebec] should be given back into the hands of his
Majesty [Louis XIII], or those empowered by him – but made no mention of the coasts of Acadia."[26]

Negotiations on these points at the state level did not prevent the
individual parties concerned from appealing to both English and French
courts in efforts to obtain disputed properties or gain favourable judg-
ments on trading rights. This was a laborious process that had been
underway almost from the time Champlain and his associates from
Quebec arrived in England with David Kirke in the autumn of 1629.
Initially, the French party expressed concerns about the charges they had

accrued, and about the limits that had been placed upon them, owing to the mistaken belief that they were prisoners of war. In fact, as they asserted before the High Court of Admiralty, they should never have been forced to surrender Quebec in the first place. The French claimed that the Kirkes had stolen part of the store of furs that had been at Quebec, while the Kirkes accused the French of exaggerating the value of the captured stores and properties.[27]

In November of 1629, Champlain and several of his adjutants made depositions before Sir Henry Marten, a judge of the Court of Admiralty. In general, they acknowledged that they had received satisfactory treatment from their captors, and admitted that, politics aside, the state of provisions at Quebec the previous summer had made its surrender a necessity.[28] The Kirkes also appeared before Marten to relate the narrative of Quebec's capture, and to report that among the other property seized, 1,713 beaver skins had been taken at the fort.[29] All the while, Champlain had been in close contact with the French ambassador, and having determined that his greatest duty lay in pushing the case for the immediate restoration of all French territories in North America before Louis XIII, he left England on 30 November to gain an audience with his king.

A chance meeting with Captain Charles Daniel, who had just returned with his prisoners (including Lord Ochiltree) from Cape Breton Island caused Champlain to learn that the Company of One Hundred Associates was prepared to grant him gubernatorial powers in Canada. This only strengthened his belief that the British should be compelled to evacuate the disputed territories as quickly as possible and he pressed this viewpoint both with government officials, and with the president of the Company of One Hundred Associates as soon as he could arrange the necessary meetings.[30]

The dispute over furs and other items that had been captured in Quebec the previous summer had still not been settled, however, especially to the satisfaction of the Compagnie Caën. Time was running out for this firm, and its directors knew it. The prospective return of Quebec to French hands would trigger the monopoly of the Company of One Hundred Associates, and the Caëns would be frozen out. Although Émery de Caën, who had been captured on the St Lawrence in the summer of 1629 and was subsequently brought to England as a prisoner, had returned to France, his cousin Guillaume took up the suit for compensation for the property his firm had lost from the capture of Quebec and arrived in England to press his firm's case against the Merchant Adventurers sometime in the spring of 1630.

That April the English Privy Council ordered the Merchant Adventurers and Guillaume de Caën to appear before the lord mayor of London. It had been determined that both sides would be permitted to bid upon the confiscated furs and property, with the lot to go to the highest bidder. On 9 April the lord mayor, Sir James Campbell wrote to Sir Henry Marten, informing him that the meeting had taken place and that Guillaume de Caën had offered 25 shillings per pound for the pelts. The Merchant Adventurers had yet to make a counter offer, but a designate was appointed to count and weigh the furs. Later that same day, Campbell reported that the French bid had been accepted.[31]

Recriminations continued to fester. The Kirkes failed to provide the necessary keys for opening the storehouse where the Quebec furs were kept. The door was finally broken down on the authorization of the lord mayor amid accusations that an agent working for the Kirkes had already removed some of the pelts. In fact, a merchant named Thomas Fitz was arrested and put in the Fleet Prison in early June 1630 on charges of "embezelling some beaver skins from a warehouse." He remained in prison until an examination before the Court of Star Chamber made possible his release upon a promise to recover the stolen pelts.[32] Caën was not at all satisfied with the number of furs he received through these actions, and claimed that of the some 1,700 skins that had been brought from Quebec, only 300 were now accounted for. He continued to badger for further compensation, and by the time he left England, he was claiming that more than 5,000 pelts had been in his company's stores when Quebec was captured.[33] Despairing of ever receiving what they thought was their due under English justice, the Compagnie de Caën in 1631 entered charges in a French court against the Merchant Adventurers and the English crown.

In the grander scheme of things, the Kirke brothers and their partners were even more concerned by the apparent willingness of their king to surrender Quebec without considering the possible benefits of taking a harder line with the French. In their petitions to the crown, for example, the partners were adamant that from a military point of view, the settlement could be held, and that by right of conquest, it was a prize to which they – and by extension, Charles himself – were due. As David Kirke wrote to the king:

> The above fort [Quebec] is so well situated that they are able to withstand ten thousand men, and will not care for them; for in winter they cannot stay in the country, soe that whosoever goes to besiege them cannot stay above three months, all in which time the musketts [mosquitoes] will tormente them that noe man is able to be abroad in centry or trench daye or night without losinge their sights at least eight dayes. So that if it please your Majesty to keep it, wee doe not care what French or any other can doe, though she have a hundred sayle of ships and ten thousand men as aforesaid.[34]

In early 1631 Charles had shown some willingness to explore ways of rewarding and compensating the Merchant Adventurers, without back-pedalling on his central promise to ensure the return of Quebec to the French. A commission was struck consisting of representatives from both English and French governments to determine what the parties with interests in Quebec in 1629 might receive.[35] In reality, this represented only one prong of the tripartite thrust of the negotiations. In all, France and the British kingdoms needed to ratify their peace agreement; the French, English, and Scottish governments needed to settle the question of the disputed territories to their satisfaction; and finally, the various competing parties would have to address their personal and commercial claims.

For the British side, a diffuse team handled the negotiating process and communicated its progresses and lapses to the king. The senior official overseeing matters from London (until his death in February 1632) was one of England's two secretaries of state, Dudley Carleton, viscount Dorchester, and the lead official in France was the English ambassador Sir Issac Wake. However, two paid agents for the English government, René Augier and Henri de Vic, conducted the lion's share of the negotiations.[36] Most of the work took place at Louis XIII's court, which in 1631 particularly, was constantly on the move, depending on the king's whims. Special envoys at court, such as Edward, lord Montagu, therefore also acted as conduits when official designates were not present.[37] At key moments, when a compromise seemed to have been reached on the payment of Henrietta Maria's dowry in September 1631, for instance, such trusted private individuals as the naturalized French financier and merchant from London named Phillip Burlamachi also became representatives for Charles I.[38] Altogether, the process moved slowly; agreement on the fate of Port Royal, payment of the dowry, and restitution for the various private interests proved to be the most contentious issues.

In pressing the claims of his company to his own government, however, Guillaume de Caën was able to obtain a special monopoly license for the 1631 season, and in the spring of that year, his cousin Émery was sent to Quebec to conduct the trade. Lewis Kirke, still in command there on behalf of the Merchant Adventurers, was initially accommodating and promised to give the Frenchman access to the natives when their fur flotillas arrived. But, as the summer wore on, he either changed his mind, or was pressured by his underlings to prevent Émery from meeting with the natives. In the end, Émery was kept waiting until August, at which point Kirke informed him that his rights would not be recognized. Caën was thus forced to withdraw to France, but not before drafting a formal protest over the English garrison's conduct in violation of the state of peace.[39]

When the Treaty of Saint-Germain-en-Laye was finally concluded on 20 March 1632, the Merchant Adventurers were confounded. To their minds, the English ambassador, Sir Isaac Wake, had made an extremely weak presentation on behalf of his countrymen and lost the best chance for them to receive financial compensation, or for their king to maintain any honour from the conquest. Because they believed an agent in their employ should have presented clear evidence to sustain their claims, Wake's alleged failure drew scathing letters from the Kirkes and Alexander, who accused him of misrepresenting them. What they found particularly galling was that Wake had not only lost the appeal on behalf of the Merchant Adventurers but had agreed to a further restitution of £14,330 to the Caëns, to be paid by the crown. But the die was cast. As secretary of state John Coke informed the ambassador: "[He was] commanded by the King to let him [Wake] know that though for the King's own honour he will not free himself from disadvantage and burden cast upon him, by disavowing openly those ministers to whom he have power, yet as to Wake ... the King disavoweth the transaction as not justifiable on your part, yet requireth you without reply immediately see it done."[40]

For the governments involved, the ratification of this treaty meant that Quebec would finally be returned to the French, and Sir William Alexander junior's colonists would now have to abandon Port Royal. As we shall see, from the point of view of the two Alexanders, this contingency had already been softened; and since the later part of 1631 they had received sufficient rewards from Charles I, that we can only infer that they had been quietly distancing themselves from their erstwhile English partners. These developments will become clearer to us if we look separately at the issues of Port Royal/Charlesfort and Sir William Alexander's wider claims to Nova Scotia. The fate of these questions rested as much on dealings within Alexander's circle of enthusiasts for Nova Scotia within Britain, as it did on more distant diplomatic manoeuvres. The other point to recognize is that when Alexander realized his wider interests were going to be protected, he slowly began to separate himself from his partners in the Merchant Adventurers to Canada.

10

Lord Ochiltree's Gamble
and the Abandonment
of Port Royal

... give ordour ... to dimolishc the Fort which was builded by your
sone there, and to remove all the peopls, goods, Ordinance, munition,
cattell, and other things belonging unto that Colonie, leaving the
boundis altogidder waist and vnpeopled.

CHARLES I TO SIR WILLIAM ALEXANDER (1631)

For most people, being given what amounts to a license to print money
would seem like a financial panacea. The elder Sir William Alexander
probably saw his own situation that way when he received what was in
essence that right from King Charles I in the summer of 1631. The
circumstances were most intriguing. For several reasons, Scotland's
monetary system was in a shambles by the time of Charles I's reign. The
first problem was that the kingdom did not mint a sufficient supply of
its own coinage. The coins that were minted were generally of higher
denominations than were practical for most transactions, and their
use fell beyond the means of most people. In reaction, people used
foreign currencies from all across Europe instead, thereby fuelling price
uncertainty and encouraging counterfeits. By 1629, however, Charles
I's government was beginning to consider minting a greater supply
of pennies, and in June 1631 royal orders were issued for the coining of
copper farthing tokens. Alexander was designated the recipient of the
crown's share of this issue, and by August, he had been granted full
authority to administer the circulation of the new money.[1]

This was not the only financial or titular windfall that Alexander enjoyed in the years framing the settlement and loss of his son's community and his own wider colonial ambitions in Nova Scotia. One of the more elaborate money-making schemes to emerge from Charles I's court commenced in the autumn of 1629 with a proposal to unite the fisheries of England, Scotland, and Ireland into a single consortium, its headquarters to be based in the northern Hebrides on the Isle of Lewis. Ever since the union of the crowns, theorists and legal scholars had been pushing for a comprehensive assertion of regal rights over Britain's waters, but differing legal interpretations, and domestic concerns in England and Scotland, had prevented the formulation of anything definitive.

In the meantime, foreign fishing in British waters and violations of domestic licensing practices had only exacerbated the sense of loss related to this potentially lucrative industry.[2] The proposed Association for the Fishing projected a massive expansion of the fishing fleets of the three British kingdoms, a scheme that would be financed through purchases of shares. If successful, all stockholders would gain from the more effective management and utilization of this key resource, and great profits were projected. Although the Association for the Fishing never materialized, efforts to make it a reality formed a key governmental impulse in the years 1630–32, and Sir William Alexander, in his capacity as secretary for Scotland and a member of the Scottish Privy Council, was heavily involved in them. He also could expect to be a major stakeholder and beneficiary if the plans were successfully carried to completion.[3]

Factors such as the money to be made from his rights in the copper coinage project, anticipated profits from the Association for the Fishing, and other rewards and sinecures that Alexander had received or anticipated receiving from the crown in these years, must be kept in mind when we consider the fate of Nova Scotia. Against the dreams, efforts, and money that Alexander had invested in his nascent colony prior to 1630 we must weigh the potentially more lucrative and tangible opportunities that his position as one of Charles I's leading courtiers offered – not to mention his ongoing priority to serve his king loyally and effectively. In the eleven years since King James VI/I had granted Alexander the charter for the planting of "New Scotland," he had seen that particular aspiration wax and wane, with the colony's greatest opportunity for permanent establishment fizzling out in the wake of the end of the 1627–29 war between the British kingdoms and France. Now, even though Alexander and his son had made efforts to protect the terms of their charter, and had even received boisterous, if belated support from the Scottish Privy Council, the installation on the Bay of Fundy called Charlesfort, on the site of the original French establishment known as Port Royal, was ultimately to be sacrificed in the pragmatic pursuit of other goals, and with it went the dream of a New Scotland.

For many years historians viewed this loss negatively; it can only have resulted from something ranging between stupidity and naked opportunism on the part of Charles I. Then, in 1977, Professor John Reid challenged that interpretation and showed that Charles's agents had used the negotiations with the French, from the signing of the Treaty of Susa to the completion of the Treaty of Saint-Germain-en-Laye, in a much more subtle fashion. Charles, he argued, had been perfectly willing to guarantee the return of Quebec and control of the St Lawrence River to the French because the Kirke brothers had technically seized those territories on behalf of their consortium, the Merchant Adventurers to Canada, during peace time. As King of England, he was therefore bound to observe the terms under which the peace treaty had been signed. The return of the Canadian territories to French hands was essentially a foregone conclusion.

Acadia/Nova Scotia was a different matter, however; that region had been granted to Sir William Alexander by the Scottish crown. For more than a year, between the early winter of 1630 and the summer of 1631, Charles and his agents tried to get the French to accept that distinction, and to decouple negotiations over that territory from the ratification of the peace agreement. Reid showed that, although they failed to win French acceptance of the distinction, Charles and his negotiators were more sincere in their efforts to maintain Nova Scotia than had previously been allowed. In fact, they had even achieved something of a compromise in getting Alexander to agree specifically to the abandonment of Port Royal/Charlesfort, while remaining vague as to ownership of the wider region. This ambiguity kept open the possibility of future plantings in

Nova Scotia under Alexander's auspices, even though such initiatives never took place.[4]

However, when we look at those negotiations in the context of Sir William Alexander's domestic career during the years 1630–32, and through the even broader prism of British politics during the same time period, yet another dimension to the fate of Nova Scotia emerges. Alexander's charter was far from being his sole priority at this time. He had already begun to shift his focus away from the nascent colony to other and potentially more lucrative undertakings that would have eliminated the debts he had accrued in his halting ventures overseas. In short, where his personal affairs were concerned, these years ultimately saw him take a path that he expected would yield greater wealth and augment the considerable authority he already enjoyed as secretary for Scotland, as a leading Scottish governmental figure, and as a trusted advisor to his king. He never forgot this latter component of his life and responsibilities, and in keeping with long-established patronage practices, Charles I was not going to abandon Alexander either. That is the key point here. In the eyes of the king, even if Alexander's colony had to be sacrificed, his servant could still be protected, compensated, and made even richer and more powerful.

Our enquiry into this evolution must begin with three integrated themes of the story, which extend over the period from early 1630 through to the surrender to the French of the territories under consideration in the summer of 1632. These are: the negotiations between British and French agents which ultimately resulted in the Treaty of Saint-Germain-en-Laye; initial efforts in Britain to decouple consideration of Nova Scotia from the return of Quebec to the French and thereby permit the young colony to remain in British hands; and domestic political developments that saw Sir William Alexander shift his priorities and interests to other fields. We shall see that the summer of 1631 marks the real turning point in terms of Charles I's and Alexander's determination to hold onto Nova Scotia, and that the reason for their shift in emphasis lies in a hitherto underrated figure in the entire story, namely Lord Ochiltree. We must begin at the ambassadorial level, however, because intergovernmental dealings present the clearest chronological and thematic pattern for understanding this element of the affair.

The Arms of Nova Scotia. Granted for the
colony and Knights Baronet of Nova Scotia
by Charles I in 1625, this is the oldest British
coat of arms outside Great Britain.

We have already shown in reference to Quebec and the St Lawrence
that the final ratification of the surrender to the French of these territories was not in serious dispute. More properly understood, it was
merely delayed. In late 1629 Charles I had tipped his hand to the French
ambassador in support of the return, and as early as February 1630 state
correspondence was treating this outcome as a *fait accompli*.[5] The explanation for the delay in ratifying that agreement and making it operative
lies in part with Louis XIII, and his personal and strategic diversions.
The other major element in the delay was Charles's initial determination
to hold onto Nova Scotia as a wider entity, and thereby protect the
integrity of Sir William Alexander's charter from the Scottish crown.

This latter component of Charles I's position was signalled first in correspondence between English secretary of state, Dudley Carleton, (Viscount Dorchester), and the ambassador in France, Sir Isaac Wake, commencing in April 1630. It appears again in letters that Charles sent to Sir William Alexander junior and the Scottish Privy Council in May and July 1630, respectively.[6] These indications of ongoing royal endorsement of the Nova Scotia project elicited strong responses from Scotland. The Scottish Convention of Estates unanimously supported the king's position and entreated Charles to remain steadfast in his claim to the region. Its members also again ratified the Order of the Knights Baronet, while on 9 September the Privy Council provided its own forceful assertion of Alexander's charter rights, tying them to expressions of their kingdom's honour and security.[7] To this point there could not have been a stronger assertion of official Scottish unity on the Nova Scotia question, and through the remainder of the year and into early 1631, both British and French negotiators worked from the premise that while Port Royal/Charlesfort would likely need to be abandoned, Scottish rights in the region would not necessarily be foresworn. There were tangible reasons for this broader Scottish position to be affirmed.

The reader will recall that the summer of 1630 had, among other things, witnessed the reinforcement of the Scottish party at Charlesfort by the arrival of Sir George Home and his shipload of new settlers from Scotland. In the parallel fiasco in the story of Claude de La Tour and his eventual rapprochement with his son Charles, Sir William Alexander junior left a reasonably secure colonial settlement when he returned to Scotland in the autumn of 1630, a burgeoning community that he believed would buttress and protect his father's charter.[8] Other activities aimed at increasing the British presence in the region were also in preparation.

Ever since his repatriation in late 1629 or early 1630 after imprisonment in France, Ochiltree had been actively appealing to Charles I on three fronts. He sought compensation for losses he claimed to have incurred the previous summer through the French capture of Fort Rosemar on Cape Breton Island; he warned the king that the French would try to assert their own claims in the wider region, and urged immediate action to oppose that impulse; and finally, he gave the strongest possible signals that he wished to serve both the king and Alexander by leading a new colonial enterprise somewhere within the disputed territory. Ochiltree's actions, and the king's responses to them, require more specific analysis than they have hitherto received. We must begin with his extrication from jail in France, and his return to Britain.

These events form a crucial, but largely unanalysed aspect of Lord Ochiltree's story as it pertains to the eventual fate of Britain's early interest in this part of North America. As we have seen, Ochiltree's career to date had featured significant moments of power and respectability, but lasting success had always eluded him. For most people in his acquaintance, he would have been best known for his many misadventures and heavy debts, not for any of the brief laurels he had won as a crown magistrate, court advisor, or colonist. As a prisoner in Dieppe, he must have cut a miserable figure, suffering from the loss of his colony and from the lingering effects of a serious illness.[9] On the insistence of Sir Thomas Edmondes, then the English ambassador in Paris, Ochiltree was brought before the Dieppe Admiralty Court sometime in the late autumn of 1629.[10] It was at this point that he seems to have realized that the loss of Cape Breton could be turned to his advantage, and that he might rise in the king's favour if he could deliver a convincing performance.

In his testimony, Ochiltree refused to concede that the French had any rights to the disputed territories in Acadia, or that his policing of the Cape Breton fishery constituted anything less than his lawful fulfilment of his king's commission.[11] Furthermore, he made every effort to construe Daniel's attack on Fort Rosemar and his subsequent maltreatment of Ochiltree and his party as direct assaults on the dignity of Charles I. If Ochiltree's account is to be believed, then Daniel had continued his political sauciness when they were back in France. He stated: "And to crowne the rest of the said captain Danyell insolences, befor the seiant maior of Deepe, Monsur Schobneall, he did call the king of Britane ane usurparer."[12] Given the strained relations that existed between the Stuart and Bourbon courts up to this point, someone who upheld the honour of Charles I in the face of such slights might well have earned his king's gratitude. Although it was never formally acknowledged or attributed to Ochiltree by either the king or Sir William Alexander, in reality,

Ochiltree was also the first of Charles I's subjects to present this forceful claim to French officials in person.

And yet, we must wonder, was Ochiltree protesting too much? Certainly his testimony was dramatic in its assertions of Daniel's treachery in the original capture of Fort Rosemar, and he made every effort to portray himself as valorous in defeat. He openly rejected any French claims in the area and subsequently tried to convince the king in a petition that he only needed Charles's co-operation to re-secure Acadia. What was more interesting, however, was a new claim, first made in Dieppe, and then repeated in petitions to the king, that he had personally lost more than £20,000 as a result of the incident.[13] As Charles had advanced him just £500 when the expedition set sail the previous spring, and considering his long history of personal debt, this figure seems wildly incongruous. Perhaps Ochiltree was trying to include in his accounting real and projected lost revenues from taxing fishermen around Cape Breton, or maybe his harsh treatment at the hands of the French had confused him. One suspects, however, that he knowingly exaggerated his losses. Whatever the reason, by the end of 1629 he had been returned to England, where he would continue to press his claims.[14]

From Ochiltree's perspective, it was vital that he immediately establish with the king his version of what had taken place at Fort Rosemar and at Dieppe. He was fortunate that one of his officers collaborated his story. As early as 9 December 1629, Captain Constance Ferrar had sent a petition to the king relating the events surrounding the loss of Fort Rosemar and reiterating the account of the mistreatment Ochiltree's party had suffered at the hands of Daniel. Ferrar was also looking for reimbursement, and claimed that he had lost £10,000 through the venture.[15]

Ochiltree began sending petitions to the king sometime in January 1630. In two separate documents, he protested the treatment he had received from the French, but turned up the rhetoric where Charles's loss of "rightful" territories in the New World was concerned. Ochiltree now claimed that more than seven thousand of Charles's subjects were living in Canada and Acadia, and that Captain Daniel was plotting a return voyage for early in the spring of 1630. He warned Charles in addition that the Jesuits were the prime movers behind the renewed French project, and that only swift action would forestall the loss of valuable territories to treacherous enemies.[16]

As it happened, Ochiltree and Ferrar (who hereafter completely disappears from the records[17]) were approaching the king and the English Privy Council at an opportune moment, and their petitions likely received careful study, even if their claimed losses were not automatically believed. As we have already mentioned, the British and French had markedly different interpretations of their respective rights in North America at this point, and events in the summer of 1629 had brought the crisis to a head.

Because the British actions had taken place after the formal cessation of hostilities, the French government was demanding that all posts and captured properties be returned before the Treaty of Susa could be ratified.[18] We now know that this factor was a matter of great importance to Charles I, because among the terms of the treaty was the requirement that the French pay the remainder of Queen Henrietta Maria's dowry – a potential replenishment of his coffers that the king desperately needed. In addition, from the autumn of 1629 until the end of 1631, the Privy Council and the English admiralty court remained occupied with efforts to mediate among the various interest groups who now claimed rights over the seized properties and trade goods from the New World. Prominent among the litigants before these bodies were the Kirkes and Sir William Alexander, represented by their company, the Merchant Adventurers to Canada, and French mercantile interests from the St Lawrence fur trading posts, specifically the Compagnie de Caen.[19]

While most evidence suggests that Charles realized he could not sustain a claim to Canada (that is, to the lands adjacent to the St Lawrence), Acadia was a different matter. In negotiating with the French, he seems to have hoped that the return of Quebec and the other St Lawrence posts would allow Alexander junior's possession of Port Royal/Charlesfort to be ratified.[20] There was considerable domestic political pressure behind this.

The elder Sir William Alexander was already hard at work in London in early 1630 trying to assemble relief for Port Royal, and in February he asked the Scottish Privy Council to supply him with a ship and men, because his solicitations in England had been unproductive.[21] More important, the king and the Scottish Privy Council had started to correspond about the maintenance of the new colony, and in May 1630 Charles wrote the aforementioned letter of endorsement urging Sir William Alexander junior to: "continow as you have begunne, that the wark may be brought to the intendit perfectione."[22]

One thing is certain about a renewed effort to retain Nova Scotia. Lord Ochiltree intended to be a part of it, and the king and Sir William Alexander supported his ongoing interest and the prospect of his return to Nova Scotia. As a mark of this, Ochiltree's name was listed on 18 April 1630 as one of the newly made Knights Baronet of Nova Scotia.[23] In keeping with his new honour, Ochiltree once more demonstrated a profitable talent for ingratiating himself with the king and for enlisting the aid of old acquaintances. To fund his new venture, Charles awarded Ochiltree a twenty-one-year lease of "all fellones landis and houses rendring [£]500 per annum." As this was an award on Scottish properties, and Ochiltree's former creditors might present claims of their own, Charles offered a further consideration in his declaration: "These ar therfor to will and requyre yow to prepair a bill readie for our signatur wheby to mak the said Lord Vchiltrie a frie denizen of this our kingdome of England and dominions therof; with this speciall caution, that it be nowayes prejudiciall to ws in our customes: And for your soe doeing these shalbe be your warrand."[24]

Finally, Ochiltree showed that he had been busy in other ways, specifically in recruiting potential colonial partners from among the ranks of his former neighbours in Ulster. This can be discovered from another letter that Charles wrote on Ochiltree's behalf, on 19 April 1631, this time to the Lords Justices of Ireland. In it, he praised the efforts of Ochiltree and three planters from Ulster, who wished to establish a new colony "near unto the river of Canada, in America." The king's support for this venture could not be mistaken:

Becaus the purpois is honorabill, and may conduce to the good of our service, Our speciall pleasur is, that from tyme to tyme, as they or any of them shall have occasion, yow grant them Commissions and warrants requisit for transporting thither such persones as shal be willing to be imployed in the plantation; and that yow licence and caus licence them, and such as shall have ther or whatsoever fitt for there vse; ffor doeing wherof, as these presents shalbe vnto yow a sufficient warrant, so we will accompt your care in forthring of them as good and acceptable service done vnto ws:[25]

This glowing affirmation of the king's ongoing support has twofold significance. First, it demonstrates that Charles was still projecting the establishment of a new British colony in the disputed territory as late as April 1631, and second, it shows that Ochiltree was making this a personal priority. Unlike Sir William Alexander, who was simultaneously mounting his coinage efforts, negotiating for the establishment of the Association for the Fishing, and performing other services on behalf of the king, Ochiltree needed the colonial venture to work. Charles's ringing endorsement of April 1631 should therefore be seen as sincere, and a further buttress to the theory that at this point, he had not abandoned the idea of retaining Nova Scotia in some form. However, these documents also mark the last time that Ochiltree would enjoy his sovereign's favour because a fresh scandal was about to emerge that would bring about Ochiltree's final disgrace and a long period of imprisonment. This in turn would dampen the ardour of Charles and Alexander for a firm stand on Nova Scotia. The events unfolded in a climate of political intrigue at the highest levels of Charles's court.

On the sixth or seventh of May 1631, Ochiltree met an old friend, Donald, lord Reay, at a public house called The Sign of the Bear, near London Bridge.[26] Reay had recently returned from the continent, where he had served in the Swedish forces under their king, Gustavus Adolphus, and he was full of gossip from the camps of the British mercenaries. In the course of their conversations he told Ochiltree about rumours he had heard of treasonous plots against Charles I, and he asked his friend's advice on whether this information should be taken to any authorities. Ochiltree may have cautioned Reay against any hasty accusations, or he may have been willing to delay judgment until he had ascertained more about the rumours. Reay soon supplied further information.

The next week, he went to visit Ochiltree in his lodgings and told him all that he knew. Reay said that the focus of the rumour was the king's close friend – and the man who was lineally next in line to the throne of Scotland – James, third marquis of Hamilton. By coincidence or not, Hamilton was just then raising troops in Scotland for service with the Protestant forces in Europe, a project for which he had the king's blessing. Reay claimed that he had been informed by another Scottish mercenary officer, Colonel David Ramsay, that the true purpose behind Hamilton's levying troops was to engineer a *coup d'état* in Scotland, through which he would seize the kingdom's principal strongholds, kidnap the royal family, execute Charles's leading advisors, Sir William Alexander among them, and proclaim himself king of Scotland.[27] Reay would later claim that the original source of the information was the earl of Seaforth.[28]

In subsequent testimonies, both men would agree that Reay apprised Ochiltree of the plot because he believed Ochiltree was better placed to judge the veracity of the rumours, and to take the information to the proper authorities at court. Reay is reported to have stated:

> Considdering it [the alleged plot] concerneit one so neir the King as the Marqueis of Hamiltoun, he thoct it not fitt that this sould at first reject it, bot it wald be fitter from some other to do it, and thairfore desyred his opinioun how to discover it. The Lord Ochiltrie advyseing any quyll said he thocht it best it wer discoverit to some of the Privie Counsell, wherupoun this examinate said that he wald not discover it to any Scottisman, bot thocht it best to reveall it to the Lord Thesaurer, becaus he thocht the Lord Thesaurer was no way in the plote.[29]

Revealing *it* to the Lord Treasurer was exactly what Ochiltree had in mind, and on the evening of 14 May, he went to the home of Richard, baron Weston, with the intention of laying the story before him. As Weston had already retired for the night, Ochiltree was forced to return the next morning. In the course of their subsequent interview, Ochiltree convinced Weston that the rumour warranted the king's attention, and that he should be permitted to lay the matter before him. Weston acquiesced, and the next day, Ochiltree and Reay were taken (separately) for audiences with Charles I at Greenwich.[30]

The historiography surrounding this incident, and Ochiltree's motive in asserting the treason charges against Hamilton, has been most inconclusive. Giovanni Soranzo, the Venetian ambassador in London, saw no personal motives against Hamilton on the parts of Ochiltree or Reay, and he indicated that they were merely acting on the rumours about Hamilton's troop-raising effort. As Soranzo observed in his regular report to the *doge* and senate: "They based their calumny upon his followers in that kingdom [Scotland] and his [Hamilton's] near blood relationship to the Crown. They suggested in particular that these levies were with that intent, and that his last journey to Scotland had no other object."[31]

Some *post facto* commentators were more certain that Ochiltree's motive was personal. Bishop Gilbert Burnet, who was a client of the Hamiltons' and who wrote a laudatory biography of the third marquis in 1677, accused Ochiltree of acting from base and jealous instincts, and this interpretation has enjoyed some resonance.[32] To be fair, the more negative view might have its merits. There is no question that Ochiltree's father had temporarily gained the earldom of Arran (some have said he usurped it) from the Hamiltons, and that it passed back to them after his fall from James VI's favour. Ochiltree himself had tried unsuccessfully to regain the title prior to 1615, and the second marquis of Hamilton had been one of Ochiltree's creditors in the early 1620s. Indeed, he had pursued Ochiltree over his debts, and this might have been one of the reasons Ochiltree fled to Ulster. Finally, if Ochiltree was thinking about his family history, he might also have recalled the fact that his father had initially gained James VI's favour through his accusation of the earl of Morton. Perhaps he believed that another timely revelation could help his own circumstances.

When all these possible elements are considered, one is struck in addition by a curious omission from Ochiltree's fragmentary history. In the surviving primary and secondary literature related to the incident, his recent experiences in the New World and France, and the fact that he was preparing to leave again for Nova Scotia in the summer of 1631,

have never been linked with the Hamilton accusations. Given the correspondence that exists between Ochiltree's revelation, the king's response,
and the subsequent alteration in policy vis-à-vis Nova Scotia, it seems that
the timing of these events is more than coincidental and that their relationship provides an additional motive whereby these seemingly reckless
charges against Hamilton can be explained. They also provide additional
context for Charles I's and Sir William Alexander's altered behaviour
regarding Nova Scotia in the summer of 1631 and afterward.

The question of Ochiltree's motives must be addressed first. It may
be that one experience with the hardships of an Atlantic crossing, the
turmoil associated with starting a colonial settlement, the humiliation of
capture by the French, and the physical deprivations he had suffered on
the return crossing and in prison meant that Ochiltree was not as eager
to return to Nova Scotia as he appeared, in spite of the aforementioned
efforts. Furthermore, he knew that the area he was proposing to settle
was a potential war zone, and that he had exaggerated the scale of the
British presence in the region appeared, in spite of the aforementioned
efforts. In short, the prospects for a renewed effort in an inhospitable
environment cannot have been very bright when he met Donald Reay in
early May 1631 and first heard the rumours about Hamilton's treason.
But, by bringing the charges forward and thereby being the agent of the
king's salvation, Ochiltree may have thought he could yet again earn his
sovereign's favour and be granted a place at court, thus being able to
forego the unpleasant option of sailing for the New World. He could
also strike a blow against an ancient family enemy in the bargain. In
short, there was much to be gained by acting on this matter "vith his accustumed bauldness." As will be seen, Ochiltree was by no means the
only figure with fledgling interests in the New World who gladly accepted
alternative rewards in Britain, in preference to the vagaries of life or fortune across the Atlantic.

What followed, however, showed that Ochiltree had taken far too
great a liberty in insisting upon laying his story before the king, in
advance of gaining any further corroboration. Charles interviewed both
Ochiltree and Reay at Greenwich on 16 May and almost immediately
deemed the charges groundless. Indeed, Charles was so sure of Hamilton's loyalty that he insisted that the marquis spend the night in his

chambers upon the latter's return to court from Scotland. Charles then made Hamilton a knight of the garter, before dispatching him to serve with Gustavus Adolphus.[33] The accusations levelled by Ochiltree could not be left unanswered, however, and Charles's response to the accuser was most instructive.

Donald Reay was made to testify further about the sources of his information, and when he reiterated that it had come from Colonel David Ramsay, that officer was also called to a hearing and was confronted by Reay. Ramsay's denials of ever starting such a rumour were so adamant that he and Reay were ordered to settle the matter in a duel. Only the king's eventual intervention prevented this, and the two officers were ultimately discharged after promising to keep the peace.[34] Ochiltree was not so lucky.

Charles was clearly enraged over the entire matter and he ensured that his former advisor would suffer accordingly for his recklessness. Ochiltree's interrogation, and the examination of related witnesses, continued until at least the end of June 1631, after which Ochiltree spent the rest of the summer in a London prison.[35] The timing of this turn of events is very important as far as the king's bargaining position on Nova Scotia was concerned. As John Reid has shown, Charles and his advisors had continued to urge their agents in France to continue asserting the claim to Acadia/Nova Scotia during negotiations in early 1631 for two reasons. One was to buttress Sir William Alexander's charter rights (and therefore, the integrity of the Scottish crown), and the other was the mistaken belief that the French did not value the region and might be satisfied with the symbolic return of Port Royal.[36] The ongoing efforts of the Alexanders to promote their colony, the expressed support of the Scottish government, and tangible efforts such as Ochiltree was providing to build new settlements somewhere else in the region, all offer evidence that the most crucial parties on the British side believed, right up to the time when Ochiltree levelled his accusations against Hamilton, that Nova Scotia could be maintained in some form. Then, things changed dramatically.

The Ochiltree storm had unfolded between mid-May and the beginning of June 1631. On 22 June Charles sent word to Sir Isaac Wake, his ambassador in France, that he was prepared to accede to the abandonment of Port Royal, "leaving these parts in the same state they were in before the peace."[37] The news was transmitted in writing (although he doubtless knew it was coming) to Sir William Alexander in the form of a royal warrant dated 10 July.[38] It specifically commanded Alexander to "give ordour to Sir George Home, knyt, or any other haveing charge from yow there, to dimolishc the Fort which was builded by your sone there, and to remove all the peopls, goods, Ordinance, munition, cattell, and other things belonging unto that Colonie, leaving the boundis alto-gidder waist and vnpeopled."[39]

The king, it seemed, wished to "have his cake and eat it too" as regards the broader question of Alexander's rights to Nova Scotia, as his treat-ment of Ochiltree demonstrated. Ochiltree had been the only other figure besides those at Port Royal/Charlesfort who was anywhere close to making a settlement effort, and Charles was now determined that he would disappear. Ochiltree was not, however, charged with anything in England that summer. On 24 September Charles sent the following cryptic orders to the Scottish Privy Council:

> The Lord Vchiltrie haveing bene examined befoir our Counsell heir
> tuitching some informations gevin by him reflecting vpon some
> nobilitie of that our kingdome, we have bene pleased to remitt him
> thither to be tryed according to the lawis therof, haveing to that
> purpois sent yow heirwith enclosed some depositions vnder his owin
> hand, and the authentik copes of others, wherof the principalls we
> cause reserve heir becaus they lykwyse concerne other persones: Our
> pleasur is, that haveing gevin ordour for receaveing and committing
> him to safe custodie, yow caus try and censure him according to our
> saids lawis befoir what Judicature and judges yow shall think fitt
> and compitent for that purpois; and, for your soe doeing these
> presents shalbe your sufficient warrand.[40]

By early November, a morose and perplexed Ochiltree had been cast into the Tolbooth Jail in Edinburgh. Deprived of legal counsel, cut-off from his family, and without ministrations from any clergy, he was in a pathetic state. Even worse, as the weeks turned to months there was still no indication when he would finally be brought to trial, or what actual charges he would face.[41] Interestingly, Ochiltree's frustration at not moving toward some resolution of his fate seems to have reflected a growing realization on Charles's part that a trial might not yield the desired result. What cannot be missed for our purposes, however, is that a man who was actively planning a new settlement in Nova Scotia in the spring of 1631 was completely removed from the equation and buried deep in a Scottish jail.

In the meantime, Charles had begun to practise a somewhat dubious obfuscation whereby Alexander's rights in Nova Scotia were asserted as a separate issue from the destruction/surrender of Port Royal/Charlesfort. Alexander may have been an accessory to this attempted sleight of hand. Just two days after sending the warrant to Alexander, Charles wrote to the Scottish Privy Council intimating that something more than Port Royal might be lost and that he wanted their help in softening the blow. His words are worth considering in depth:

> Our pleasur is, that yow seriouslie consider ather amongst yow all
> or by a Committie of such as ar best affectionat towards that work,
> how it may be best brought to perfection (whatever contraversie be
> about it) from quyting our title to New Scotland and Canada, that
> we wilbe verie carefull to manteane all our good subjects who doe
> plant themselffis ther, and lett none of the barronets anyway be pre-
> judged in in the honour and priviledges conteynit in ther patantes,
> by punisching of all that dare to presume wrong therin, that other
> may be encouraged to tak the lyk course as the more acceptable
> vnto ws, and the nearer to the title of Nobilitie, wherevnto that
> of barrontes is the nixt degrie.[42]

Given that the only Scottish settlement in the region had been ordered destroyed and abandoned, and that the leader of the only other tangible effort was now in prison, the short-term priorities were made clear. The integrity of the Knights Baronet as a social order in Scotland was to be reiterated and protected, and Sir William Alexander was to be compensated with additional favours. That process had already begun. The previous September Charles had prepared a patent elevating Alexander to the peerage as "Viscount Stirling." The granting of this honour was

formally delivered to the Privy Council on 5 July, in advance of the order
to demolish Port Royal/Charlesfort and the call to the Privy Council to
consider the wider ramification of an abandonment of the claims to Nova
Scotia and Canada.

On the same day that the warrant ordering the destruction of Port
Royal/Charlesfort was issued, two other events took place: the new
viscount Stirling was appointed to the bench of the court of session in
Scotland, and the orders assigning him the profits from minting the copper coins was sent to the lord treasurer. Finally, on 12 July, the deputy
treasurer for Scotland received blanket orders to cover Stirling's debts:

> Being verie desyreous in regard of the good service and *daylie atten-*
> *dance* [my italics – Alexander's access to the king, and foreknowl-
> edge of his orders should not be underestimated] of our trustie and
> weilbloved Sir Wm Alexanderer, our Secretarie for that our king-
> dome, that he should enjoy the whole benefite belongling vnto his
> place, and that no ther have any part therof; And yit being loath to
> tak from any other that which they justlie posses, without giveing
> them reasonable satisfaction, Our will is that yow vse your best
> meanes to mediat agriement with any persone that is interested that
> way, and that what ever yow shall find by a just value (efter due
> consideratioun) fitt to be bestowed for the effect whereby our said
> servad may come to the whole benefite of this place, this shalbe
> a warrant vnto youw to pay the same.[43]

Yet another reward that Stirling enjoyed that year was a renewed
license to print and sell a revised translation of the Psalms of David that
he had produced in conjunction with King James VI/I and had first been
printed in Oxford.[44] Now, however, that favour was expanded to an
order that the Psalms be purchased for use by all schools and churches
in England, Scotland, and Ireland, with the resulting royalties to go to
viscount Stirling.[45]

The juxtaposition of Stirling's rewards and favours with Ochiltree's
treatment and imprisonment is significant. Stirling did nothing to mediate on behalf of his erstwhile associate and did not affix his name to any
correspondence dealing with Ochiltree's charges, imprisonment, or pos-

sible trial. Although the specific reasons for this are unclear, it can be assumed that if Charles was insincere about planting any new colonies in Nova Scotia and, for an unrelated political reason, wanted the man who was closest to establishing a settlement put out of the way, then Stirling was well advised to distance himself from Ochiltree. With the royal will pertaining to testing his case in a trial still unsettled, Ochiltree was left to continue his incarceration in Edinburgh.

Ultimately, the king does not seem to have believed that the Scottish courts would judge Ochiltree as harshly as he had hoped. Accordingly, on 14 March 1632, he wrote personally to William, earl of Strathern, the president of the Privy Council, and instructed him not to bring Ochiltree to trial: "Because i see by what ye haue towld me that Oghltrie is not lyke to receaue suche a sentence as his falte deserues, therefore I comman yow (for this and manie other reasons,) not to bring [him] to his tryall, but command him that he com not within 50 myles of my Court, upon paine of my hauiest displesure; for all which this is your warrent."[46]

Throughout 1632 Ochiltree nevertheless remained in the Tolbooth. As the *Register of the Privy Council of Scotland* indicates, the prospect of a trial did not completely disappear, but some excuse was always found to delay the proceedings. Finally, in May 1633, while he was on his coronation visit to Scotland, the king ordered that: "the said Lord Uchiltrie [be] transported fra the tolbuith of Edinburgh, where he now remaines, to the castell of Blacknes be the shireff of Edinburgh ... and to committ him to waird within the said castell and to keepe and deteane him therein till he understands forder of his Majesteis will and pleasure concerning him."[47]

Ochiltree had been put away and could cause no further trouble. There would be no new settlement venture within Stirling's chartered territories to muddy the negotiations with the French. Stirling was receiving compensatory rewards and further advancement, and although he, the king, and the Scottish government continued to pay lip service to the notion that "New Scotland" remained a serious prospect, protected by a royal charter, there were plenty of reasons by this point to doubt their commitment. Perhaps the most revealing instance of Stirling's acceptance that

Blackness Castle, Scotland. Lord Ochiltree was kept here as a prisoner from
1633 until 1651.

Nova Scotia's fate was a foregone conclusion was his sale of the Largs
property, which was to have been the new Scottish supply port for the
colony on the River Clyde, in late July for £12,000.[48] However, Stirling
remained in partnership with the Kirke brothers, and others, in the consortium known as the Merchant Adventurers to Canada. Their collective
fates, and the ultimate surrenders of Quebec and Port Royal/Charlesfort,
are the subject of our final chapter.

11

The Treaty of
Saint-Germain-en-Laye
and the End of a Partnership

He's vow'd to mourne in Beaver skins
Because his pattron, as ye know,
Became Knight Beaver longe agoe.

ANONYMOUS (1640)

Between 10 July 1631 and the announcement of the signing of the Treaty of Saint-Germain-en-Laye on 29 March 1632, Sir William Alexander, now raised to the peerage as Viscount Stirling, received significant rewards and honours from Charles I, clearly intended to compensate him for his quiet abandonment of the Nova Scotia project.[1] We have noted, however, that Nova Scotia and the St Lawrence River region, particularly the main trading installation at Quebec, represented a separate commercial and diplomatic entity in the negotiations between the French and British representatives who hammered out the relevant treaty. Although Charles I had already given his own tacit agreement to the surrender of Quebec, the main British interests in the question lay with the Merchant Adventurers to Canada and, in particular, with the Kirke brothers, who had forced the taking of Quebec in the first place. Did they also receive cushions against Charles I's diplomatic priorities that could compare to those awarded to Sir William Alexander? And did their partnership, which owed its origins to the circumstances of the late war, endure throughout this period?

Charles did try to reward the brothers, who had led the only successful British military expedition against French interests in 1628 and 1629.
Indeed, the trappings associated with a military victory were present at
key stages in the negotiation process. From the beginning of 1631 the
British negotiators in France had pressed for a repeal of the outlaw status the French crown had assigned the Kirke brothers. Louis XIII's agents
soon complied, and the Kirkes were free to resume their trade in and out
of French ports.[2]

It is interesting to juxtapose the honours that Sir William Alexander
received in anticipation of the surrender of Port Royal – and his quiet
acceptance that a colony in Nova Scotia was not in the offing – against
his relations with his partners in the Merchant Adventurers. The year
1631 began for the company with a petition to the English Admiralty
reminding it that the company alone possessed a monopoly to trade for
furs along the St Lawrence, and complaining that they knew of "divers
ships ... particularly the Whale of London, masters Rich. Brewerton
and Wolston Goslyn," who were violating that privilege. They asked the
Admiralty to use all its authority to prevent these ships from sailing; and
the government complied by issuing a warrant against unauthorized
voyages dated 29 February.[3]

That spring and summer David Kirke was particularly involved with
preparing the company's legal case, and he made several written and oral
presentations before various authorities recounting how Quebec had
been taken and what commodities had been captured there, and updat-
ing their financial claims. He seems to have been somewhat successful
in achieving ratification of the company's trading rights, as several
more assertions of governmental support came from the Privy Council.
A typical example was the 14 October warrant against specific skippers
who were attempting to trade in Canada without a license or permission
from the Merchant Adventurers.[4]

This flurry of official correspondence, and the now public knowledge
that Charles I had agreed to the surrender of Quebec and Port Royal, to
take effect in the summer of 1632, was evidently a topic of gossip. Some
merchants on both sides of the Atlantic rushed to make the most of a
final chance to undercut the Merchant Adventurers. We can infer this
from a letter dated 26 December 1631 sent by a London resident named

Francis Kirby to John Winthrop, governor of the Massachusetts Bay colony. Kirby related: "Captain Bruton who was imployed by my cozen Moris Thomson and company for the trade of bever in the river of Canada is now arrived heer ... he hath brough in heer about 3000 lb weight of bever, and they are now hasteninge to set forth a small ship only for that river hopinge to be there before Captain Kerke whom (I hear) is to fetch his men from Quibeck and yield up the Castle againe to the French this next somer."[5]

On 1 December 1631 the king issued a declaration citing the valour of David, Lewis, Thomas, and James Kirke in conducting their operations on the St Lawrence in the summers of 1628 and 1629. To honour their capture of the fleet led by the sieur de Roquemont, they were awarded his coat of arms, to be added to their own family's coat of arms, in perpetuity.[6] The reader will recall that Roquemont had been captured in the summer of 1628, when the war was still on. Thus, in making this award, Charles took pains to separate the Kirkes' actions of that year from those of 1629, when peace had formally been declared. That distinction aside, these new honours did not completely take the sting out of the looming loss of Quebec for the Kirke brothers; nor did they mollify the shareholders of the Merchant Adventurers to Canada who still wished to exercise their rights to trade on the St Lawrence.

The authorities seem to have recognized that some distinction needed to be made between the Kirkes' military achievement in taking Quebec under letters of marque from the king, and the fact that the installation was now held under the authority of a chartered company, the Merchant Adventurers. That the Merchant Adventurers as a commercial entity would be temporarily decoupled from the Kirke brothers as conquerors can be inferred from the king's order of 12 June 1632 to Sir William Alexander, Robert Charlton, and William Berkeley,[7] making them commissioners for Canada charged with overseeing the surrender of Quebec back to the French.[8] Had Charles wished, he could simply have ordered Lewis Kirke to make the surrender, as he had done in issuing a personal order to Alexander to ensure the return of Port Royal/Charlesfort.

The impending surrender notwithstanding, it is also clear that during the summer and autumn of 1632 the partnership between Alexander and the English interests who comprised the Merchant Adventurers was still in place. They were still meeting and planning trade expeditions, and appear to have been preparing to assert their British monopoly rights to trade along the St Lawrence, even if they would not, in the future, be able to use Quebec as a base for their North American operations. They clearly believed – or hoped – that the Treaty of Saint-Germain-en-Laye did not stipulate exclusive commercial control of the region by the French. Furthermore, in petitioning the Privy Council for ongoing ratification of their monopoly rights, Alexander and his partners also indicated a desire to establish some new settlement to support the Canadian trade. They had in mind the lands in the most northerly part of Alexander's original charter from James VI/I along the south banks of the St Lawrence. Specifically, they wanted "sole trading in the Gulfe and River of Canada, and partes thereunto adjacent, and to place a Colony and fortresse there if they thinke fit, from the latitude of fourty foure degrees to the latitude fifty foure degrees for one and thirty yeares."[9]

The French government, for its part, had also been wrestling with counterclaims where Quebec was concerned. The region lay technically within the monopoly jurisdiction of the Company of One Hundred Associates, although trading rights were still the subject of compensatory demands on the part of the Compagnie de Caën. By the spring of 1632, however, a compromise was reached, and the Compagnie de Caën was granted trading rights at Quebec for the remainder of that season. Thus, it was Émery de Caën, no doubt enjoying the opportunity to exact a measure of revenge on Lewis Kirke for Kirke's refusal to allow him to trade the previous summer, who was given the right to receive the surrender of Quebec. This took place on 13 July.[10]

Plans were also unfolding for the surrender of Port Royal/Charlesfort, and for the assertion of the Company of One Hundred Associates' monopoly in Acadia. Isaac de Razilly had already been designated to lead this process. Charles de La Tour, with an eye to the future, had decided to turn over Cape Sable to new settlers sent out by the Hundred Associates and to relocate his settlement to Fort Sainte-Marie at the mouth of the Saint John River, across the Bay of Fundy from the Scottish settlement. Word had also now reached Port Royal/Charlesfort that the residents there would have to abandon their settlement. Sir George

Home, whom Sir William Alexander junior had left in charge in 1630, had by this time returned to Britain, and a military officer named Andrew Forrester now led the Scottish community.

In spite of the fact that the terms of the Treaty of Saint-Germain-en-Laye were now known, Forrester seems to have determined independently to exploit the ambiguities encouraged by distance one final time. On 18 September he led a force of twenty-five men in an attack against Charles de La Tour's new settlement on the Saint John River. In an incident reminiscent of Captain Charles Daniel's ruse at Fort Rosemar in 1629, Forrester and his men entered the installation with claims of peaceful intercourse but then produced arms, imprisoned the residents, and tortured the agent of the Company of One Hundred Associates until he revealed the whereabouts of that season's haul from the fur trade. Forrester and company then ransacked the premises, took everything they could find of value, and returned to Port Royal/Charlesfort. They ended the raid by transporting their captives to the authority of English officials at Fort Pentagouet on the Penobscot River.

Forrester and his accomplices were evidently able to escape serious retribution for their unprovoked and illegal actions against the French settlement. When Isaac de Razilly arrived at Port Royal/Charlesfort to complete its surrender in December, Forrester was there to represent the Scottish party. Razilly must have been unaware of what had transpired in September because he provided a return passage to England in one of the Hundred Associates' ships for the forty-one settlers, Forrester among them, who were forced to leave.[11]

Charles de La Tour, meanwhile, had gone to France to seek clarification of his rights and authority vis-à-vis Razilly and the Company of One Hundred Associates. He was instructed that he might remain at his new establishment, and for the most part, he and the settlers he brought out from France coexisted peacefully with Razilly's new community. However, when Razilly transferred his rights to his cousin, Claude d'Aulnay, disputes between d'Aulnay and La Tour soon arose. Before long, these escalated into all out hostilities between the two factions and a virtual civil war that would last for more than a fifteen years.[12]

Even though 1632 had seen the return of the disputed territories in the
New World into French hands, the Merchant Adventurers continued into
1633 to press for a reassertion of their commercial rights and for compensation they believed was owed them by the Compagnie de Caën to
cover the cost of evacuating Quebec and transporting home those who
had settled there as part of their company. On 11 May the English Privy
Council issued yet another patent to Viscount Stirling (although in the
document he is referred to as Sir William Alexander) and his partners
covering trade on the St Lawrence.[13] The timing of this patent is important because it shows that in the spring of 1633 the Anglo-Scottish partners who had formed the Merchant Adventurers to Canada were still
asserting common cause. As late as 17 June they had together filed an af-
fidavit with Secretary Coke, outlining the £4,417, 2s, 6d compensation
they sought from the Compagnie de Caën, which had agreed to cover
expenses related to the evacuation of Quebec.[14] Cracks in the partnership
soon became evident, however.

Later in June (although the exact date is not specified) officers of the
Merchant Adventurers resident in London, including David Kirke and
William Berkeley, sent a petition to the king via Sir John Coke. They
asked again for ratification of the company's trading rights, but then
noted: "Our suit is that your Majesty will be graciously pleased to give
order to Mr. Secretary Coke to deliver the said patent to pass the great
seal, and *that the difference betwixt my Lord Stirling and your petitioners* [my italics] be referred to at the return of your Majesty out of
Scotland."[15] There is no other correspondence to indicate what the
source of this difference was, but two possibilities may be surmised. The
first is that in spite of his participation in the firm's petitions, actions,
and projections up to that point, Stirling developed some sort of
eleventh-hour desire to preserve the exclusivity of his old patent, and
thus wished to dispense with his erstwhile partners, or make them agree
to additional conditions that would benefit him exclusively. The other
possibility is that he, like the king, had since July 1631 only been paying lip service to the idea of resettling his former territories, and that
further assertiveness on the part of the Merchant Adventurers might
now cause him problems as he moved to distance himself from active
colonial speculation.

Viscount Stirling had continued to prosper under Charles I's patronage throughout 1632. In March he was granted a coat of arms "quartered with the Armes of Clan Allaster, who hath acknowledged him for cheiff of ther familie [and] the Armes of the Cuntrie of New Scotland in ane Inscutchione, as in a badge of his endeavours in the interprysing of the work of that plantation, which doe tend so much to hour honour and the benefite of our subjects of that our kingdome."[16] Further signs of his elevated status soon followed. During the summer his son Anthony, a noted architect, made a start on the construction of a very opulent baronial residence for his father in the burgh of Stirling.[17]

It is not known whether Stirling's partners in the Merchant Adventurers were aware of this accrual of fortune and patronage, or, if so, whether they had cause to resent it. However, in the course of the most important event of the summer of 1633, the rift between Stirling and his partners was known within the king's circle. In June Charles I made his long-awaited procession to Scotland to formally receive his coronation in Edinburgh. Among those who were privileged to travel with him as part of the royal carriage were Stirling, who had laid much of the groundwork for the visit, and David Kirke. By tradition, such royal visits, particularly for a ceremony as important as a coronation, occasioned the dispensation of many honours and rewards from the king. Kirke was not forgotten. For his recent services in the New World he received a knighthood.[18] Stirling, as might be expected, given the depth and breadth of his service to the king, was the recipient of an even greater honour – another elevation in the peerage, this time as earl of Stirling.[19]

The new earl of Stirling remained in Scotland after Charles's departure and in October his master proclaimed once more that any debts Stirling owed were the result of shortfalls in payments from the king, and that the Court of Session was to shield him. As Charles made clear: "It is our pleasur, to the effect that he may not suffer for so much as is hue by ws, yow certifie ws what course ye think best for the tyme, ather for payment of the principall to his creditours, or of some part therof; and that youw tak such course as yow think best to satisfie them for ther forbearing the same, that they may not charge him till we appoynt his payment some other way, which we warrand yow heirby to allow out of the benefite arrysing out of the copper coyne, that he may reap the benefite we intend for him."[20]

The previously mentioned petition, sent in June to the king from the Merchant Adventurers, had been cleared by Sir John Coke during Charles's visit to Scotland, and it had specifically called for the king to deal with their rift with Stirling when he returned to London. We can therefore assume that something had caused the division to emerge either just before the royal departure for Scotland, or during the journey, when both David Kirke and Stirling were part of the royal procession. By the end of 1633, Coke had received another petition, asking the king to judge in favour of "the patent to Captain Kirk *and against* [my italics] the patent to Sir Wm. Alexander under the Great Seal of Scotland."[21] Whatever the cause of the quarrel, the partnership that had been fostered by the king and forged to meet to the exigencies of war in early 1629 had come to an end.

———————

But what of the lives of our protagonists after the end of the partnership in 1633? What happened to them after their convergence, occasioned by the politics of early Stuart Britain, the aspirations associated with nascent colonial and mercantile ventures across the Atlantic, and the war of 1627–29? Our story can be continued, by way of dénouement, by tracing what is known of their lives, projects, and reputations as they followed their respective trajectories to their final days.

The earl of Stirling and his eldest son, Sir William Alexander junior, continued to enjoy Charles I's favour and patronage. The younger Alexander's service to his king – and to his father – ensured his political future. He was appointed as one of Scotland's extraordinary lords of session and, like his father, served for a time on the board of the Council of New England. In 1637 he was named deputy secretary of state for Scotland at a yearly salary of £300. He died the next year, however, aged just thirty-six years.[22] His father believed his untimely death was the result of a fever the young man had first contracted in Nova Scotia.[23] Others have remarked that, unlike his father, when Sir William Alexander junior died, his estate was solvent.

William Alexander senior, earl of Stirling, also enjoyed escalating political powers and royal favour following his separation from the Merchant Adventurers to Canada. Thomas McGrail, his biographer, notes that the years after 1633 saw him reach the height of his powers as a force in Scottish affairs and as an advisor and courtier to Charles I. He was a dogged supporter of the king's religious policies as Charles tried, clumsily and unsuccessfully, to harmonize religious practices between England and Scotland during the 1630s. This initiative would ultimately lead to rebellion against the king in Scotland, and to wars and revolutions that would see the temporary fall of the Stuart monarchy in the British kingdoms. The earl of Stirling did not live to see the worst of that.

In addition to his governmental responsibilities in the 1630s, he maintained an arm's-length interest in potential colonial ventures overseas. His service on the board for the Council of New England was one example; so also were conveyances he received for lands in New England, one of which included his right to plant settlements on Long Island. The obfuscation regarding Nova Scotia continued up to the end, with periodic assertions of the integrity of his original charter from James VI. No further ventures were attempted, however.

What did endure, after a fashion, was the noble order that had been created to help finance the colonial venture, the Order of Knights Baronet of Nova Scotia. In an effort to make some money from the scheme, subscription rights were opened in 1633 to include English and Irish applicants but, as with the Scots, very few takers were ever found. By 1639 officials in Britain and New England were noting that the designation carried no weight, and recommended that Alexander not be empowered to create any new Knights Baronet, should he attempt to do so for properties he held in the New World. Nonetheless, patents for the order continued to be issued right up until the first decade of the eighteenth century, and requests to wear the orange silk ribbon that had been a badge of the order extended into Victorian times. In 1901 it was even suggested that the order be revived to help settle the more remote parts of Canada.[24]

Until the day of his death, 12 February 1640, William Alexander, earl of Stirling, lived as he had since his introduction to James VI's court in Edinburgh thirty-seven years earlier. To our eyes, it may look all too much like what we call a "credit card lifestyle," with lavish trappings masking heavy debts. Historians have often pointed out that when

Menstrie Castle, Menstrie, Scotland. Sir William Alexander's residence, completed in the early 1630s.

Stirling was on his deathbed, his numerous creditors were already at his home seeking restitution. How, we may wonder, could a man who exercised so much power, and enjoyed such access to and favours from his sovereigns, have allowed himself to fall into such a state?

The context of Alexander's society and times, however, permits us to see things differently. If we remember that he lived in an age when belief in the possibilities of alchemy and the workings of the supernatural was strong, faith that one's king would deliver on his promises is not so hard to comprehend. Service to his king and the promise of royal favour and patronage were the strands that ran consistently through Alexander's life. What might be seen as his illusions of grandeur did not recommend him to posterity, however.

After he had died, contemporaries lampooned him as a ridiculous figure, laid low by his extravagant dreams of founding an empire – a latter-day Icarus who had flown too close to the sun. As one piece of doggerel put it:

The reassone, no man can denay it,
Whay that ther buriall was so quiet;
Because there Landes beyond ye lyne
Layes so far off, as I devyne,
Ther subjects in ye winter wither,
Could not conveniently come hither.
Yet [Victire] quhen ye spring begins,
He's vow'd to mourne in Beaver skins
Because his pattron, as ye know,
Became Knight Beaver longe agoe.

[and in the final stanzas]

An Earle, A Viscount, and a Lord,
With such poore sytlles will not accord
Yet to conclude, 'twill make a verse
Vpon My Lord hes father's hearse.[25]

Historians have largely shared in entrenching this interpretation of Alexander, and only in the last thirty years has his reputation been reconsidered, especially in terms of his contributions to British colonial/imperial history. John Reid, who has done the most to revise Alexander's image put it best: "Alexander was a transitional figure: more knowledgeable and sophisticated than an earlier generation of colonizers in North America, but soon overtaken by newer approaches. Even a transitional figure can merit historical analysis, however, and the career of Sir William Alexander, first earl of Stirling, ending with his death some [370] years ago, is a revealing one not only for the historian of Nova Scotia but also for the historian of wider questions of European approaches to North America in the early seventeenth century."[26]

A major purpose of this study has been to shed some additional light on this last aspect of Reid's analysis of Alexander's colonizing ambitions. In particular I have hoped to draw attention to the vital importance of seeing these and other contemporary North Atlantic and North American ventures in the context of contemporary social, political, and military issues and patterns. For Alexander especially, any consideration of success or failure (according to one's interpretation) must be undertaken not in the light of Nova Scotia's fate alone, but rather in the context of his lengthy career in the service of Britain's first two Stuart monarchs. That this career of service was of vital and central importance becomes even clearer when Alexander's final years are compared with those of his old associate, Lord Ochiltree, who had fallen so spectacularly afoul of Charles I.

Ochiltree, we recall, had been taken to Blackness Castle at Linlith-gow outside Edinburgh in the spring of 1633, beginning a period of in-carceration that would last until 1652. For those two decades his name nearly disappeared from the public record. In the intervening years, however, Charles I would alienate significant factions in all his king-doms, and by 1642, all three of them were in rebellion against him. In the face of this opposition, the fate of a single prisoner cannot have been much of a priority. Ochiltree unfailingly insisted on his innocence, but as Scotland sank deeper into civil war, he continued to languish in prison.[27] Because he and his family lacked resources, he was sometimes compelled to appeal to the Scottish Parliament for relief, as this 1644 remonstrance indicated: "[As] my cryes cannot reach [the] kinges Mātie neither are they of force with him My adress to [the] Counsell and other Judicatories have not prevailed ... A poore prisoner sine Crimine (give me live to say so until I be convict) ... his Dyeing cryes receave no heir-ing My humbe desyre therefore is The premis being considdered that all my bygone meanes and arreires wherof I have bene this Longe tyme frustrat may be givine me and fair and certane way prescribed for my estir Liveing."[28]

By this point Charles I had lost his northern kingdom, and the Scottish parliament, evidently sympathetic to Ochiltree, responded by granting him a backdated allowance that averaged £4 per year.[29] It appears, however, that payments were irregular, and Ochiltree continued to experience financial hardship while in prison. In January 1649 he was again forced to appeal to parliament: "Litle or no paiment hes beene made since the 20 of July 1644."[30] His original allowance was then re-confirmed, and he was granted freedom of movement within a three-mile radius of his place of confinement.[31]

The end of Lord Ochiltree's story gives us a final glimpse of a man who had spent most of his life mired in controversy and had searched unsuccessfully for an elusive personal triumph. When Oliver Cromwell's officials finally released him from his confinement in 1652, a penniless Ochiltree had to find some means to provide for himself up to the time of his death in 1659. According to Sir John Scot of Scotstarvet, his old colleague from the Revocation days, once Ochiltree was freed, "[he] took himself to be a Doctor of Medicine, by which means he sustains himself and his family."[32] Since nothing in Ochiltree's background prior to his imprisonment suggests that he had any medical training, this fascinating piece of information indicates that he must have taken an interest in medical study during his years of confinement in Blackness. Whatever the truth may be, we can only assume from his known history that if James Stewart of Killeith, fourth lord Ochiltree, practised medicine "vith his accustumed bauldness," we may have reason to feel some residual concern for the fate of his patients. In the end, his services to the Nova Scotia enterprise, his king, and his misguided warnings about treason had done nothing for him.

The fates of the main English partners in the Merchant Adventurers to Canada lay somewhere in between the earl of Stirling's uninterrupted royal favour and Lord Ochiltree's abject disgrace. The Merchant Adventurers' suits against the Compagnie de Caën and the French government for compensation were never resolved; nor did the English government ever grant them the level of financial recompense they believed they deserved. Over time, however, the suits ceased to derive from the defunct company, and were mounted instead by the Kirke brothers and their families. As late as 1683, David Kirke's surviving relatives were still petitioning Charles II for funds they believed the family was owed.[33] Nevertheless, these attempts at recovery did not prevent the principals from continuing to serve their sovereign in customary fashions.

Lewis and Thomas Kirke entered the royal navy in the 1630s, and when the English Civil War erupted in 1642, both men pledged their allegiance to Charles I. For Lewis the outbreak of the war and the king's need for experienced and loyal officers seems to have come as a reprieve, because in 1641 he had been convicted as accessory to the murder of a militia officer.[34] Charles must have been happy to have him, however, because Lewis Kirke was with the king during the siege of Gloucester and at the Battle of Newbury in September 1643. As a mark of the king's

gratitude for his valour, Lewis was granted a knighthood.[35] Thomas
Kirke also fought bravely for the royalist side and was wounded in 1642
while helping to take Knock Castle in Ireland. Thereafter, his name
disappears from the records and it is likely that he died without having
married, leaving no direct heirs.[36]

The William Berkeley who had been named a commissioner for
Canada to oversee Quebec's surrender in 1632, initially came the closest
to enjoying considerable royal favour. He was made a gentleman of the
king's privy chamber in 1633 and seems to have turned to literary pur-
suits. His tragi-comedy *The Lost Lady* was published in 1638 and may
have been performed in London playhouses prior to the outbreak of the
Civil War. Berkeley was spared an active role in that conflict, however,
because in 1641 he was appointed governor of Virginia. From there he
tried to provide a refuge for royalists, but after Charles's defeat, Parliament forced his resignation. He was permitted to remain in the colony
and was reappointed governor by Charles II after the Restoration. In
1676 he returned to England, where he died the following year.[37]

Like his brothers, David Kirke had apparently not had enough of sailing the North Atlantic. At an unspecified time between 1633 and 1635
he made the voyage to Newfoundland and published a description of the
island.[38] In the years since Lord Baltimore had left Ferryland in 1629 (see
chapter 6), the island had suffered from a lack of authority and governance, and many old problems associated with disputes between the
island's residents and seasonal fishermen, piracy, and general lawlessness
were still festering. Accordingly, in 1637 David Kirke was granted a
patent for the island of Newfoundland and was charged with restoring
order.[39] The crown's intent was reminiscent of James VI's efforts to bring
authority to peripheral regions in Scotland such as the Highlands and
Islands, and Orkney and Shetland, three decades earlier. Ironically, David
Kirke's co-proprietor to the island of Newfoundland was the marquis
of Hamilton, the nobleman whom Ochiltree had wrongfully accused of
treason in 1631.[40]

David Kirke moved into Baltimore's old "Mansion House" and began
policing unlicensed fishermen and other interlopers. He was successful in
encouraging about a hundred settlers to join him in Newfoundland prior

Portrait of David Kirke(?) Unknown artist.

to the outbreak of the Civil War, and he established a number of fortifications – and even taverns – across the island. However, disputes with
English fishermen who claimed rights to fish on the Grand Banks, and a
conflict with the second lord Baltimore, who tried to reassert his father's
original charter, led to court actions. When the Civil War began, it was
common knowledge that David Kirke, like his brothers, was a royalist,
but he did not actively participate in any fighting. Instead, he remained
in Newfoundland, from where he offered Charles I a refuge in 1647, and
where he raised a naval force to support Prince Rupert in 1648. Following Charles's execution in 1649, the new parliamentary regime recalled
Kirke to England, where he faced charges that he had withheld taxes
from the government. Newfoundland was placed under the authority of
a commission. David Kirke now faced additional harassment from the

government and renewed suits from Lord Baltimore. His estate was sequestered, his movements were curtailed, and he was imprisoned. He died, a prisoner, in late January 1654.[41]

Although his widow and other members of the family would continue to seek legal redress during the Restoration, the story of David Kirke and his brothers, their partnership with Sir William Alexander, and their fleeting empire in Canada faded into the pages of history. Over time, even historians of early Canada found the convergence of events and themes that brought these individuals together was either too complex, or too short-lived, to warrant much attention. For many, it was simply easier to leave the Kirke brothers and Sir William Alexander out of the narrative. My hope is that room can now be found for them.

Epilogue:

Not as Strangers

In the spring of 1632, Émery de Caën led an expedition to recover Quebec from Lewis Kirke and the agents of the Merchant Adventurers to Canada who had held the site since the summer of 1629. They were not pleased with what they found, particularly the fact that the English seemed to have destroyed many of the garrison's dwelling places.[1] This scorched-earth action on the part of Kirke and his functionaries may have been less a concern for Émery than it was for two of the men who accompanied him, Charles Du Plessis-Bochart, agent of the Company of One Hundred Associates, and Father Paul Le Jeune, the new superior of the Jesuit mission in Canada. Émery had only the remainder of 1632 and the first part of 1633 to engage in trade on behalf of his family's company. He knew well that in the spring he would have to cede control to Du Plessis-Bochart on behalf of the Company of One Hundred Associates. The transfer was duly made on 22 May 1633, after which, Émery de Caën left Canada for the final time.[2]

His departure coincided with the return from France of Samuel de Champlain, who carried with him for the first time what amounted to gubernatorial powers and clear authority from the crown that he had never previously enjoyed in the colony.[3] He oversaw the rebuilding of the fort at Quebec and laid the groundwork for new settlements on the Isle de Richelieu and at Trois-Rivières. He also wrestled with renewed hostilities from the Iroquois and ongoing English attempts to trade on the St Lawrence. He died on Christmas Day 1635 and was buried in an unmarked grave. Its location has never been discovered.[4]

Champlain's story is one of almost unwavering belief in the potential
of New France. Captain Charles Daniel, by contrast, would serve his
king wherever the needs of state might take him. In the wake of his
actions on Cape Breton Island in 1629, he had worked mainly for the
Company of One Hundred Associates and led supply missions to Fort
Saint-Anne and Cape Sable in 1630 and 1631. He developed his own
trading interests on Cape Breton Island during the 1630s, having parted
with the Company of One Hundred Associates. Thereafter, he served
successfully in the French navy and was eventually elevated to the
nobility in recognition of his long years of service to the Crown. He died
in 1661, no doubt satisfied in the knowledge that his actions on Cape
Breton Island in 1629 had helped to save New France.[5] He had been a
man of action.

Father Jean de Brébeuf, by contrast, was a man of God who had dedicated himself to bringing salvation to the native peoples of New France.
He returned to the colony with Champlain in the spring of 1633, and the
next year, he was able to fulfil his promise to return to the land of the
Huron. Indeed, he had told them that "he and his companions were
eager to come to them and were determined to spend the rest of their
lives with them, not as strangers but as brothers."[6]

It was a prophetic statement. When he returned to Huronia in 1634,
Father Antoine Daniel, the brother of Captain Charles Daniel, accompanied him. Together they would help to lead and expand the Jesuit
mission in North America, their work culminating in the construction
of a central mission headquarters, Sainte-Marie among the Hurons, in
1639. They would meet their ends in Huronia as two of the eight North
American martyrs – Daniel in 1648, and Brébeuf in 1649.[7]

The Huron Confederacy was also destroyed, the victim of epidemics,
internal divisions between Christians and non-Christians, and sustained
warfare with the Iroquois. The Jesuits decided to abandon their permanent missionary headquarters in Huronia and a once mighty civilization
was in its death throes. In 1650 spring would not bring its customary
rebirth and regeneration to the people and fields of the lands adjacent to
Georgian Bay.

Conclusion

In 1824 a former schoolmaster and son of a merchant from Birmingham named Alexander Humphreys obtained legal permission to change his surname to Alexander. Although it is not clear whether he was clinically delusional – or even criminally motivated – the renamed Alexander Humphreys Alexander claimed lineal descent on his mother's side from the original patentee for Nova Scotia, coveted the title earl of Stirling and Dovan, and most of all, demanded rights to, or compensation for, lands in the by then British colony.[1] By 1830 he was openly using these titles, creating new Knights Baronet and brokering deals for property in Nova Scotia through a London office. Furthermore, his pestering of crown officials reached the highest levels. In an October 1831 petition to Lord Grey, First Lord Commissioner of the Treasury, he made clear his modest terms for making peace with the government:

> I, the said Alexander Earl of Stirling and Dovan, do hereby also protest against the possession or exercise of any of the High Heredi-tary Offices, to which reference has herein been made by any person or persons whomsoever, other than by such person or persons as by me may have been previously nominated or appointed to act as and for my deputy therein; and I ... do hereby also protest against the appropriations, grants, and assignations of lands, mainlands, islands, mines, parts, portions, or pertinents of the country, domin-ion and territories herein also before referred to, which may at any time have been made, otherwise than by my immediate predecessors,

the lawful heirs of Sir William Alexander, within the legal term or prescription, to the prejudice of my right or rights of inheritance.[2] [He was probably unaware of his "ancestor's" license to coin money for Scotland.]

Although the House of Lords tried as early as 1832 to put a stop to his pretensions, particularly his use of the lapsed noble titles and his efforts to sell lands in the colony, his charade continued until 1839 when he was charged with using forged and false documents to buttress his claims. The trial before Edinburgh's High Court of Justiciary took five days and resulted in a verdict of "Not Proven." The would-be earl of Stirling faded from public view and was never heard from again.[3]

This story shows two things. The first is an ongoing romanticism about the riches to be obtained through colonial speculation that lasted into the age of railways and steamships; the second is a telling ignorance about what the original earl of Stirling's Nova Scotia had been, and how he had dealt with it. Modern historians have had few illusions regarding Sir William Alexander and his grand designs for "New Scotland." however. Tom Devine, author of a massive recent study of the role of Scots and Scotland in the history of the British Empire, mentions him only in his first two pages of more than four hundred.[4] Bruce Lenman, another distinguished Scottish historian, wrote of Alexander in his 2001 study of the growth of English colonialism: "The Earl of Stirling's efforts were those of an undercapitalised court projector whose ignorance led to disaster. His death in 1640 was a shrewd career move, as the disruption of his funeral at Stirling by frustrated and enraged creditors showed."[5] As Lenman also asserted, however, the fate of Alexander's colony was tied to Charles I's foreign policy. Echoing John Reid's rehabilitation of Alexander among some historians, Lenman allowed that while it lasted as a colony, Nova Scotia was just as successful as some contemporaries, and more successful than other efforts.[6]

From the perspective of historiography, this re-evaluation suggests that a sense of "what if ...?" can be applied to the venture as it moved forward. That question enriches the story of both the colonial factor and his would-be colony. The present study has been an attempt to both build upon and modify that approach, and thereby to reconsider some forgotten aspects of the early history of European ventures in North America.

As I have tried to demonstrate, the customary surveys of early Canadian and American history, which focus primarily on colonial developments foreshadowing the emergence of new states, can miss the significance of events and personalities that defy established narrative patterns. We have seen, however, that the possibilities of a British presence and dominance along the St Lawrence River, or in Acadia/Nova Scotia, were real and tangible in the late 1620s and early 1630s, and that a very different history of North America might have unfolded, had Charles I determined to hold onto these early gains.

This story has also shown that domestic and diplomatic priorities both made these possessions something worth bargaining away, and to that extent, the North American theatre of the late war with France demands greater notice than it tends to receive in the study of British history generally, and in studies of Charles I's policies specifically, for the years in question. For those reasons, the "Atlantic History" paradigm offers an additional and topical lens through which to examine the combined stories.

The preceding story has also shown that individual choices and actions matter a great deal in understanding the unfolding of events in history. And this is true not only of kings. Sir William Alexander is here seen in a much different light, for example, than he is usually seen in studies of early European colonial initiatives, because our emphasis here has been on his domestic political career in early Stuart Britain, rather than solely on his aspirations to found a colony. We can now view his acquiescence in his king's decision to surrender Nova Scotia as the studied and pragmatic choice of a seasoned courtier, rather than as a sign of abject failure for a would-be colonial factor who was out of his depth.

Ultimately, while Alexander's interest in founding a "New Scotland" should be seen as sincere until at least the summer of 1632, this skilled and influential courtier also knew where his proverbial bread was buttered. Accordingly, he understood that if he did not inhibit his master's diplomatic priorities in the name of his nascent colony, royal favour and patronage would continue to flow his way. Service to his monarch was his major and lifelong priority, and Alexander's ability to navigate the interplay of loyalty and patronage was the key to his political, if not ultimately financial, success. It was a game played by many contemporaries of his social and political class.

Not all the protagonists we have met in this story were as fortunate as Alexander in their ease of access to the king or the confidence they could place in the king's consistent support and largesse. Lord Ochiltree spent a lifetime on the fringes of power and prestige, and at first glance, his enlistment to the Cape Breton colonial venture in the spring of 1629 seems merely to define him as someone who looked to the New World as a place where his fortunes could be reversed. Clearly, he hoped that might be the case but, as historical hindsight has demonstrated, what was a misguided attempt to protect the king – and perhaps a desperate effort to salvage his fortune at home – proved to be his undoing. Again, the favour of his king was a prize that necessitated playing a dangerous game. That Ochiltree's liberty would be taken from him, and that he would suffer extra-legal treatment at the hands of a vengeful Charles I, shows that both his domestic political impact and his profile of a would-be colonizer have been underplayed until now.

We can also now look at the Kirke brothers and their story in a new light and elevate them from the walk-on roles they play in Canadian History survey texts. They were merchants and mariners who turned to privateering only because war interrupted their business in the wine trade between France and England. Although they knew that Quebec and the Canadian fur trade were viable targets, they cannot have anticipated that their modest successes in 1628 and 1629 would excite popular acclaim, and ultimately bring them into partnership with one of Charles I's most powerful courtiers.

The Alexander-Kirke partnership that led to the creation of the Merchant Adventurers to Canada, and which advanced the further tasks of planting colonies on Cape Breton Island and in Nova Scotia, was unique in the annals of early British overseas ventures in that it tied commerce and colonization with a strategic vision and agenda born of wartime circumstances. The Kirkes would receive their rewards and payments for this, but when the strategic imperatives that brought them to prominence disappeared, and their partnership with Alexander ceased to serve his or the king's interests, they faded from view – at least as far as their usual treatment in the early History of Canada is concerned.

As we have seen, Lewis and Thomas Kirke remained loyal to Charles I, and when civil war in the 1640s caused his subjects to choose sides, they were once again willing to serve him and to align their fates with his. David Kirke demonstrated an even clearer pattern of looking to court connections – and the fate of the king – to forge his own destiny. In Newfoundland in the later 1630s and into the 1640s, he prospered both through association with powerful courtiers like the marquis of Hamilton, and also through his enforcement of the king's licenses and decrees. In short, he had been redefined – no longer was he a mere merchant or privateer. Now he was a knight, and royal governor of Newfoundland to boot. However, service to Charles I entailed hard choices in the 1640s, and although David Kirke avoided fighting in the civil wars, his loyalty to the king attracted the notice of the new regime and was one of the reasons that he battled lawsuits and died in prison.

What ultimately unites the likes of Alexander, Ochiltree, and the Kirke brothers is that the "spoyles" they wished to obtain were not to be found in "strange nationes"[7] they hoped to colonize, but rather in their own nations, and through the person and entity that mattered most of all – their king. Although that might mean projecting their own ambitions into distant theatres, the thread that runs through their combined stories is a desire to win and sustain royal favour, and thereby prosper. Such ambitions can be hazardous, however, because kings are human and will pursue their own ends – ends that do not always embrace the fates of loyal subjects.

Years earlier, a much younger William Alexander had foreshadowed as much in the *Tragedy of Darius*, the poem that brought him to the notice of James VI:

Long smooth'd of all, whilst I (pale cares despis'd)
In fortunes lap asleep, of greatnesse dream'd,
Even in that calme, my state a storme surpris'd,
And ere I wak't, my ruine was proclaim'd.

Ironically, ruin was in the end the fate of all our major protagonists, a fate each of them would share with the king he had tried to serve and please.

————————

NOTES

INTRODUCTION

1 George W. Brown, *Building the Canadian Nation*, 39.
2 Bernard Allaire, "The Occupation of Quebec by the Kirke Brothers," in Raymonde Litalien and Denis Vaugeois, eds., *Champlain: The Birth of French America*, 245.
3 Past works that come closest to combining the stories include: Francis Parkman, *Pioneers of France in the New World*; H.P. Biggar, *The Early Trading Companies of New France*; G.P. Insh, *Scottish Colonial Schemes 1620–1686*; and John G. Reid, *Acadia, Maine, and New Scotland: Marginal Colonies in the Seventeenth Century*.
4 Consideration of lesser-known colonial British ventures in the broader context of early North American History begins with John G. Reid, *Acadia, Maine, and New Scotland*.
5 Reid has been similarly dogged in arguing that Alexander should not be underestimated as an early colonial factor. See John G. Reid, *Sir William Alexander and North American Colonization: A Reappraisal*. We are in agreement on this point, and the importance of Professor Reid's work in shaping this study will be obvious. Where we diverge is in observing a different emphasis in Alexander's political priorities in Charles I's regime and his colonial venture. That dichotomy will unfold in chapters 3 and 4 especially.
6 For another variation on this theme see Jane H. Ohlmeyer, "'Civilizinge of those rude partes': Colonization within Britain and Ireland, 1580s–1640s," in Nicholas Canny, ed., *The Origins of Empire*, 124–47.
7 Nicholas Canny, "Writing Atlantic History; or, Reconfiguring the History of Colonial British America," 1095.
8 A brief summary of major works in the field is offered in Alison Games, "Introduction, Definitions, and Historiography: What Is Atlantic

History?," OHA *Magazine of History*, April 2004, 3–7. Other examples can be found in the Endnotes of this study.

9 See, for example, the discussion in Bernard Bailyn, *Atlantic History: Concept and Contours*, 44.

10 For a fuller consideration of this assertion see Carole Shammas, "Introduction," in Elizabeth Mancke and Carole Shammas, eds., *The Creation of the British Atlantic World*, 4; and Philippa Levine, ed., *Gender and Empire*, passim.

11 J.G.A. Pocock, "The New British History in Atlantic Perspective"; Nicholas Canny, "Writing Atlantic History," 1107.

12 J.C. Beckett, *The Making of Modern Ireland, 1603–1623*; J.G.A. Pocock, "British History."

13 This approach has not always been welcomed. See Willy Maley's review of Brendan Bradshaw and John Morrill, eds., *The British Problem c. 1534–1707: State Formation in the Atlantic Archipelago* in *History Ireland* 4 (Winter 1996): 53–5, and Alexander Grant and Keith Stringer, eds., *Uniting the Kingdom?: The Making of British History*, referenced in Jane Ohlmeyer, "Seventeenth-Century Ireland and the New British and Atlantic Histories," 446.

14 Jenny Wormald, "The Union of 1603," in Roger Mason, ed., *Scots and Britons: Scottish Political Thought and the Union of 1603*, 33.

15 Andrew D. Nicholls, *The Jacobean Union: A Reconsideration of British Civil Policies Under the Early Stuarts*.

16 Peter Donald, *An Uncounselled King: Charles I and the Scottish Troubles, 1637–1641*; Allan Macinnes, *Charles I and the Making of the Covenanting Movement 1625–1641*; Conrad Russell, *The Causes of the English Civil War*; *The Fall of the British Monarchies 1637–1642*.

17 The etymology and usage of the term "plantation" must be clarified. As historians for this period are always at pains to explain, the term should not be confused with the more sinister connotation that would later be associated with the slave-based plantations of places like the American south. In the early seventeenth century the term was almost interchangeable with "colony" while "planter" referred to those who held charters for specific territories.

18 Jane Ohlmeyer, "Seventeenth-Century Ireland," 460–1.

19 Sir William Alexander, *An Encouragement to Colonies*, in Edmund F. Slafter, ed., *Sir William Alexander and American Colonization*, 159.

20 Jack P. Greene, *Peripheries and Center: Constitutional Development in the Extended Polities of the British Empire and the United States, 1607–1788*; Allan I. Macinnes, *Clanship, Commerce and the House of Stuart, 1603–1788*; Jane Ohlmeyer, "Civilizinge of those rude partes," 124–47; Ned C. Landsman, ed., *Nation and Province in the First British Empire: Scotland and the Americas, 1600–1800*.

21 J.H. Elliott, *Empires of the Atlantic World: Britain and Spain in America 1492–1830*, 53–4.

22 Thomas H. McGrail, *Sir William Alexander, First Earl of Stirling: A Biographical Study*; D.C. Harvey, "Sir William Alexander," in DCB, 1: 50–4; Reid, *Sir William Alexander*.

23 The inducement was modelled on contemporary rewards for Britons who emigrated to Ulster. Reid, *Sir William Alexander*, 4.

24 John C. Appleby, "War, Politics, and Colonization, 1558–1625," in Nicholas Canny, ed., *The Origins of Empire*, 77–8.

25 For a discussion of the wider interplay among natives of the British kingdoms overseas, and what he refers to as "pan-British" initiatives prior to the Union of 1707, see David Dobson, "Seventeenth-century Scottish Communities in the Americas," in Alexia Grosjean and Steve Murdoch, eds., *Scottish Communities Abroad in the Early Modern Period*, 105–32.

26 Kevin Sharpe, *The Personal Rule of Charles I*, 44.

27 Reid, *Sir William Alexander*, 12–13.

28 This issue is explored in John G. Reid, "The Scots Crown and the Restitution of Port Royal, 1629–32."

CHAPTER ONE

1 See generally: Elizabeth Tooker, *Ethnography of the Huron Indians, 1615–1649*; Bruce G. Trigger, *Huron Farmers of the North*, and *The Children of Aataensic: A History of the Huron People to 1660*. It has been pointedly suggested that the fur trade was transformative for aboriginal peoples in another sense. Carol Devens argues that native men became commercial individualists rather hunter-providers for the wider community, while contacts with missionaries would also cause native women to be marginalized and recast into roles akin to womens' places in Christian society. See: Carol Devens, *Countering Colonization: Native American Women and the Great Lakes Missions, 1630–1900*, 15–18.

2 For a discussion of the Hurons' determination to protect their role in the fur trade with the French see Bruce Trigger, *Natives and Newcomers*, chapter 4, "Traders and Colonizers."

3 This interpretation does not enjoy universal acceptance. See: W.J. Eccles, *France in America*, 21. It has been defended more recently by Denys Delânge, "The Fur Trade of New France," in Benjamin, Hall, and Rutherford, eds., *The Atlantic World in the Age of Empire*, 140–1.

4 H.P. Biggar, ed., Samuel de Champlain, *Works of Samuel de Champlain*, 2: 99–100. (Hereafter, Champlain, *Works*).

5 Champlain himself believed that the expedition had been a failure, since his allies had acquired neither territory nor booty. See: William Englebrecht, *Iroquoisa: The Development of a Native World*, 147.

6 Olga Jurgens, "Étienne Brûlé," *Dictionary of Canadian Biography*, 1:, 131. (Hereafter, *DCB*). Champlain does not, in fact, name either of these individuals. See Champlain, *Works*, 2: 186.

7 Delânge, "The Fur Trade of New France," in Benjamin, Hall, and Rutherford, eds., *The Atlantic World in the Age of Empire*, 142–3.

8 H.P. Biggar, *The Early Trading Companies of New France*, 69. Challenges to the monopoly also came from fur wholesalers, many of which whom were based in the Netherlands, and from Paris-based hat makers. Neither group wanted to be subject to or dependent on a single supplier of furs. See: Bernard Barbiche, "Henri IV and the World Overseas: A Decisive Ttime in the History of New France," in: Raymond Litalien and Denis Vaugeois, eds., *Champlain: The Birth of French America*, 30.

9 Gervaisse Carpin has argued that for many merchants, it was not the price of sending out and supplying settlers *per se* that detracted from settlement effort; it was fears over ongoing and permanent expenses that would be accrued in helping to run a colony. Carpin, "Migrations to New France in Champlain's Time," in Litalien and Vaugeois, eds., *Champlain*, Ibid., 165.

10 Dominique Deslandres, "Samuel de Champlain and Religion," in Litalien and Vaugeois, eds., *Champlain*, in Litalien and Vaugeois eds., *Champlain*, 194–5.

11 Champlain, *Works*, 2: 199–200.

12 Englebrecht, *Iroquoisa*, 44–5, 55, 127.

13 Champlain, *Works*, 1: 214–15. It has been forcefully asserted that the Hurons only accepted the missionaries as a necessary cost of doing business. See Trigger, *Natives and Newcomers*, passim.

14 Champlain, *Works*, 3: 4–6.

15 Biggar, *Early Trading Companies*, 69–93.

16 Gervase Carpin, "Migrations to New France in Champlain's Time," Litalien and Vaugeois eds., *Champlain*, 169–70.

17 Ironically, the 1614 assembly would be the last meeting of the Estates General prior to Louis XVI's ill-fated summons in 1789.

18 P.F.X. de Charlevoix, *History and General Description of New France*, 2: 25.

19 Morris Bishop, *Champlain: The Life of Fortitude*, 193–4.

20 Ibid., 199–231.

21 Champlain, *Works*, 4: 358–70. On Champlain's proposal to the king and the Chamber of Commerce, see Carpin, "Migrations to New France in Champlain's Time," 176–7.

22 Frédéric Gingras, "Joseph Le Caron," *DCB*, 1: 436–8. The main source is Gabriel Sagard, *The Long Journey to the Country of the Hurons*.

23 James B. Conacher ed., *The History of Canada or New France by Father François du Creux, S.J.*, (Toronto, 1951), 1: 26. (Hereafter, Du Creux, *History of Canada*.)

24 See: Sagard, *Long Journey to the Country of the Hurons*, 157.

25 For analyses of the challenges inherent in translating the native tongues, see Marianne Mithun, "The Synchronic and Diachronic Behavior of Plops, Squeaks, Croaks, Sighs, and Moans," *International Journal of American Linguistics* 48, no. 1 (Jan., 1982), 49–58; and, "Untangling the Huron and the Iroquois," ibid., 51, no. 4 (Oct. 1985), 504–7. See also Du Creux, *History of Canada*, 1: 137–43.

26 Josesph P. Donnelly, *Jean de Brébeuf, 1593–1649*, 56. See also Sagard's description of how he tried to learn terms useful in religious instruction, Sagard, *Long Journey*, 73.

27 Denys Delâge, "The Fur Trade of New France," in Benjamin, Hall, and Rutherford, eds., *The Atlantic World in the Age of Empires*, 139.

28 Donnelly, *Brébeuf*, 12–13.

29 Ibid., 50–1.

30 Reuben Gold Thwaites, ed., *Jesuit Relations and Allied Documents*, 4: 211–13.

31 Edwin John Pratt, *E.J. Pratt on His Life and Poetry*, 117.

32 Donnelly, *Brébeuf*, 65–7; Champlain, *Works*, 5: 233.

33 A.J. Macdougall, ed., *The Huron Relation of 1635 by Jean de Brébeuf*, 8–9.

34 P.F.X. de Charlevoixs, *History and General Description of New France*, 2: 38.

35 For the story of early Acadia see: Elizabeth Jones, *Gentlemen and Jesuits: Quests for Glory and Adventure in the Early Days of New France*, passim.

36 Marcel Trudel, *The Beginnings of New France*, 164–5.

37 Champlain, *Works*, 4: 29–30.

38 Trudel, 170–1.

39 Charter of the Company of New France, better known as the Company of One Hundred Associates, in J.H. Stewart Reid, Kenneth McNaught, and Harry S. Crowe, eds. *A Source-book of Canadian History*, 30.

40 N.E. Dionne, *Champlain*, 171–2; Henry Kirke, *First English Conquest*, 71–2.

41 J.R. Jones, *Britain and Europe in the Seventeenth Century*, 20; Geoffrey Parker ed., *The Thirty Years' War*, 105; Roger Lockyer, *The Early Stuarts*, 24–30.

42 Andrew D. Nicholls, *The Jacobean Union: A Reconsideration of British Civil Policies Under the Early Stuarts*, 94–6.

43 Privateers were private individuals, consortiums, or skippers licensed by a government under letters of marque to attack a hostile nation's ships. For the etymology of the term in Tudor England see N.A.M. Rodger, *The Safeguard of the Sea*, 199–200.

44 Champlain, *Works*, 5: 279–82.

45 "The State of the Business of Canada or New France, 1628," Historical

Manuscripts Commission (hereafter HMC), Coke MSS, Papers of the Earl Cowper, 374–6.

46 Champlain, Works, 6: 46–7; also quoted in Donnelly, *Brébeuf*, 72.

47 Ibid.

CHAPTER TWO

1 Sir Humphrey Gilbert, *A Discourse of a discoverie for a new passage to Cataia*, 88.

2 Theodore A. Rabb, *Enterprise and Empire, 1575–1630*, 104; David Loades, *England's Maritime Empire: Seapower, Commerce and Policy 1490–1690*, 117.

3 John Thornton, "The Birth of an Atlantic World," in Benjamin, Hall, and Rutherford, eds., *The Atlantic World in the Age of Empire*, 18–28.

4 John Dee, *General and rare memorials pertayning to the perfect arte of nauigation annexed to the paradoxal cumpas, in playne: now first published: 24. yeres, after the first inuention thereof* (London, 1577), 63. That Tudor England had not heretofore featured anything like this sort of naval capacity is explained in N.A.M. Rodger, *The Safeguard of the Sea: A Naval History of Britain 660–1649*, 221–37.

5 John Guy, "Tudor Monarchy and Political Culture," in John Morrill, ed., *The Oxford Illustrated History of Tudor and Stuart Britain*, 232.

6 He was inspired by his lawyer cousin (Richard Hakluyt the elder), who wrote and translated cartographical, geographical, and navigational tracts.

7 See David Armitage, *The Ideological Origins of the British Empire*, 61–95. Some modern scholars have cautioned against over estimating the impacts and audiences that these authors enjoyed. See Bruce Lenman, *England's Colonial Wars 1550–1688*, 90–4.

8 A notable contemporary example is Martin Frobisher's failed effort to mine for gold on Baffin Island. He had first reconnoitred Baffin Island in 1576 while searching for the Northwest Passage in Arctic waters, and had returned to England with a captured Inuit. He then proceeded to fuel speculative imaginations about gold deposits on the island from ore samples he had brought back. Excitement grew, and a new venture, the Cathay Company, was chartered, with Queen Elizabeth herself among the backers. Frobisher returned to Baffin Island in 1577 with an enlarged contingent, and mined some thousand tonnes of ore. Almost immediately upon his return to England scientific opinions started to appear with findings against his discoveries, and, despite a return mining effort in 1579, Frobisher was ruined. An expedition that proved to be more long-lasting in its results was John Davis's 1587 exploration of the strait that now bears his name. The effect of Davis's exploration was to prove the existence of the Northwest Passage. For Davis, see Margaret Montgomery Larner, "John Davis," DCB, 1: 251–2.

9   Susan Brigden, *New Worlds, Lost Worlds: The Rule of the Tudors,*
    1485–1603, 279–80; J.H. Elliott, *Empires of the Atlantic World,* 31–2.

10 See, for example, the undated dialogue entitled "Mr. Herritt and Mr.
    Hayes's discourses concerning the discovery of Newfoundland," Lands-
    downe MS, Vol. /100, f. 83. For a more general assessment of contem-
    porary English nautical advances see: Rodger, *Safeguard of the Seas,*
    238–53.

11 By the time of Gilbert's death this rivalry had shifted. The end of the
    Avis line of Portuguese monarchs in 1580 created an opening for Philip
    II of Spain to annex both the kingdom of Portugal, and the Portuguese
    empire, a process he had completed by 1583. See J.H. Elliott, *Europe*
    Divided 1559–1598, 276–83.

12 J.H. Parry, *The Age of Reconnaissance: Discovery, Exploration and*
    Settlement 1450 to 1650, 152–4.

13 Ibid.

14 J.A. Williamson, *The Cabot Voyages and Bristol Discovery under Henry*
    VII; D.B. Quinn, *England and the Discovery of America, 1481–1620*;
    G.T. Cell, *English Enterprise in Newfoundland, 1577–1660.* It was
    Hakluyt who anglicized the spelling of Cabot's surname.

15 David M. Loades, *England's Maritime Empire,* 32–3.

16 David Harris Sacks, *The Widening Gate: Bristol and the Atlantic Econ-*
    omy, 1450–1700, 34–5; Mark Kurlansky, *Cod: A Biography of the Fish*
    That Changed the World, 50–6.

17 The distinction between governmental and private or corporate endeav-
    ours in the emerging Atlantic World is an important one for the histori-
    ography of the wider field. As the editors of one recent collection on the
    subject have noted: "This New World was not discovered but assembled
    by sailors, traders, mapmakers, soldiers, natives, colonists, slaves, mis-
    sionaries, bankers, monarchs, and many other varied participants."
    Thomas Benjamin, Timothy Hall, and David Rutherford, eds., *The*
    Atlantic World in the Age of Empires, 1.

18 G.R. Elton, *England Under the Tudors,* 333; Loades, *England's*
    Maritime Empire, passim.

19 William F.E. Morley, "Verrazzano ("Janus Verrazanus,") DCB, 1:
    657–60.

20 W.J. Eccles, *France in America,* 4.

21 Ibid., 4–12. Cartier's accounts of his voyages were first published in
    English in 1580.

22 The two primary sources for the Hore voyage, including the more fan-
    tastic account by Oliver Dawbeny that alleges cannibalism, are found in
    Richard Hakluyt, *Principal Navigations,* 8: 3–7. The Dawbeny version
    of the story has, unfortunately, been kept alive most recently in: Don
    Gillmore and Pierre Turgeon, *Canada: A People's History,* 1: 27–8,
    where it is retold without qualification. See instead E.G.R. Taylor,

"Master Hore's Voyage of 1536," and D. B. Quinn, "Richard Hore,"
DCB, 1: 371–2.

23 John C. Appleby, "War, Politics, and Colonization," in Nicholas Canny,
ed., *The Origins of the British Empire*, 56–61.

24 Elton, *England Under the Tudors*, 340–1.

25 Arthur Herman, *To Rule the Waves: How the British Navy Shaped the
Modern World*, 50–2.

26 R.B. Wernham, *The Making of Elizabethan Foreign Policy, 1558–1603*,
34–70.

27 Peter Pope, *Fish into Wine: The Newfoundland Plantation in the Seventeenth Century*, 22.

28 Sacks, *The Widening Gate*, 49. For a chronology of the works in English
that first mentioned or attempted to describe Newfoundland, see:
Gillian T. Cell, *English Enterprise in Newfoundland 1577–1660*, 34–6.
The manuscript reference is "Anthony Parkhurst's account of advan-
tages arising from encouraging traffic at Newfoundland," Landsdowne
MS, Vol. 100, f. 95.

29 John C. Appleby, "War, Politics, and Colonization, 1558–1625," in
Nicholas Canny, ed., *The Origins of Empire*, 64.

30 Loades, *England's Maritime Empire*, 118–19.

31 Bruce Lenman, *England's Colonial Wars, 1550–1688*, 149.

32 The entire notion question of how or if profit should be pursued was
by no means an easy one. For a variety of Elizabethan and early Stuart
thinkers, the pursuit of profits suggested a moral failing. Could one,
for instance, please God by making a profit through the sale of grain to
regions experiencing famine? Did profits come dangerously close to the
sin of usury? These issues are explored by Mark Valeri, "Puritans in
the Marketplace," in Bremer and Botelho, eds., *The World of John
Winthrop*, 147–86.

33 Lenman, *England's Colonial Wars*, 141–2.

34 *Calendar of State Papers Colonial Series*, 1: 1574–1660, 4 (hereafter,
Cal. S.P. Colonial).

35 Elizabeth Jones, *Gentlemen and Jesuits*, 228–34.

36 *Cal. S.P. Colonial*, 1: 15.

37 Ibid., 3–4. Gorges' plans covered lands stretching from the 34th parallel
of latitude in the south, to the 45th degree in the north, and running
fifty miles inland.

38 Baxter, James Phinney, ed., *Sir Ferdinando Gorges and His Province of
Maine*, 68.

39 "Sir Ferdinando Gorges," *Dictionary of National Biography* (DNB), 1:
242–3.

40 "The Mayflower Compact," 1620. "[We] solemnly and mutually, in the
Presence of God and one another, covenant and combine ourselves together into a civil Body Politick, for our better Ordering and Preserva-

tion, and Furtherance of the Ends aforesaid: And by Virtue hereof do enact, constitute, and frame, such just and equal Laws, Ordinances, Acts, Constitutions, and Officers, from time to time, as shall be thought most meet and convenient for the general Good of the Colony; unto which we promise all due Submission and Obedience."

41 *Sir Ferdinando Gorges*, 115–21; John G. Reid, *Acadia, Maine, and New Scotland*, 30.

42 Guy had visited Newfoundland in 1608 and appears to have chosen the protected site for the new colony based on that reconnaissance. See Cell, *English Enterprise*, 63.

43 Peter Pope, "Adventures in the Sack Trade: London Merchants in the Canada and Newfoundland Trades, 1627–1648," 2, finds that there were comparatively few English sack ships before 1640.

44 Sack ships earned their names from having previously been used in the wine, or sack trade. See Cell, *English Enterprise*, 6. For a detailed description of the logistics of sack voyages see Peter E. Pope, *Fish into Wine: The Newfoundland Plantation in the Seventeenth Century*, 104–16.

45 Gillian Cell, ed., *Newfoundland Discovered: English Attempts at Colonisation, 1610–1630*, 12.

46 The pamphlet can be found in Cell, ed., *Newfoundland Discovered*, 89–99. For Mason's appointment as governor see Cell, *English Enterprise*, 73–4.

47 Cell, *Newfoundland Discovered*, 17–18.

48 Ibid., 16–23.

49 Carl Schuster, "Into the Great Bay: Henry Hudson's Mysterious Final Voyage," *The Beaver*, August/September, 1999, 8–15.

50 Pope, *Fish into Wine*, 52–3.

51 Luca Codignola, *The Coldest Harbour of the Land: Simon Stock and Lord Baltimore's Colony in Newfoundland, 1621–1649*, 10.

52 Pope, *Fish into Wine*, 53–4.

53 Codignola, *The Coldest Harbour of the Land*, 12–13.

54 Cell, *Newfoundland Discovered*, 44–9.

55 *Cal. S.P. Colonial*, 1 (1574–1660): 25.

56 Karen Ordhahl Kupperman, "The Beehive as a Model for Colonial Design," in Kupperman, ed., *America in European Consciousness*, 272–92.

CHAPTER THREE

1 Susan Brigden, *New Worlds, Lost Worlds*, 355–6. Contemporary observers differed as to whether in her last days Elizabeth indicated a preference for James. See C.H. Firth, ed., *The Stuart Tracts*, ix–x.

2 Brigden, *New Worlds, Lost Worlds*, 356; Maurice Lee, *Great Britain's Solomon: James VI/I in His Three Kingdoms*, 102–5.

3 G.R. Elton, ed., *The Tudor Constitution: Documents and Commentary*, 3.

4 John Guy, *The True Life of Mary Stuart, Queen of Scots*, 479–83.

5 For James's early life see Maurice Lee, *Great Britain's Solomon*, 31–58. For the Andrew Melville anecdote see Thomas M'Crie, *The Life of Andrew Melville, Containing Illustrations of Ecclesiastical and Literary History*, 391.

6 Sir Robert Carey, "Account of the Death of Queen Elizabeth; and of His Ride to King James at Edinburgh, 1603," in Firth, ed., *Stuart Tracts, 1603–1693*, 7–8.

7 Bruce Galloway, *The Union of England and Scotland, 1603–1608*, passim.

8 This subject is assessed in Andrew D. Nicholls, *The Jacobean Union: A Reconsideration of British Civil Policies Under the Early Stuarts*, passim.

9 See, for example, James VI to Elizabeth, 10 May 1586, in G.P.V. Akrigg, ed., *Letters of James VI and I*, 69.

10 Nicholls, *The Jacobean Union*, 83–4.

11 *Register of the Privy Council of Scotland* (RPCS), 9: 1610–13, xxvi. Although historians have tended to see the Highlands and Islands as the focus of encompassing policies, it has been stressed more recently that the Scottish government varied the specifics of its efforts according to finer, regional details. See Julian Goodare, "The Statutes of Iona in Context." See also Lee, *Great Britain's Solomon*, 196–226.

12 See Jane H. Ohlmeyer, "'Civilizinge those rude partes': Colonization within Britain and Ireland, 1580s–1640s," in Canny, ed., *The Origins of Empire: British Overseas Enterprise to the Close of the Seventeenth Century*, 124–47. This analysis of fissures caused within the British Kingdoms by the Stuart dynasty's efforts to centralize was not confined to the Gaelic periphery. As Karen Ordahl Kupperman has pointed out, both James VI/I and Charles I alienated the English gentry by attempting to dilute this class's predominance in local government via reliance on crown-appointed lords lieutenant. See Kupperman, "The Beehive as a Model for Colonial Design," in Kupperman, ed., *America in European Consciousness*, 281; and more specifically, Anthony Fletcher, *Reform in the Provinces: The Government of Stuart England*, passim.

13 See Peter Pope, *Fish into Wine: The Newfoundland Plantation in the Seventeenth Century*, 1.

14 James VI, *Basilikon Doron*, in C.H. McIllwain, ed., *The Political Works of James I*, 22; Lee, *Great Britain's Solomon*, 199.

15 Michael Perceval-Maxwell, "The Ulster Plantation: Scotland's First Colonial Venture," 1–2; *Acts of the Parliament of Scotland*, 4: 139, 160–4; RPCS, 1604–07, 87, 89–90, 314, 465, 504, 528.

16 Maurice Lee, "James VI's government of Scotland," 50.

17 James MacDonnell had been poisoned, probably by English agents, in 1601. Michael Perceval-Maxwell, *The Scottish Migration to Ulster in the Reign of James VI*, 8–9.

18 Modern scholarship has dramatically altered our understanding of the workings of the clan system, and has demonstrated the prejudices with which the central government approached the Highlands and Islands. See Allan I. Macinnes, *Clanship, Commerce and the House of Stuart, 1603–1788*, 30–52.

19 Lee, "James VI's government of Scotland," 50.

20 Through the 1590s, the third lord Ochiltree had served as a privy counsellor, and eventually rose to become first lord of the bedchamber, governor of Edinburgh Castle, and keeper of ordnance. In November 1597, James VI appointed Ochiltree warden of the West March in the Borders. Despite the general culture of lawlessness that existed in this region, Ochiltree was relatively successful in asserting some measure of order within his area of jurisdiction. According to one contemporary observer, he "hangit and slew thriescore with the moir of notable thiefes" and was generally credited with keeping the country peaceful. See Keith Brown, *Bloodfeud in Scotland, 1573–1625: Violence, Justice, and Politics in Early Modern Society* (Edinburgh: John Donald, 1896), 222; David Moysie, burgess of Edinburgh, quoted in T.I. Rae, *The Administration of the Scottish Frontier 1513–1603*, 219.

21 *RPCS*, 8: 1607–1610, 512–19; Nicholls, *The Jacobean Union*, 86.

22 Donald Gregory, *The History of the Western Highlands and Isles of Scotland*, 318–26.

23 *RPCS*, 1st series, 8: 1607–1610, 173–5, 521–26; *RPCS*, 1st series, 10: 1613–1616, 68–9; Maurice Lee, *Government by Pen: Scotland under James VI*, 107, n. 46; James Balfour-Paul, *The Scots Peerage*, 6: 516–17.

24 See "Sir Thomas Hamilton to James VI, 7 April 1613," in John Maidment, ed., *State Papers and Miscellaneous Correspondence of Thomas, Earl of Melros*, 1: 103–4. His efforts to provide the sort of example in Ireland that the king envisioned, did not always meet royal expectations, however. In 1615, James complained to lord deputy Sir Arthur Chichester, that Ochiltree had been one of several MPs who failed to attend that year's session of the Irish Parliament. See "James I to lord deputy Chichester, 25 March, 1615," in Charles Russell and John Prendergast, eds. *Calendar of State Papers Ireland* (James I), 5: 1615–1625, 24.

25 Perceval-Maxwell, *Scottish Migration to Ulster*, 107

26 *RPCS*, 10: 1613–1616, 333–4; John Nichols, *The Progresses, Processions, and Magnificent Festivities of King James the First*, 3: 581; George Hill, *An historical account of the plantation of Ulster at the commencement of the seventeenth century, 1608–1630*, 140; 546–8.

27 Balfour-Paul, *The Scots Peerage*, 6: 516.

28 "Statutes of Iona," in Gordon Donaldson, ed., *Scottish Historical Documents*, 171–5.

29 *RPCS*, 9: 16, 18, 30–3, 569–70.

30 Perceval-Maxwell, "The Ulster Plantation," 13.

31 Perceval-Maxwell, *Scottish Migration to Ulster*, 260.

32 Ibid.

33 Ibid. Perceval-Maxwell's favourable portrayal of Knox's work in Raphoe is far different from Archbishop Ussher's findings during his metropolitan visitation of 1629, when apparently, he found "all out of order." F.R. Bolton, *The Caroline Tradition in the Church of Ireland, with Particular Reference to Bishop Jeremy Taylor*, 6.

34 Perceval-Maxwell, *Scottish Migration*, 260; *Calendar of State Papers, Ireland, 1611–14*, 149.

35 Gillian T. Cell, "John Mason," DCB, 1: 496.

36 John Ward Dean, ed., *Captain John Mason, the Founder of New Hampshire*, 10.

37 Ibid. See also "Mason's Surrender of His Ship," Scottish Privy Council notice, 23 August 1615, in J.W. Dean, *Captain John Mason*, 219–20.

38 Mason to Sir John Scot of Scotstarvet, 31 August 1617, in Dean, *Captain John Mason*, 220–1.

39 Ibid.

40 John Mason, "A Briefe Discourse of the Newfoundland," in Cell, ed., *Newfoundland Discovered: English Attempts at Colonisation, 1610–1630*, 90–9.

41 Bishop Andrew Knox exemplifies this as well. RPCS, 9: 16, 18, 30–3, 569–70; Michael Perceval-Maxwell, *Scottish Migration to Ulster*, 260.

42 Gillian T. Cell, "Richard Whitbourne," DCB, 1: 668.

43 Cell, *Newfoundland Discovered*, 31.

44 A brief summary of the tracts on Newfoundland from this period can be found in Luca Codignola, *Coldest Harbour in the Land: Simon Stock and Lord Baltimore's Colony in Newfoundland, 1621–1649*, 16–17.

45 Reference sources conflict over the year of his birth. Gordon Donaldson, *A Dictionary of Scottish History*, 5, lists it as c. 1567. Donaldson and Robert Morpeth repeat this in *Who's Who in Scottish History*, 117. D.C. Harvey's entry for Alexander in the DCB lists his birth year as c. 1577, 50.

46 E.F. Slafter, *Sir William Alexander and American Colonization*, 2.

47 Alexander also enjoyed access to Scotland's high political circle, and James' court, through his marriage to Janet Erskine, a kinswoman of the seventh earl of Mar. See John G. Reid, *Sir William Alexander*, 2.

48 Macinnes, *Clanship, Commerce and the House of Stuart*, 58–61.

49 D.C. Harvey, "William Alexander, Earl of Stirling," DCB, 1: 50–4.

50 Bruce Lenman, *England's Colonial Wars, 1550–1688*, 175.

51 William Alexander of Menstrie, "The monarchick tragedies" (London, 1604).

52 Gillian T. Cell, *English Enterprise in Newfoundland 1577–1660*, 73, 95.

53 RPCS, 1st series, 12: 1618–22, 774.

54 William Alexander, *Encouragement to Colonies*, 32, in David Laing, ed., *Royal Letters, Charters and Tracts Relating to the Colonization of New Scotland*.

55 In actuality Alexander's grant overlapped with that of Gorges, and the latter had to approve the new delineation for New Scotland. See J.P. Baxter, ed., *Sir Ferdinando Gorges and His Province of Maine*, 55–6.

56 Alexander, *Encouragement to Colonies*, 1.

57 Ibid., 30–5.

CHAPTER FOUR

1 The well-known allusion was Francis Drake's, in reference to his 1587 raid on Cadiz where he destroyed Philip II's first incarnation of the Armada. See "Francis Drake to Amyas Leigh," in Charles Kingsley ed., *Westward Ho: The Voyages and Adventures of Sir Amyas Leigh*, 519–20; Colin Martin and Geoffrey Parker, *The Spanish Armada*, xviii; N.A.M. Rodger, *Safeguard of the Sea: A Naval History Of Britain 1660–1649*, 253.

2 Sir Walter Raleigh, "Letter to My Lord Careyy Touching Guiana," *Apologie for his voyage to Guiana* (London, 1650), 67.

3 John C. Appleby, "War, Politics, and Colonization," in Nicholas Canny ed., *The Origins of Empire: British Overseas Enterprise to the Close of the Seventeenth Century*, 68; Karen Ordahl Kupperman, "The Changing Definition of America," in Kupperman, ed., *America in European Consciousness*, 15–16.

4 See the contrast drawn between Alexander and Sir Robert Gordon of Lochinvar by G.P. Insh, *Scottish Colonial Schemes*, 91.

5 Quoted in John G. Reid, *Sir William Alexander and American Colonization: A Reappraisal*, 9.

6 D.C. Harvey, "Sir William Alexander," *DCB*, 1: 51.

7 Keith M. Brown, *Noble Society in Scotland: Wealth, Family and Culture, from Reformation to Revolution* (Edinburgh, 2000), 20.

8 Ibid., plate one.

9 David Stevenson, *Highland Warrior: Alasdair Mac Colla and the Civil Wars*, 27.

10 Charles Slafter, *Sir William Alexander and American Colonization, Including Three Royal Charters*, 3; D.C. Harvey, "Sir William Alexander," 50–1.

11 *RPCS*, 1st series, 10: 622.

12 Sir William Alexander, "An Elegie on the Death of Prince Henrie" (London, 1612).

13 Charles Rogers ed., *The Earl of Stirling's Register of Royal Letters Relative to Scotland and Nova Scotia*, 1: 3.

14 In instituting the changes required by the Five Articles, Alexander

sometimes had to investigate the actions of religious opponents as a member of *ad hoc* boards of inquiry. For one example see "A Relation of James Cathkin His Imprisonment and Examination About Printing of the Nullitie of Perth Assemblie by Himself," in W. Scott, D. Laing, and T. Thomson, eds., 1: 199–210.

15 The most thorough description of Alexander's services to the crown during these years is Thomas H. McGrail, *Sir William Alexander, First Earl of Stirling: A Biographical Study*, chapter 3.

16 Mason to Scot of Scotstarvet, August 1617, John Ward Dean, ed., *Captain John Mason, the Founder of New Hampshire*, 221.

17 See James VI to Sir James Cunningham, Nov. 1617, in Sir George Birdwood and William Foster, eds., *The Register of Letters &c. of the Governor and Company of the Merchants of London Trading Into the East Indies*, 490–1.

18 Nicholas Canny, "England's New World and the Old," in Canny, ed., *The Origins of Empire: British Overseas Enterprise to the Close of the Seventeenth Century*, 164.

19 Maurice Lee, *Great Britain's Solomon: King James VI and I in His Three Kingdoms*, 262.

20 See James VI to the Scottish Privy Council, June 1617, in Adam Anderson, ed., *Letters and State Papers during the Reign of King James the Sixth. Chiefly from the Manuscript Collections of Sir James Balfour of Denmyln* (Edinburgh: Abbotsford Club, 1839), 303; RPCS, 1st series, 11 (1616–1619): 157; Andrew D. Nicholls, *Jacobean Union*, 35–7.

21 Charter in Favour of Sir William Alexander, Knight etc., 10 September 1621, in E.F. Slafter, ed., *Sir William Alexander and American Colonization*, 127.

22 David Laing, ed., *Royal Letters, charters and tracts relating to the colonization of New Scotland*, 116–21; Insh, *Scottish Colonial Schemes*, 91–3; H.P. Biggar, *The Early Trading Companies of New France*, 122–3.

23 Sir William Alexander, *Encouragement to Colonies*, 33.

24 Ibid., 32–3; RPCS, 13: 258.

25 Ibid., 33; Reid, *Sir William Alexander*, 4.

26 RPCS, 13: 14–15; McGrail, *Sir William Alexander*, 84–8.

27 *Cal. S.P. Colonial*, 1 (1574–1660), 60–1; McGrail, *Sir William Alexander*, 85–6. Alexander acknowledged the pedigree of these claims. See *Encouragement to Colonies*, 15–16.

28 Roger Lockyer, *The Early Stuarts*, 15–16.

29 Ibid., 20–1.

30 David L. Smith, *The Stuart Parliaments*, 110.

31 Mark Kishlansky, *A Monarchy Transformed: Britain, 1603–1714*, 102–6.

32 Letter of Friar Giacinto da Casale to Cardinal Francesco Barberini,

Brussels, June 20, 1624 in McGrail, *Sir William Alexander*, Appendix F, 1: 240–51. See also *Cal. S.P. Domestic* (1623–1625), 151, 159.

33 McGrail, *Sir William Alexander*, 126–7.

34 Ibid., Appendix F, "Documents concerning Alexander's Dealings with the See of Rome (translated from the Italian), 250–1.

35 Ibid., 127; *Cal. S.P. Domestic* (1623–1625), 151, 159.

36 McGrail, *Sir William Alexander*, Appendix F, 252–3.

37 Ibid., 127.

38 Alexander, *Encouragement to Colonies*, 4.

39 J.H. Elliott, *Empires of the Atlantic World*, 100; Alexander, *Encouragement to Colonies*, 7.

40 Ibid., 44.

41 A Scottish *merk* was the equivalent of 13 shillings, 4 pence, in contemporary English currency. McGrail, *Sir William Alexander*, 91, n. 2.

42 *RPCS*, 1st series, 13 (1622–1625): 616, 634, 650–1.

43 Alexander, *Encouragement to Colonies*, 46–7.

44 McGrail, *Sir William Alexander*, 127; *Melros Papers*, 2: 590.

CHAPTER FIVE

1 "John Williams," *DNB*, 1: 61, 416; Maurice Lee, *Great Britain's Solomon: King James VI and I In His Three Kingdoms*, 186. Arminians were the followers of the Dutch theologian, Jacobus Arminius, who rejected Calvin's doctrine of predestination and asserted that salvation could be earned during one's lifetime. For an accessible summary, see Mark Kishlansky, *A Monarchy Transformed, Britain 1603–1714*, 127.

2 John Heneage Jesse, *Memoirs of the Court of England During the Reign of the Stuarts, Including the Protectorate*, 1: 86.

3 For a brief discussion of the historiography relating to James VI/I, see Maurice Lee, *Great Britain's Solomon: King James VI and I in His Three Kingdoms*, xi–xv.

4 The funeral sermon and the parallels Williams drew between Solomon and James caused immediate debate. Within days of the official publication of the sermon, critical editions were also published taking Williams to task for his perceived misuse of the Old Testament account of Solomon, especially Second Chronicles x: 29–31. See Thomas Fuller, *The Church History of Britain from the Birth of Jesus Christ Until the Year MDCXLVIII*, 3: 333–4.

5 John Hope, ed., *State Papers and Miscellaneous Correspondence of Thomas, Earl of Melros*, 2: 590.

6 John Williams, "Great Britain's Solomon / Funeral Sermon of King James," 7 May 1625 in Walter Scott, ed., *Somers Tracts*, 2: 48.

7 Paul Lucas, *American Odyssey, 1607–1789*, 36.

8 Charles and Henrietta Maria had already been married, by proxy, at

Notre Dame Cathedral, on 1 May 1625. This was their first meeting as a married couple. See Pauline Gregg, *King Charles I*, 114–15.

9 Roger Lockyer, *The Early Stuarts*, 24.

10 Kevin Sharpe, *The Personal Rule of Charles I*, 3–59.

11 Kishlansky, *A Monarchy Transformed*, 108.

12 Ibid., 108–12.

13 Buckingham had been staying at an inn in Portsmouth called the Greyhound, while he made preparations for a renewed effort to relieve La Rochelle. Ironically for this story, the owner of the Greyhound was none other than Captain John·Mason, former governor of Newfoundland. See Roger Lockyer, *Buckingham: The Life and Political Career of George Villiers, First Duke of Buckingham 1592–1628*, 452.

14 Kishlansky, *A Monarchy Transformed*, 89–90.

15 Thomas H. McGrail, *Sir William Alexander, First Earl of Stirling: A Biographical Study*, 128.

16 For more complete analyses see Maurice Lee, *The Road to Revolution: Scotland under Charles I, 1625–37*, 17–18, 20–4, chap. 2, passim; Peter Donald, *An Uncounselled King: Charles I and the Scottish Troubles, 1637–1641*, 16–20; Allan I. Macinnes, *Charles I and the Making of the Covenanting Movement*, 42–64.

17 McGrail, *Sir William Alexander*, 128–9; RPCS, 2nd series, 1: 187, 205, 337–8.

18 The examples of favours Charles I tried to do for Alexander over the course of his career are numerous. One of the more touching ones is the king's endorsement of the meals Alexander was permitted to enjoy in his household at royal expense. For a dynasty that took the enforcement of sumptuary laws seriously, this was no mean allowance: "Whereas we are pleased to allow a new dyett of seaven dishes evrie meale, according to the vsuall faire of our household, vnto Sir William Alexander, Knight, Secretarie for our kingdome of Scotland, and are further pleased for the defraying of the charge of the sayd dyett that ane allowance of fyve hundred pounds yearlie shalbe made by way of encrease of assignment vunto the Cofferer or Cofferers of our sayd household for the tyme being." Charles I to William, Earl of Pembrook, Lord Steuart of our House, 24 October 1627, Charles Rogers, ed., *The Earl of Stirling's Register of Royal Letters*, 1: 225–6.

19 John G. Reid, *Sir William Alexander and North American Colonization: A Reappraisal*, 4; RPCS, 1st series, 13: 650–1.

20 RPCS, 2nd series, 1: 261–3.

21 McGrail, *Sir William Alexander*, 97–9; RPCS, 2nd series, 1: 96, 344, 412. Sometime in 1626 Alexander had a conversation about his difficulties with all aspects of his colonial scheme with William Vaughan, the erstwhile colonial factor who had employed Richard Whitbourne in

Newfoundland. Vaughan published the dialogue as part of a metaphorical description of Newfoundland he had written called *The Golden
Fleece*. Excerpts, including the conversation between Vaughan and
Alexander, form Appendix B of McGrail, *Sir William Alexander*,
224–30.

22 D.C. Harvey, "Sir William Alexander (the younger)," DCB, 1: 54.

23 James Morrin (ed.), *Calendar of Patent and Close Rolls of Chancery
in Ireland, Charles I*, 277.

24 APC, 41 (1626), 271. See also Andrew D. Nicholls, *Jacobean Union*,
94–5.

25 Sir John Coke, "A proposition for the settling of his Maties affairs,"
PRO SP Domestic, Charles I, 16/527, fo. 104v.

26 See for example the discussion of guarding against enemy privateers and
the stated need to consult Alexander, in Viscount Conway to Sir John
Coke, 30 August 1627, HMC *Cowper*, 1: 318.

27 Quoted in G.P. Insh, *Scottish Colonial Schemes, 1620–1686*, 66.

28 For discussions on the evolution of privateering policies, tactics, and
logistics see Kenneth R. Andrews, *Elizabethan Privateering: English Privateering During the Spanish War 1585–1603*, and *Ships, Money and
Politics: Seafaring and Naval Enterprise in the Reign of Charles I*.

29 Insh, *Scottish Colonial Schemes*, 105.

30 David Laing, ed., *Royal Letters, Charters, and Tracts Relating to the
Colonization of New Scotland*, 41.

31 Insh, *Scottish Colonial Schemes*, 66.

32 RPCS, 2nd series, 4: 375.

33 *Dumbarton Burgh Records, 1627–1746*, 18.

34 Ibid., 24.

35 McGrail, *Sir William Alexander*, 109; RPCS, 2nd series, 2: 313–14.

36 Alexander to William, earl of Menteith, 18 November 1628 in William
Fraser, ed., *The Red Book of Menteith*, 2: 98.

37 William Maxwell to Sir John Maxwell, 23 November 1628 in William
Fraser, ed., *Memoirs of the Maxwells of Pollok*, 2: 199.

38 Henry Kirke, *The First English Conquest of Canada*, 34. Kirke based his
assertion about his ancestor's place of birth on his examination of parish
records noting the marriage of Gervase Kirke's parents, Thurstan Kirke
and Frances Blythe, and Gervase's birth. There has always been confusion about the ancestry and lineage of the Kirke brothers, however.
Champlain mistakenly recorded that their father (Gervase) was a Scot.
See Champlain, *Works*, 6: 71. This error has endured in a number of
publications. See, for example, Samuel Eliot Morison, *Samuel de Champlain*, 191; N.A.M. Rodger, *Safeguard of the Sea: A Naval History of
Britain 660–1649*, 469.

39 Leon E. Trakman, *The Law Merchant: The Evolution of Commercial Law*, 15–16.

40 Kirke, *First English Conquest of Canada*, 33–6; 41–2; John S. Moir, "David Kirke," DCB, 1: 404–6.

41 Moir, "David Kirke," 404–6.

42 "House of Lords Journal, 3: 1 March 1621," *Journal of the House of Lords: volume 3: 1620–1628* (1802), 31–3. URL: http://www.british-history.ac.uk/report.asp?compid=30275&strquery=David%20Kirke. Date accessed: 18 August 2007.

43 Champlain, *Works*, 6: 71. Champlain states, incorrectly, that the Kirkes' father was Scottish.

44 Richelieu believed that the privileges and protections the Huguenots enjoyed under the terms of the Edict of Nantes (1599) made them prone to disloyalty to the crown, and therefore, potential rebels against central authority. See William F. Church, *Richelieu and the Reasons of State*, 186–91.

45 For one instance of the firm's activities in the wine trade see "Arrêt de compte entre David (Kirke) et Nicolas Réveillaud, pour fournitures de marchandises et de 95 tonneaux de vin," New Rochelle, 1624, accessed from NAC MSS0457 (website), 19 August 2007.

46 I believe that the pursuit of booty, or perhaps the choice of the Canadian fur trade as an alternative to the wine trade, is a more likely explanation for this alteration. It is unlikely that in the course of a war against both France and Spain Britain's wine market was glutted, as suggested by Peter Pope in "Adventures in the Sack Trade," 4. The difficulties that were being experienced by English wine merchants in these years can be discerned from HMC Cowper, 1: 377. Indeed, the French seizure of the English and Scottish wine fleets at Bordeaux in January 1627 was one of the triggers for the war. Not surprisingly, this act created a severe wine shortage in the British kingdoms in 1627 and 1628 especially. See also Robert Davies, ed., *The Life of Marmaduke Rawdon of York*, 6–7; Thomas Birch, ed., *Court and Times of Charles I*, 1: 180; S.R. Gardiner, *History of England from the Accession of James I to the Outbreak of the Civil War, 1603–1642*, 6: 147.

47 This was suggested in a 1630 petition to the king, in which the Merchant Adventurers to Canada stated that they "first sent out Capt. Kirke in 1627 to plant and trade there." *Cal. S.P. Colonial*, 1: 106.

48 *Acts of the Privy Council of England*, 1626, 41, 271.

49 Kirke, *The First English Conquest of Canada*, 80; McGrail, *Sir William Alexander*, 108; Moir, "David Kirke," 405; John G. Reid, *Acadia, Maine, and New Scotland: Marginal Colonies in the Seventeenth Century*, 31; Bernard Allaire, "The Occupation of Quebec by the Kirke Brothers," in Litalien and Vaugeois, eds., *Champlain*, 245. There has

always been confusion about what happened in the 1628 voyages and what took place in 1629. See Reid, *Acadia, Maine, and Nova Scotia*, 31, and "The Scots Crown and the Restitution of Port Royal, 1629–1632," 44.

50 Charles Rogers was almost certainly mistaken in his suggestion that David Kertch (sic), approached Alexander about forging an alliance in 1627. See Rogers, ed., *The Earl of Stirling's Register of Royal Letters*, 1: xxvi.

51 D.C. Harvey, "Sir William Alexander, the younger," *DCB*, 1: 54.

52 Alexander to William, earl of Menteith, 18 November 1628, in William Fraser, ed., *The Red Book of Menteith*, 2: 98.

53 Sir George Hay, Viscount Dupplin and, from 1633, first earl of Kinnoull. He served as Lord Chancellor of Scotland from 1622–34. *DNB*, 9: 259–60.

54 Petition of Edward Lord Newburgh and his partners to the king, *Cal. S.P. Colonial*, 9: 70.

55 Reports of what had happened in New France were certainly circulating by the late autumn of 1628, but the facts were muddled to say the least. The Suffolk MP and diarist John Rous recorded on 16 November: "The former newes for Nova Francia was thus, as is reported: One captain Kirke, conducting some English soldiers through France, received fowle discurtesies of the French, and being come home, he vowed to be revenged; of which the French hearing, sent five ships of warre for defense of the theire plantation in America; for Kirke, by helpe of a rich father in London and some partners in the adventure, prepared two ships and a pinnace." This is the only reference that suggests that David Kirke had some sort of military experience against the French prior to the 1628 voyage. See Mary Anne Everett Green, ed., *The Diary of John Rous*, 32.

56 HMC, *Cowper*, 1: 376.

57 McGrail was incorrect in styling him the "earl of Newburgh." Sir James Livingstone was born in either 1622 or 1623, and in 1647 was created first viscount Newburgh. In 1660, following the Restoration of Charles II, he was elevated, becoming the *first* (my italics) earl of Newburgh. His family, the Livingstones of Kinnaird, were a cadet branch of the family headed by the earls of Linlithgow. The eventual earl of Newburgh's father, Sir John Livingstone of Kinnaird, had been a gentleman of the bedchamber to James VI/I, and Charles I. See William Anderson, *The Scottish Nation: Or, The Surnames, Families, Literature, Honours, and Biographical History ...*, 248; John Bernard Burke, *Vicissitudes of Families*, 66; Matthew Foster Connolly, *Biographical Dictionary of Eminent Men of Fife: Natives of the County, Or Connected with it ...*, 298.

58 McGrail, *Sir William Alexander*, 111–12.

59 *RPCS*, 2nd series, 2: 489.

60 C.H. Firth and S.C. Lomas eds., *Notes on the Diplomatic Relations of England and France*, 8–9.
61 William Laud, *Works*, 7: 81–2.
62 Laing, ed., *Register of Royal Letters*, 122; E.F. Slafter, ed., *Sir William Alexander and American Colonization, Including Three Royal Charters*, 235.
63 HMC, *Cowper*, 1: 376.
64 Ibid.
65 Ibid.
66 Laing, ed., *Register of Royal Letters*, 122.

CHAPTER SIX
1 Champlain, *Works*, 5: 240–5.
2 Denys Delâge, *Bitter Feast: Amerindians and Europeans in Northeastern North America, 1600–64*, 176.
3 Champlain, *Works*, 4: 329; Samuel Eliot Morison, *Champlain*, 173.
4 P.F.X. de Charlevoix, *History and General Description of New France*, 2: 37.
5 In 1610 Champlain, who was then in his early forties (his birth date is not known) was betrothed to Hélène Boullé, the daughter of a secretary in King Henry IV's household. Owing to Champlain's travels and the priority he placed on affairs in Canada, they did not begin to cohabitate until 1620. She spent four dreary years at Quebec before returning to France. Her brother, Eustache Boullé was a trusted lieutenant to Champlain during this period. Following Champlain's death in 1635, Mme Champlain, who had converted to Catholicism after her marriage, determined to enter a convent. She became an Ursuline nun in 1645, and died in 1654. See Marie-Emmanuel Chabot, "Hélène Boulléz,' DCB, 1: 110. It is unfortunate that the tenor of our times causes suspicions. This makes it necessary to relate that with regard to Champlain's wardship of the three Montagnais girls, there has never been the slightest hint of impropriety.
6 Champlain, *Works*, 5: 260–73.
7 Du Creux, François, *History of Canada or New France*, 1: 40.
8 This was not the first time that a ruse of this nature would be employed. See pages 134–5.
9 Champlain, *Works*, 5: 274–9; Lucien Campeau, "Foucher," DCB, 1: 311.
10 Champlain, *Works*, 5: 279–82.
11 Ibid., 283–5.
12 François du Creux, *History of Canada*, 1: 40, claimed that the Caëns had informed the Kirkes about the efforts of the Company of One Hundred Associates to relieve Quebec. This seems unlikely.
13 These events are described in Champlain, *Works*, 5: 285–96; Du Creux,

History of Canada, 1: 41–3; Marcel Trudel, "Claude de Brisson, Roquemont," DCB, 1: 579.

14 HMC Cowper, 1: 376.

15 Champlain noted himself that if supply ships did not reach him before the summer of 1629, he would be forced to surrender Quebec if the Kirkes returned. *Works*, 5: 302.

16 Ibid., 297–302.

17 Henry Kirke, *The First English Conquest of Canada*, 79.

18 Du Creux, *History of Canada*, I, 47.

19 The entire ballad can be read at website of the National Library of Canada: http://www.nlc.-bnc.ca/1/1/n1-224-e.html.

20 See pages 78, 81.

21 Thomas H. McGrail, *Sir William Alexander, First Earl of Stirling: A Biographical Study*, 132-3; RPCS, 2nd series, 2: 107-10.

22 Ibid., 366.

23 HMC, *Mar and Kellie Papers*, 168.

24 See Alexander to the earl of Menteith, 15 November 1628, in William Fraser ed., *The Red Book of Menteith*, 2: 95-6; McGrail, *Sir William Alexander*, 136–7.

25 Alexander to Menteith, 27 September 1628, Fraser ed., *Red Book of Menteith*, 2: 93; McGrail, *Sir William Alexander*, 137.

26 George, lord Baltimore to the King, 25 August 1628, and George, lord Baltimore to the duke of Buckingham, 25 August 1628, *Cal. SP Colonial*, 1: 93.

27 Ibid., 94–5.

28 Ibid., 96; PRO SP CO 1/5, no. 2. That Charles had taken an active role in forming this partnership is inferred from HMC Cowper, 2: 42, and Charles's subsequent grants to lord Ochiltree, where his personal interest in the enterprise is stated.

29 Andrew D. Nicholls, "'The purpois is honorabill, and may conduce to the good of our service': Lord Ochiltree and the Cape Breton Colony, 1629–1631," 115.

30 La Tour had married one of Henrietta Maria's French ladies-in-waiting, and eventually accepted a knight-baronetcy of Scotland as a mark of his alliance with Alexander. This did not impress or persuade his son Charles, who continued his allegiance to the French crown, from his base in Acadia. As Samuel de Champlain remarked: "He [Charles de La Tour] had not allowed himself to yield to the persuasions of his father, who was with the English; for he would rather have died than consent to such baseness as to betray his King." Biggar, ed., *The Works of Samuel de Champlain*, 6: 173.

31 'Notes on the preparation of French shipping for raids on North America and the West Indies', PRO SP CO 1/5, 3.

32 The Dutch were established in their colonies on Manhattan Island and

at Albany. At this point they were still allied with the British Kingdoms. See Cornelius Jaenen, "Champlain and the Dutch," in Litalien and Vaugeois, eds., *Champlain: The Birth of French America*, 239–44. The English Privy Council differentiated between ventures it believed would succeed, and those that appeared to be overly speculative, even in the face of the war. See the exchanges between the Council and a Frenchman (presumably a Huguenot) named Monsieur Belanvene for the settling of a colony in Florida, to attack Spanish shipping. PRP C/O 1/5, nos. 18, 19, 21, *Cal. S.P. Colonial*, 1: 99.

CHAPTER SEVEN

1 Stewart's claim to legitimacy in regard to this grant stemmed from his descent from a daughter of the first Hamilton earl of Arran. *DNB*, "Stewart, James of Bothwellmuir," Gordon Donaldson, *Scotland: James V–VII*, 173.

2 Ibid.

3 See also Samuel Cowan, *The Lord Chancellors of Scotland: From the Institution of the Office to the Treaty of Union*, 2: 122–39.

4 David Calderwood, *The History of the Church of Scotland*, 3: 596.

5 See above, 42–3.

6 James Balfour-Paul, *The Scots Peerage*, 6: 517–18.

7 Ibid., 518; Maurice Lee, *Government by Pen: Scotland under James VI*, 135.

8 *RPCS*, 10: 1613–1616, 239–41, 298, 320.

9 *RPCS*, 11: 1616–1619, 156–7.

10 Ibid., 431, 434.

11 Ibid., 10: 1613–1619, 516; 12: 1619–1622, 379.

12 George Barry, *The History of the Orkney Islands: in Which is Comprehended an Account of their Ancient State …*, 349–50.

13 Privy Council to James VI, 20 July 1620, in John Maidment, ed., *State Papers and Miscellaneous Correspondence of Thomas, Earl of Melros*, 2: 365–6.

14 Earl of Melrose to James Douglas, 8 August, 1621, ibid., 428.

15 *RPCS*, 13: 1622–1625, 760.

16 Ibid., 714–15; Barry, *History of the Orkney Islands*, 250.

17 *RPCS*, 13: 1622–1625, 818–819.

18 Keith M. Brown, *Noble Society in Scotland: Wealth Family and Culture, From Reformation to Revolution*, 92–104.

19 Ibid., 65–6.

20 John Spottiswood, *The History of the Church and State of Scotland to 1625*, 541.

21 Thomas, Earl of Kellie, to John, Earl of Mar, 5 October 1625, in HMC, *Supplementary Report on the Manuscripts of the Earl of Mar and Kellie*, 234.

22 For more complete analyses see Maurice Lee, *The Road to Revolution: Scotland under Charles I, 1625–37*, 17–18, 20–4, chap. 2, passim; Peter Donald, *An Uncounselled King: Charles I and the Scottish Troubles, 1637–1641*, 16–20; Allan I. Macinnes, *Charles I and the Making of the Covenanting Movement*, 42–64.

23 HMC, *Mar and Kellie Papers*, 134.

24 Ibid., 140.

25 Ibid.

26 Ibid., 136, 142.

27 Macinnes, *Charles I and the Making of the Covenanting Movement*, 77.

28 Donald, *An Uncounselled King*, 18–21; Macinnes, *Charles I and the Making of the Covenanting Movement*, 77–89.

29 Ibid., 97n3.

30 See, for example, Charles I's July 1626 letters to the Scottish Privy Council and Nithsdale, dealing with the provisioning and dispatch of ships "for the defence of our subjects and of that our kingdom of Scotland" in Charles Rogers, ed., *The Earl of Stirling's Register of Royal Letters Relative to Scotland and Nova Scotia*, 1: 56–7.

31 For a discussion of the primacy attached to strong social leadership for a prospective colony, see Kupperman, "The Beehive as a Model for Colonial Design," in Kupperman, ed., *America in European Consciousness*, 273.

32 See above, 28, 75.

33 Public Record Office, State Papers (Colonial), (hereafter: PRO, SP, CO) 1/5, nos. 2, 3.

34 Rogers, ed., *The Earl of Stirling's Register of Royal Letters*, 1: 403.

35 H.P. Biggar, *Early Trading Companies of New France*, 147; John G. Reid, *Sir William Alexander and North American Colonization: A Reappraisal*, 12. This surmise is problematic. As we have seen, the few surviving references relating the fourth lord Ochiltree's ventures in Ulster suggest that they were a financial disaster. It is unlikely that Alexander could have seen Ochiltree as a proven colonizer.

36 Sir William Alexander, *Encouragement to Colonies*, 4.

37 Richard Guthry, "A Relation of the Voyage and Plantation of the Scots Colony in New Scotland under the Conduct of Sr Wm Alexander younger 1629." National Archives of Scotland, GD 90/3/23, 4–5.

38 Ibid., 6.

39 Champlain, *Works*, 5: 280; George McBeath, "Saint-Étienne de La Tour, Claude de," DCB, 1.

40 Ibid., DCB, 1: 596–7. G.P. Insh, *Scottish Colonial Schemes, 1620–1686*, 83–4.

41 Notes on the preparation of French shipping for raids on North America and the West Indies, PRO SP CO 1/5, 3.

CHAPTER EIGHT

1 Thomas H. McGrail, *Sir William Alexander, First Earl of Stirling: A Biographical Study* 108–9 (he misdates the voyage to 1628); Mark Finnan, *The First Nova Scotian*, 120–1.

2 *Cal. S.P. Colonial*, 1: 103.

3 Richard Guthry, *A Relation of the voyage and plantation of the Scots Colony in New Scotland under the conduct of Sr Wm Alex younger 1629*, National Archives of Scotland, GD90/3/23. This document has now been published. See N.E.S. Griffiths and John G. Reid, eds., "New Evidence on New Scotland, 1629." The author is working with a facsimile copy of the original. All additional references to Guthry are to that document, unless otherwise indicated.

4 They were the *Abigail*, the *William*, the *George*, and the *Gervase*, as listed in Henry Kirke, *First English Conquest of Canada*, 80. There are also a number of references in Champlain, *Works*, 6: 53–143.

5 Guthry, *Relation*, 2–3.

6 See above, 94.

7 *François Du Creux, The History of Canada or New France*, 1: 47; Charles Daniel, "Narrative of the Voyage Made by Captain Daniel of Dieppe to New France in the present year, 1629." This is reprinted in English in Champlain, *Works*, 6: 153–61, and in Richard Brown, *A History of the Island of Cape Breton*, 74–8. It is reprinted in French in Julien Félix, ed., *Voyage à la Nouvelle-France du Capitaine Charles Daniel de Dieppe*, 1–9. Unless otherwise indicated, future references will be to the version in Champlain, *Works*, 6.

8 *Cal. S.P. Colonial*, 1: 96.

9 Charles Daniel, "Narrative" in Champlain, *Works*, 6: 153–4.

10 Kevin Sharpe, *The Personal Rule of Charles I*, 65–6; *Cal. S.P. Venetian*, 1628–1629, 266, 273, 308, 313. On 16 June 1629 the French crown completed the Peace of Alais with representatives of the Huguenot community. It ratified the guarantees contained in the Edict of Nantes regarding religious practice, but removed guaranteed political rights and the right to maintain fortified towns and cities. See A.D. Lublinskaya, *French Absolutism: The Crucial Phase, 1620–1629*, 219.

11 The articles of peace agreed vpon, betwixt the two crownes of Great Brittaine and of France Date: 1629 Reel position: STC/1378:13. In a sad footnote to this episode, Queen Henrietta Maria, who evidently took great pride in the part she had played in drawing her husband and brother into the diplomatic accord, suffered a miscarriage shortly after the publication of the treaty in London. See S.R. Gardiner, *History of England*, 7: 1629–1635, 99–101.

12 George MacBeath, "Isaac de Razilly, *DCB*, 1: 567–8; Champlain, *Works*, 6: 97.

13 Daniel, "Narrative," 153–4.

14 *Cal. S.P. Colonial*, 1: 103.

15 Champlain, *Works*, 6: 27–51; Du Creux, *History*, 1: 46–7.

16 Champlain, *Works*, 6: 39–41; Du Creux, *History*, 1: 46.

17 Champlain, *Works*, 6: 53–4.

18 Ibid., 54–5.

19 Ibid., 56–69. The third native girl, Faith, had already returned to her people.

20 Ibid., 63–5.

21 Ibid., 67. François Du Creux, whose account of the surrender is extrapolated from Champlain's, states that the Kirkes hoisted a "British" flag. This is possible. During James VI/I's reign, the first incarnation of the Union Jack had been designed, and in 1606 a proclamation was issued ordering all ships in royal service to fly the new flag. James pushed others to follow this precedent, and in 1634 Charles I issued a proclamation of his own, this time designating that only ships in royal service were to fly the "Union Flagge." See Andrew D. Nicholls, *Jacobean Union*, 151.

22 Champlain, *Works*, 6: 72–3.

23 Champlain and Du Creux both offer more expansive and colourful accounts of the engagement. The latter focuses on Émery de Caën's ineptitude in the fight, while Champlain asserts that Thomas Kirke showed a concern for his personal safety, bordering on cowardice, during the engagement. The veracity of Champlain's story is debatable, because he had previously stated that Kirke had sent him below decks, before the fight ensued. Champlain, *Works*, 6: 76–80; Du Creux, *History*, 1: 54–5.

24 Champlain, *Works*, 6: 90–94; Du Creux, *History*, 1: 55.

25 H.P. Biggar, *Early Trading Companies of New France*, 119, 133–6; Champlain, *Works*, 6: 84–6.

26 Champlain relates an argument between David Kirke and Jean de Brébeuf, in which the former, in the presence of Michel, accused the Jesuits of complicity in the trampling of the de Caëns' monopoly rights. Ibid., 137.

27 Ibid., 130, 133.

28 Ibid., 133.

29 Ibid., 138–9.

30 Ibid., 104–22; Du Creux, *History*, 1: 57–61.

31 Champlain, *Works*, 6: 142.

32 Ibid., 143–6.

33 Ibid., 155–7; Andrew D. Nicholls, "Showdown at Fort Rosemar," 30–2.

34 See above, 115–16, 118; also, Andrew D. Nicholls, "'The purpois is honorabill, and may conduce to the good of our service': Lord Ochiltree and the Cape Breton Colony, 1629–1631."

35 Diligent research efforts from a number of quarters have even failed to discover his first name. See Griffiths and Reid, eds., "New Evidence on New Scotland," 502n50. There are three documented possibilities. A George Ogilvie of Carnous[t]ie had subscribed as a Knight Baronet of Nova Scotia in April 1626, while Sir John Ogilvie of Innerquhartie had subscribed in September. They were joined by a George Ogilvie of Banff in July 1627. It should be clear, however, that subscription to the Order of Knights Baronet did not necessarily mean that the individuals in question intended to go to the New World immediately; nor did not subscribing preclude joining a colony. Lord Ochiltree, for example, was not yet a Knight Baronet when he went to Cape Breton in 1629. It should be noted that Guthry in his *Relation* spells the surname "Ogilivy" and "Ogilvie" within a few lines in the same document. This is not an uncommon occurrence in historical manuscripts – a test sent to vex researchers!

36 C. Bruce Fergusson, "Constance Ferrar," DCB, 1: 305. In the only document known to have been written by Ferrar, he identifies himself as someone who had "fought in the Low Countries" under the command of an officer whose name is illegible. PRO SP C/O 1/5, no. 41.

37 "Memorial of Lord Ochiltree to the King," PRO SP C/O 1/5, no. 46. For an inventory of the party's goods and equipment see National Library of Scotland (hereafter NLS) MS 2061.

38 Guthry, "Relation," 5.

39 Ibid., 4.

40 Ibid., 4–6. Significantly, Guthry relates that he performed a marriage ceremony on Cape Breton Island. He makes no mention of any other clergy being with him, and does not say that the settlement Ochiltree founded had obtained a minister. See also "Memorial of Lord Ochiltrie to the King," PRO SP C/O 1/5, no. 46.

41 "Narrative of the Voyage Made by Captain Daniel ...," Champlain, *Works*, 6: 156–9; Julien Félix, ed., *Voyage à la Nouvelle-France du capitaine Charles Daniel de Dieppe*, 8–9.

42 Ibid. (both references).

43 André Malapart, "La prise d'un seigneur escossais ...," in Félix, ed., *Voyage à la Nouvelle-France*, 12–23.

44 Lord Ochiltree, "The barbarous and perfidius cariage of the Frenche ...," 6–7; "Memorial of Lord Ochiltree to the King," PRO SP C/O 1/5, no. 46.

45 "Petition of Captain Constance Ferrar to the King," PRO SP C/O 1/5, no. 41.

46 John G. Reid, *Acadia, Maine, and New Scotland: Marginal Colonies in the Seventeenth Century*, 82.

47 Ochiltree, "The barbarous and perfidius cariage of the Frenche ...," 9.

48 Ibid., 11–12.

CHAPTER NINE

1 Richard Guthry, "Relation," 6–8.
2 N.E.S. Griffiths and John G. Reid, eds., "New Evidence on New Scotland," 504–55nn55–6.
3 See above, chapter 8, n35.
4 Guthry, "Relation," 9.
5 The classic analysis of this problem is Edmund S. Morgan, "The Labor Problem at Jamestown, 1607–18."
6 For two contemporary accounts see Thomas Birch, ed., *The Court and Times of Charles I*, 2: 54, 60; and G.P. Insh, *Scottish Colonial Schemes*, 80–1; also, D.C. Harvey, "Segipt," *DCB*, 1: 605; Thomas McGrail, *Sir William Alexander, First Earl of Stirling: A Biographical Study*, 113. The most interesting account is provided by the Reverend Joseph Mead in a letter of 12 February 1630 to Sir Martin Stuteville: "The King [Segipt] comes to be of our king's religion, and to submit his kingdom to him, and become his homager for the sam, that he may be protected against the French of Canada. Those savages arrived at Plymouth were a while entertained at my Lord Poulet's in Somersetshire, much made of, especially my lade of the savage queen: she came with her to the coach when they were to come to London, put a chain about her neck with a diamond valued by some at near £20. The savages took all in good part, but for thanks or acknowledgement made no sign or expression at all." Thomas Birch, ed., *Court and Times of Charles I, etc*, 2: 60.
7 Insh, *Scottish Colonial Schemes*, 81–82; McGrail, *Sir William Alexander*, 113; Mark Finnan, *The First Nova Scotian*, 124.
8 Insh, *Scottish Colonial Schemes*, 83.
9 *RPCS*, 2nd series, 3: 1629–1630, 392–4; Insh, *Scottish Colonial Schemes*, 83.
10 *RPCS*, 2nd series, 3: 1629–1630, 488.
11 Quoted in, McGrail, *Sir William Alexander*, 114. The full text is in William Fraser, ed., *The Red Book of Menteith*, 2: 111.
12 La Tour is listed as having subscribed as a Knight Baronet of Nova Scotia on 30 November 1629. See David Laing, ed., *Register of Royal Letters*, 122.
13 *RPCS*, 2nd series, 3: 1629–1630, 543.
14 Champlain, *Works*, 6, 171–7.
15 Ibid.
16 *Cal. S.P. Colonial*, 1: 106–7.
17 Champlain, *Works*, 6: 170–4.
18 Ibid., 184.
19 *Cal. S.P. Colonial*, 1: 139; PRO C/O 1/6, no. 38.
20 *Acts of the Privy Council*, 1: 160, doc. 267.
21 Champlain, *Works*, 6: 184–5.
22 Ibid., 217.

23 Memorial of the French Ambassador, *Cal. S.P. Colonial*, 107; PRO C/O
   1/5, no. 50. See also Champlain, *Works*, 6: 210.
24 John G. Reid, "The Scots Crown and the Restitution of Port Royal,"
   49–51; *Cal. S.P. Colonial*, 1: 107.
25 Ibid.
26 Champlain, *Works*, 6: 168.
27 Marcel Trudel, *The Beginnings of New France*, 177. Champlain, it will
   be recalled, had asserted that Monsieur Le Baillif of Amiens had burgled
   the warehouse of the Compagnie de Cäen when Quebec was seized. No
   further exploration of this accusation appears. See Champlain, *Works*,
   6: 184–5.
28 *Cal. S.P. Colonial*, 1: 102.
29 Ibid., 103.
30 Champlain, *Works*, 6: 148–52; 167–9; H.P. Biggar, *The Early Trading
   Companies of New France*, 150.
31 *Cal. S.P. Colonial*, 1: 112; PRO SP CO 1/5, no. 81.
32 *Cal. S.P. Colonial*, 1: 117–18; PRO SP CO 1/5, no. 97.
33 Champlain essentially corroborated this figure when recalling the surrender of Quebec, and the seizure of the Caëns' warehouse by the
   Frenchman Le Baillif. Champlain, *Works*, 6, 63–4.
34 Henry Kirke, *The First British Conquest*, 102–3; *Cal. S.P. Colonial*, 1:
   139; PRO C/O 1/6, no. 38.
35 Biggar, *Early Trading Companies*, 161.
36 John G. Reid, "The Scots Crown and the Restitution of Port Royal,"
   50–2; C.H. Firth and S.C. Lomas, *Notes on the Diplomatic Relations
   of England and France*, 10–11.
37 Biggar, *Early Trading Companies*, 156.
38 Burlamachi had undertaken diplomatic missions for the English crown
   beginning in James's reign. He had organized much of the private funding in Britain that was sent to support Frederick of the Palatinate, Count
   Mansfeld's army, and Buckingham's expeditions during the wars with
   Spain and France. He had been promised in 1625 that partial repayment
   for advances he had made to the crown over a period of years would
   come from Henrietta Maria's dowry. By the mid-1630s his largesse to
   the crown and other parties forced him into bankruptcy, although he
   was protected by Charles I. Like Sir William Alexander, he is a prime
   example of how individuals would incur deep personal debts, in anticipation of tangible rewards and patronage from the crown. It was an all
   too common form of political, speculative investment. See A.V. Judges,
   "Philip Burlamachi: A Financier of the Thirty Years' War."
39 Champlain, *Works*, 6: 214–17; *Cal. S.P. Colonial*, 1: 134; PRO SP CO
   1/6, no. 23.
40 *Cal. S.P. Colonial*, 1: 142; PRO SP CO 1/6, no. 45.

CHAPTER TEN

1 Thomas H. McGrail, *Sir William Alexander, First Earl of Stirling: A Biographical Study*, 146–7; RPCS, 2nd series, 4, xxv–xxviii; xxii; 323–6.

2 Nicholls, *The Jacobean Union*, 156–8.

3 See "Instructions ... anent the erectioun of a generall fishing," APS, 5, 221–3; "Instructions ... anent the erecting of a commoun fishing," idem., 232; RPCS, 2nd series, 4: xix; PRO SP/16/172/78. Another North Atlantic veteran of our acquaintance, Captain John Mason, was also a director of the association.

4 John G. Reid, "The Scots Crown and the Restitution of Port Royal," passim.

5 *Cal. S.P. Colonial*, 1: 107; PRO CO 1/5, no. 51.

6 Reid, "The Scots Crown and the Restitution of Port Royal," 50–1.

7 Ibid., 51; RPCS, 2nd series, 4: 46–7.

8 See above, 140.

9 Champlain recorded that, in his testimony before the Dieppe Admiralty Court, Ochiltree had claimed to be a relative of the king of England. Champlain, *Works*, 6: 151. Given Ochiltree's career and antecedents, such an exaggeration on his part was possible. On the other hand, none of the other documents relating to this case repeat the claim. It should probably be read as an error on Champlain's part, or an instance of third hand innuendo.

10 *Cal. S.P. Colonial*, 1: 105–6; PRO CO 1/5, no. 46.

11 Although Ochiltree would not likely have been aware of the scheme, arguments about the king's rights vis-à-vis fisheries were becoming highly topical, in light of the projected Association for the Fishing.

12 *Cal. S.P. Colonial*, 1: 105–6; PRO CO 1/5, nos. 46, 47.

13 Ibid., both references.

14 Conflicting evidence exists over the exact month in which Ochiltree was returned. When Constance Ferrar petitioned the Privy Council on 9 December 1629, he assumed that Ochiltree was still imprisoned in Dieppe. Sir Isaac Wake, writing from Paris in January, stated that his complaints over the treatment Ochiltree was receiving in prison had already led to his release. Ochiltree seems to have been in London by late January, as he began to petition the king and the Privy Council. See: PRO SP CO 1/5, nos. 41, 46, 47; *Cal. S.P. Domestic, Charles I, 1631–33*, 5: 164.

15 PRO SP CO 1/5, no. 41.

16 PRO SP CO 1/5, nos. 46, 47. There had already been one ill-fated 1629 attempt by the Jesuits to send relief to Quebec. It had been organized and led by Father Philibert Noyrot, who had chartered a supply ship that sailed with Charles Daniel's squadron. It will be recalled that Daniel mentioned having been separated from his fleet in the Gulf of St

Lawrence, and that this was what led him to Cape Breton Island and his encounter with Ochiltree's party. Noyrot's ship was nearly captured by David Kirke as it tried to enter the St Lawrence. It escaped, but was sunk in a gale in the Strait of Canseau between Cape Breton Island and Nova Scotia. Noyrot drowned, but several members of the party survived, including the former Jesuit Superior at Quebec, Father Charles Lalement. He was rescued by the crew of a Basque fishing vessel, but had to survive yet another shipwreck on the homeward voyage, this time off the coast of Spain. See the accounts in Champlain, *Works*, 6: 161–7; François Du Creux, *History of Canada*, 1: 62–8; Reuben Thwaites, ed., *Jesuit Relations*, 4: 229–44; Léon Pouliot, "Charles Lalemant," *DCB*, 1: 411–12; Jacques Monet, "Philibert Noyrot," *DCB*, 1: 521.

17 The only other reference to a Constance Ferrar that I have discovered cites a letter from one Constance Ferrar to the Earl of Stamford, who, during the English Civil War, had issued an invitation to Ferrar to join his parliamentary regiment from Hereford. Ferrar's letter reads: "Sir, I received a letter that bears your name, inviting me to such an act of baseness as (these must tell you), I hold in highest disdain; for never yet did my necessity (or ever shall) put me one tittle off my fidelity, or inforce me to violate my honour, which, notwithstanding the offer you make from his Excellency. I shall still endeavour (as hitherto I have done) entirely to preserve. As for his Majesty's pardon, I conceive not myself to stand in need of it, my service and employment being only for the preservation of the true Protestant religion, the safety of his Majesty's person, the defence of the laws of the land, the liberty of the subject, and privilege of Parliament, whereunto, I am persuaded, all true Englishmen are conscientiously obliged. For your undoubted power to reduce the rebels in Hereford (as you term them), doubt not Sir, when you come, you shall receive the entertainment of a soldier. CONSTANCE FERRAR." Transcribed from: Paul Rollinson, "Sir John Birch, His Regiment in the Civil War in Herefordshire," http://www.colbirch.org.uk/pages/hereford.php

18 See "Memoir of the French Ambassador, 1 February 1630," in Laing, ed., *Royal Letters, Charters and Tracts Relating to the Colonization of New Scotland*, 53–4.

19 PRO SP CO 1/5, nos. 16, 20, 33–6, 38, 49, 51.

20 For a complete exploration of this possibility, see Reid, "The Scots Crown and the Restitution of Port Royal," 39–63.

21 See Alexander to the Earl of Menteith, 9 February 1630, in William Fraser, ed., *The Red Book of Menteith*, 2: 111–13.

22 *RPCS*, 2nd. series, 3: 1629–1630, 45–6; Charles I to Sir William Alexander, junior, 13 May 1630, in Charles Rogers, ed., *Earl of Stirling's Regis-*

ter of Royal Letters, 2: 439; Reid, "The Scots Crown and the Restitution of Port Royal," 47.

23 Roll of Baronets of Nova Scotia, in Laing, ed., *Royal Letters, Charters*, 122.

24 Charles I to the Scottish Privy Council, 19 April 1631, in Rogers, ed., *Earl of Stirling's Register*, 2: 513.

25 Charles I to the Justices of Ireland, 19 April 1631, ibid., 514.

26 "The Examinatioun of James, Lord Ocheltrie, Takin 20 Junij, 1631," in HMC, *Mar and Kellie*, 184.

27 Ibid., 185.

28 "Examination of Donald, Lord Ray, Taken 21 June 1631," ibid., 189.

29 Ibid., 188.

30 "The Examinatioun of James, Lord Ocheltrie, Takin 20 Junij, 1631," ibid., 185.

31 Giovanni Soranzo to the Doge and Senate, 18 July 1631, in: *Cal. S.P. Venetian*, 22: 526–7.

32 Gilbert Burnet, *Memoirs of the Lives and Actions of James and William, dukes of Hamilton and Castleherald*, 4–8. This view is echoed by G.P. Insh, *Scottish Colonial Schemes*, 111–12, and by Hamilton's most recent biographer. See Hilary L. Rubinstein, *Captain Luckless: James, First Duke of Hamilton, 1606–1649*, 29–30. Maurice Lee is less certain, noting simply that it is difficult to ascertain why Ochiltree acted as he did, although jealousy of Hamilton may have been a factor. See Maurice Lee, *Road to Revolution: Scotland under Charles I, 1625–37*, 88–9.

33 Rubinstein, *Captain Luckless*, 30–1.

34 HMC, *Mar and Kellie*, 191; Rubinstein, *Captain Luckless*, 30. Both sources suggest that the original date for the duel was set for 12 April 1631. Rubinstein further states that a court of chivalry discharged them on 12 May 1631. These dates cannot be correct, as Ochiltree did not even learn of the rumour from Reay until early May, and did not meet with Charles until 16 May.

35 See, for example, "Depositions by Lieutenant Colonel Alexander Stewart and Captain William Stewart, in reference to Lord Ochiltree's Plot," HMC, *Laing Manuscripts*, 1: 187.

36 Reid, "The Scots Crown and the Restitution of Port Royal," 53.

37 PRO SP 78/89, f. 210. Quoted in Reid, "The Scots Crown and the Restitution of Port Royal," 54.

38 The king's *Act for the Abandonment of Port Royal* was drafted in early June and sent to Louis XIII in a Latin document dated 4 June 1631. Alexander was likely aware of this document as well. *Cal. S.P. Colonial*, 1: 132; PRO CO 1/6, no. 17.

39 Warrant, Greenwich, 10 July 1631, in Rogers, ed., *The Earl of Stirling's Register*, 2: 544.

40 Charles I to the Scottish Privy Council, 24 September 1631, in Rogers, ed., *The Earl of Stirling's Register*, 2: 555–6.

41 See RPCS, 2nd series, 4: 1630–1632, 263, 269, 348, 352–3, 358, 398, 627, 629.

42 Charles to the Scottish Privy Council, 12 July 1631, in Rogers, ed., *The Earl of Stirling's Register*, 2: 545.

43 Charles to the Treasaurer Depute (sic.) 12 July 1631, ibid., 546.

44 McGrail, *Sir William Alexander*, 165.

45 Ibid.; Rogers, ed., *The Earl of Stirling's Register*, 2: 537–8.

46 Charles I to William, Earl of Strathern, 14 March 1632, in Fraser, ed., *The Red Book of Menteith* (Edinburgh: 1880), 2: 41. On 30 August, the king reiterated these instructions. Ibid., 43.

47 Warrant from his Majest for the removal of Lord Ochiltree from the Tolbooth of Edinburgh to the Castle of Blackness, 20 May 1633, in RPCS, 2nd series, 5: 1633–1635, 101.

48 McGrail, *Sir William Alexander*, 144.

CHAPTER ELEVEN

1 The war with Spain had concluded in November 1630 with the signing of the Treaty of Madrid.

2 H.P. Biggar, *The Early Trading Companies of New France*, 155.

3 *Cal. S.P. Colonial*, 1: 128; PRO C/O 1/6 nos. 4, 5. It is interesting to note that in spite of the unclear status surrounding of trading rights and British possessions in the region at this stage, certain individuals were still intent on mounting speculative expeditions, and Charles I was willing to grant licenses in return for a cut of any profits. On 1 March 1631 one Daniel Gookin, gentleman, petitioned the king for monopolies monopoly rights to mine on an island "...between 50 and 55 deg N.L. distant about 300 leagues from the Blasques in Ireland, which has been discovered in part and named by Saint Brandon, or the Isle de Verd, likely to produce many valuable commodities." Gookin specifically wanted: "...a patent under the Great Seal for planting and enjoying that island and any others adjacent, with similar privileges to those granted to Sir William Alexander." Secretary of State Sir James Coke recorded that the king would grant the license, and then in an act of great magnanimity, added: "the King to take but the 10th part of silver or gold mines discovered." *Cal. S.P. Colonial*, 1: 128–9.

4 *Cal. S.P. Colonial*, 1: 130–5; PRO C/O 1/6, nos. 12, 15, 23, 27.

5 Francis Kirby to John Winthrop, 26 December 1631. Cited in Horace E. Ware, "An Incident in Winthrop's Voyage to New England," 107.

6 *Cal. S.P. Colonial*, 1: 137; PRO C/O 1/6, no. 33.

7 Berkeley's exact identity, and his connection with the Merchant Adventurers prior to 1629 is uncertain. Peter Pope (*Fish into Wine*) asserts that

William Berkeley, also stylled "Barkeley," "Barkly," and "Bartly," had
been in partnership in the wine trade with Gervase Kirk prior to the war
with France. As Pope shows definitively, a William Barkeley, merchant
of St Helen's, Bishop's Gate, was indeed in partnership with the Kirke
brothers in various ventures in the later 1630s. This partnership was
maintained until the early 1650s. Barkeley died in 1653. Pope's evidence
is corroborated in several sources, notably doc. 224, *Acts of the Privy
Council*, 25 March 1629, where William Barkeley and Gervase Kirke
are named as co-defendants in a suit brought by the sieur de Roquemont
surrounding in regard to charges the latter had accrued while in David
Kirke's custody. The William Berkeley who was named as one of the
commissioners for Canada in 1632 seems instead to have been a
younger man, recently returned from Europe, but whose family had extensive connections at court, and were long-standing investors in the
Virginia Company. Eventually, he was knighted, and would go on to be
governor of Virginia. See above, 182. The identity of this William Berkeley is asserted by the editors of the *Calendar of State Papers Colonial*,
the *Acts of the Privy Council*, and the editor of the original *Dictionary
of National Biography*. For the genealogy of the Berkeleys as it relates to
the New World, see Henry J. Berkley, "The Berkeley-Berkley Family and
Their Kindred in the Colonization of Virginia and Maryland." For Governor William Berkeley specifically, see Marcia Brownell Bready, "A
Cavalier in Virginia–? The Right Hon. Sir Wm. Berkeley,
His Majesty's Governor."

8 *Cal. S.P. Colonial*, I, 1: 151; PRO c/o 1/6, no. 55.
9 *Acts of the Privy Council*, 1: 180, doc. 298, 21 November 1632.
10 Champlain, *Works*, 6: 219; Reuben Thwaites, *Jesuit Relations*, 5: 39,
   41, 49; Biggar, *Early Trading Companies*, 164–5.
11 George MacBeath, "Andrew Forrester," DCB, 1: 311; John G. Reid, *Acadia, Maine, and New Scotland: Marginal Colonies in the Seventeenth
   Century*, 82; Naomi E. S. Griffiths, *From Migrant to Acadian: A North
   American Border People, 1604–1755*, 49. It is possible that this attack
   was not completely unprovoked. John Winthrop refers to a raid made
   by a French party against Fort Pentagouet in the spring or summer of
   1632. He states that: "The French came in a pinnace to Penobscot, and
   rifled a trucking house belonging to Plymouth, carrying thence three
   hundred weight of beaver and other goods. They took also one Dixy
   Bull and his shallop and goods." See: James Kendall Hosmer, ed.,
   Winthrop's Journal: History of New England 1630–1649, 1: 82.
12 George MacBeath, "Charles Sainte-Étienne de La Tour," DCB, 1: 592–6;
   Griffiths, *From Migrant to Acadian*, 49–70.
13 *Cal. S.P. Colonial*, 1: 165; PRO SP CO 1/6, no. 74.
14 *Cal. S.P. Colonial*, 1: 166, PRO SP CO 1/6, no. 75.

15 HMC Cowper, 2: 42.
16 Charles I to Sir James Balfour, Lyon King at Armes, 15 March 1632, in: Charles Rogers, ed., *The Earl of Stirling's Register of Royal Letters*, 2: 582.
17 Thomas McGrail, *Sir William Alexander, First Earl of Stirling: A Biographical Study*, 153–4
18 Henry Kirke, *The First English Conquest of Canada*, 108.
19 McGrail, *Sir William Alexander*, 156–7; William Fraser, ed., *The Red Book of Menteith*, 2: 54.
20 "Charles I to the Court of Session, 18 October 1633," in Rogers, ed., *The Earl of Stirling's Register of Royal Letters*, 2: 693.
21 HMC Cowper ,3: 155.
22 D.C. Harvey, "Sir William Alexander, the younger," DCB, 1: 54.
23 McGrail, *Sir William Alexander*, 180.
24 Ibid., 102–3; David Laing, ed., *Register of Royal Letters, Charters, and Tracts*, 81; *Cal. S.P. Domestic*, 1639, 71; D.C. Harvey, "Sir William Alexander," DCB, 1: 53–4.
25 Printed in McGrail, *Sir William Alexander*, 186–7.
26 John G. Reid, *Sir William Alexander and North American Colonization: A Reappraisal*, 14.
27 On at least one occasion, he seems to have been granted permission to leave prison for several days to attend to personal business. See "Discharge of James Stewart, Lord Uchiltrie, 20 Oct., 1637." National Archives of Scotland, GD90/2/70.
28 *APS*, 6: pt. on1e, 1643–1647, 181.
29 Ibid.
30 Ibid., 6: pt.2, 1648–1660, 151.
31 Ibid., 215–16. In a report to Cromwell in August 1657, General Monck and the council of Scotland related that among their expenses had been a payment: "To the Lord Ochiltree one hundred twentie one pounds thirteen shillings and fower pence." "General Monck and the council of Scotland to the Protector, 20 August 1657, in," ibid., 911.
32 Scot of Scotstarvet, quoted in: Laing, ed., *Royal Letters, Charters, and Tracts*, 55.
33 *Cal. S.P. Colonial*, 1: 381; 9: 197
34 John S. Moir, "Lewis Kirke," DCB, 1: 407.
35 Ibid.; Ware, "An Incident in Winthrop's Voyage," 109; Kirke, *The First English Conquest*, 177–9.
36 John S. Moir, "Thomas Kirke," DCB 1: 408.
37 DCB, 1: 368–9.
38 John S. Moir, "David Kirke," DCB, 1: 405.
39 Pope, *Fish Into Wine*, 122–30.
40 *Acts of the Privy Council*, 1: 278, no. 460.

41 *Cal. S.P. Colonial*, 1: 363, 371, 372, 373, 381; Kirke, *The First English Conquest*, 174–81; Moir, "David Kirke," 405–6.

EPILOGUE

1 Reuben Thwaites, *Jesuit Relations*, 5: 39, 41, 49.
2 Marcel Trudel, "Emery de Caën," DCB, 1: 159.
3 His specific titles were: Captain of the Royal Navy, Lieutenant General of New France, Lieutenant for the St Lawrence Valley, and chief representative of the Company of One Hundred Associates. See David Hackett Fischer, *Champlain's Dream*, 445–6.
4 Morris Bishop, *Champlain*, 293–301.
5 René Baudry, "Charles Daniel," DCB, 1: 247–8.
6 Brébeuf, quoted in: François Du Creux, *History of Canada*, 1: 150.
7 Léon Pouliot, "Antoine Daniel," DCB, 1: 246–7; René Latourelle, "Jean de Brébeuf," ibid., 1: 236.

CONCLUSION

1 Nova Scotia had been formally ceded to Britain in 1713 under the terms of the Treaty of Utrecht.
2 Archibald Swinton, ed., *Report of the Trial of Alexander Humphreys or Alexander Claiming the Title of Earl of Stirling Before the High Court of Justiciary at Edinburgh for the Crime of Forgery*, Appendix, lxxxi.
3 Ibid., passim; Anonymous, *Celebrated Claimants from Perkin Warbeck to Arthur Orton*, 117–21.
4 Tom Devine, *Scotland's Empire 1600–1815* (London, 2003), 1–2.
5 Bruce Lenman, *England's Colonial Wars 1550–1688*, 177.
6 Ibid.; John G. Reid, *Sir William Alexander*, 14.
7 See the stanza from Alexander's *The Tragedy of Julius Caesar* immediately preceding the Prologue.

BIBLIOGRAPHY

MANUSCRIPT SOURCES
National Archives of Scotland, GD 90/3/23.
National Library of Scotland, MS 2061.
Public Record Office (PRO), State Papers Domestic, Charles I, 16/527,
f. 104v.

MANUSCRIPT SOURCES (from microfilm)
Public Record Office (PRO) State Papers Colonial Series
PRO, SP, CO, 1: Vols. 1 6; 10–12; 14–15; 16–17; 21–22; 24–25; 34;
44; 66.

MANUSCRIPT SOURCES FROM STATE PAPERS ONLINE (Gale)
Landsdowne MS Vol. /100 f. 83. (Gale document number MC4305008477)
Landsdowne MS Vol/100 f. 95. (Gale document number MC4305008478)

PUBLISHED SOURCES
Akrigg, G.P.V., ed. *Letters of James VI and I*. Berkeley: University of
   California Press, 1984.
Anderson, Adam, ed. *Letters and State Papers during the Reign of King
   James the Sixth. Chiefly from the Manuscript Collections of Sir James
   Balfour of Denmyln*. Edinburgh: Abbotsford Club, 1839.
Anderson, William. *The Scottish Nation: Or, The Surnames, Families,
   Literature, Honours, and Biographical History ...* Edinburgh: Fullerton,
   1863.
Andrews, Kenneth R. *Elizabethan Privateering: English Privateering During
   the Spanish War, 1585–1603*. Cambridge: Cambridge University Press,
   1964.
– *Ships, Money and Politics: Seafaring and Naval Enterprise in the Reign of
   Charles I*. Cambridge: Cambridge University Press, 1991.

Armitage, David. *The Ideological Origins of the British Empire*. Cambridge: Cambridge University Press, 2000.

Bailyn, Bernard, *Atlantic History: Concept and Contours*. Cambridge: Harvard University Press, 2005.

Bain, Joseph, ed. *Calendar of Letters and Papers Relating to the Affairs of the Borders of England and Scotland*. Edinburgh: General Register House, 1896.

Balfour-Paul, James. *The Scots Peerage*. 9 vols. Edinburgh: T. and A. Constable, 1904–1914.

Banks, Christopher Thomas, ed. *Baronia Anglica Concentrata or A Concentrated Account of All the Baronies Commissioned Baronies in Fee, etc.* Ripon, Yorkshire: William Harrison, 1843.

Barry, George. *The History of the Orkney Islands: in Which is Comprehended an Account of their Ancient State...* Edinburgh: Archibald Constable and Company, 1805.

Baxter, James Phinney, ed., *Sir Ferdinando Gorges and His Province of Maine*. Boston: The Prince Society, 1890.

Beckett, J.C. *The Making of Modern Ireland, 1603–1623*. London: Routledge, 1966.

Benjamin, Thomas, Timothy Hall. and David Rutherford, eds., *The Atlantic World in the Age of Empire*. Boston: Houghton Mifflin, 2001.

Berkley, Henry J. "The Berkeley-Berkley Family and Their Kindred in the Colonization of Virginia and Maryland," *William and Mary Quarterly*, 2nd Ser., 3, no. 3 (July., 1923): 180–99.

Biggar, H.P. *The Early Trading Companies of New France*. Toronto: University of Toronto Library, 1901.

– ed., *Works of Samuel de Champlain*, Vols. 1–6. Toronto: Champlain Society, 1922–36.

Birch, Thomas ed., *The Court and Times of Charles I, etc.* 2 Vols. London: Henry Colbourn, 1848.

Birdwood, George, and William Foster, eds., *The Register of Letters &c. of the Governor and Company of the Merchants of London Trading Into the East Indies*. London: B. Quartich, 1893.

Bishop, Morris. *Champlain: The Life of Fortitude*. Toronto: McClelland & Stewart, 1964.

Bolton, F.R. *The Caroline Tradition in the Church of Ireland, with particular reference to Bishop Jeremy Taylor*. London: Church Historical Society, 1958

Bready, Marcia Brownell. "A Cavalier in Virginia—? The Right Hon. Sir Wm. Berkeley, His Majesty's Governor," *William and Mary College Quarterly Historical Magazine*18, no. 2 . (Oct., 1909): 115–29.

Brebner, J.B. *New England's Outpost: Acadia Before the Conquest of Canada*. Hamden, Connecticut: Archon Books, 1965.

Bremer, Francis J., and Lynn A. Botehlo, eds., *The World of John Winthrop: Essays on England and New England 1588–1649*. Boston: Massachusetts Historical Society, 2005.

Brigden, Susan. *New Worlds, Lost Worlds: The Rule of the Tudors, 1485–1603*. New York: Viking, 2000.

Brown, George W. *Building the Canadian Nation*. Toronto: J.M. Dent, 1942.

Brown, Keith M. *Noble Society in Scotland: Wealth Family and Culture, From Reformation to Revolution*. Edinburgh: Edinburgh University Press, 2000.

Brown, P. Hume, ed. *Registers of the Privy Council of Scotland*. Second Series, 8 vols. Edinburgh: General Register House, 1899–1908.

Brown, Richard. *A History of the Island of Cape Breton*. London: Sampson and Low, 1869.

Bruce, John, ed. *Letters of Queen Elizabeth and King James VI of Scotland*. London: Camden Society, 1859.

– *Correspondence of King James VI of Scotland with Sir Robert Cecil and Others*. London: Camden Society, 1861.

– and William Hamilton, eds., *Calendar of State Papers Domestic Series, of the Reign of Charles I, 1625–1649*. 23 Vols. Nendeln, Liechtenstein: Kraus Reprint, 1967.

Burke, John Bernard. *Vicissitudes of Families*. Oxford: Oxford University Press, 1863.

Burnet, Gilbert. *Memoirs of the Lives and Actions of James and William, dukes of Hamilton and Castleherald*. London, 1677.

Burton, J. H., and D. Masson, eds. *Registers of the Privy Council of Scotland*. First series, 14 vols. Edinburgh: General Register House, 1877–98.

Calderwood, David. *The History of the Church of Scotland*. 8 vols. Edinburgh: Woodrow Society, 1849.

Canny, Nicholas. "Writing Atlantic History; or, Reconfiguring the History of Colonial British America," *Journal of American History* 86, no. 3, (Dec., 1999): 1095.

– ed. *The Origins of Empire: British Overseas Enterprise to the Close of the Seventeenth Century*. Oxford: Oxford University Press, 1998.

Cell, Gillian T. *English Enterprise in Newfoundland, 1577–1660*. Toronto: University of Toronto Press, 1969.

– ed. *Newfoundland Discovered: English Attempts at Colonisation, 1610–1630*. London: Hakluyt Society, 2nd Ser., Vol. 160, 1982.

Charlevoix, P.F.X. de. *History and General Description of New France*, Vol. 2. New York: John Gilmary Shea, 1870.

Chrimes, S.B. *Henry VII*. Berkeley: University of California Press, 1972.

Church, William F. *Richelieu and the Reasons of State*. Princeton: Princeton University Press, 1972.

Codignola, Luca. *The Coldest Harbour of the Land: Simon Stock and Lord Baltimore's Colony in Newfoundland, 1621–1649*. Montreal: McGill-Queen's University Press, 1988.

Conacher, James B. ed. *The History of Canada or New France by Father François Du Creux, S.J.* Toronto: Champlain Society, 1951. 2 vols.

Connolly, Matthew Foster *Biographical Dictionary of Eminent Men of Fife: Natives of the County, Or Connected with it ...* Edinburgh: Inglis and Jack, 1866.

Cowan, Samuel. *The Lord Chancellors of Scotland: From The Institution of the Office to the Treaty of Union*. Edinburgh: W. & A.K. Johnston, Limited, 1891.

Davies, Robert, ed. *The Life and Times of Marmaduke Rawdon of York*. London: Camden Society, 1863.

Dean, John Ward ed., *Capt. John Mason, the Founder of New Hampshire*. Boston: The Prince Society, 1887.

Dee, John. *General and rare memorials pertayning to the perfect arte of nauigation annexed to the paradoxal cumpas, in playne: now first published: 24. yeres, after the first inuention thereof*. London, 1577.

Delâge, Denys. *Bitter Feast: Amerindians and Europeans in Northeastern North America, 1600–64*. Vancouver: University of British Columbia Press, 1993.

Devens, Carol. *Countering Colonization: Native American Women and the Great Lakes Missions, 1630–1900*. Berkeley: University of California Press, 1992.

Dionne, N.E. *Champlain*. Toronto: Morang and Company, 1963.

Donald, Peter. *An Uncounselled King: Charles I and the Scottish Troubles, 1637–1641*. Cambridge: Cambridge University Press, 1990.

Donaldson, Gordon ed., *Scottish Historical Documents*. Glasgow: Neil Wilson Publishing, 1974.

– *Scotland: James V–VII*. Edinburgh: Mercat Press, 1990.

– ed. *A Dictionary of Scottish History*. Edinburgh: John Donald, 1977.

– and Robert Morpeth, eds. *Who's Who in Scottish History*. Cardiff: Welsh Academic Press, 1996.

Donnelly, Josesph P. *Jean de Brébeuf 1593–1649*. Chicago: Loyola University Press, 1975.

Dumbarton. *Dumbarton Burgh Records, 1627–1746*. Dumbarton, 1890.

Eccles, W.J. *France in America*. Markham, Ontario: Fitzhenry and Whiteside, 1990.

Elliott, J.H. *Europe Divided, 1559–1598*. London: Fontana, 1968.

– *Empires of the Atlantic World: Britain and Spain in America 1492–1830*. New Haven: Yale University Press, 2006.

Elton, G.R. *England Under the Tudors*. London: Methuen and Company, 1974.

– ed., *The Tudor Constitution: Documents and Commentary*. Cambridge: Cambridge University Press, 1982.

Félix, Julien, ed. *La Prise d'un seigneur escossois et de ses gens qui pilloient ...* Rouen, 1880.

– ed., *Voyage à la Nouvelle-France du Capitaine Charles Daniel de Dieppe*. Rouen, 1880,

Finnan, Mark. *The First Nova Scotian: The Story of Sir William Alexander and His Lost Colony of Charlesfort, Nova Scotia's First English-speaking Settlement*. Halifax: Formac Publishing Company, 1997.

Firth, C.H., ed., *The Stuart Tracts 1603–1693*. Westminster: Archibald Constable and Co., 1903.

– and S.C. Lomas, eds. *Notes on the Diplomatic Relations of England and France, 1603–1688: Lists of Ambassadors from England to France and from France to England*. Oxford: Basil Blackwell, 1906.

Fischer, David Hackett. *Champlain's Dream*. Toronto: Alfred A. Knopf, 2008.

Fletcher, Anthony, *Reform in the Provinces: The Government of Stuart England*. New Haven: Yale University Press, 1986,

Fraser, William, ed., *The Red Book of Menteith*. 2 vols. Edinburgh: 1888.

Fuller, Thomas. *The Church History of Britain from the Birth of Jesus Christ Until the Year MDCXLVIII*. London: Thomas Tegg, 1842.

Galloway, Bruce. *The Union of England and Scotland, 1603–1608*. Edinburgh: John Donald, 1986.

Gardiner, S.R. *History of England from the Accession of James I to the Outbreak of the Civil War, 1603–1642*. 10 vols. London: Longmans, Green and Co., 1894.

Gilbert, Sir Humphrey. *A Discourse of a Discoverie for a New Passage to Cataia*. London, 1574.

Gillmore, Don, and Pierre Turgeon. *Canada: A People's History*. Toronto: McClelland & Stewart, 2000.

Goodare, Julian. "The Statutes of Iona in Context," *Scottish Historical Review*, Volume 77, No. 203, April 1998, 31–57.

Grant, Alexander, and Keith Stringer, eds. *Uniting the Kingdom?: The Making of British History*. London, 1995.

Grant, W.L., and James Munro. *Acts of the Privy Council of England. Colonial Series, Vol. I.* A.D. *1613–1680*. London: HMSO, 1908. Nendeln, Liechtenstein: Kraus Reprint, 1967.

Green, Mary Anne E. *Diary of John Rous*. London: Camden Society, 1856.

– *Calendar of State Papers Domestic Series of the Reign of James I*. Vols. 8–12, 1603–1625. Nendeln, Liechtenstein: Kraus Reprint, 1967.

Greene, Jack P. *Peripheries and Center: Constitutional Development in the Extended Polities of the British Empire and the United States, 1607–1788*. Athens, Georgia: University of Georgia Press, 1986.

Gregg, Pauline. *King Charles I*. London: J.M. Dent and Sons, 1981.

Gregory, Donald. *The History of the Western Highlands and Isles of Scotland: From A.D. 1493 to A.D. 1625*. London: Longman, 1881.

Griffiths, Naomi E.S. *From Migrant to Acadian: A North American Border People, 1604–1755*. Montreal: McGill-Queen's University Press, 2005.

– and John G. Reid, eds. "New Evidence on New Scotland, 1629," *William and Mary Quarterly*, 3d Series, Vol. 49, July, 1992, 492–508.

Grosjean, Alexia and Steve Murdoch, eds., *Scottish Communities Abroad in the Early Modern Period*. Leiden: Brill, 2005.

Guy, John. *The True Life of Mary Stuart, Queen of Scots*. Boston: Mariner Books, 2004.

Hakluyt, Richard. *The principal navigations, voyages, traffiques & discoveries of the English nations, made by sea or overland to the remote and farthest distant quarters of the earth at any time within the compasse of these 1600 yeares, by Richard Hakluyt*. London: J.M. Dent & sons. 7 vols., 1907.

Hill, George. *An historical account of the plantation of Ulster at the commencement of the seventeenth century, 1608–1630*. Belfast: M'Caw, Stevenson, and Orr, 1877.

Historical Manuscripts Commission, Coke MSS, Papers of the Earl Cowper. London: HMSO, 1888.

Historical Manuscripts Commission. *Supplementary Report on the Manuscripts of the Earl of Mar and Kellie*. London: HMSO, 1930.

Hosmer, James Kendall ed. *Winthrop's Journal: History of New England 1630–1649*, 2 Vols. New York: Charles Scribner's Sons, 1908.

Insh, G.P. *Scottish Colonial Schemes 1620–1686*. Glasgow: MacLehose, Jackson & Co., 1922.

Jesse, John Heneage, ed. *Memoirs of the Court of England During the Reign of the Stuarts, Including the Protectorate*. London: Richard Bentley, 1855.

Jones, Elizabeth. *Gentlemen and Jesuits: Quests for Glory and Adventure in the Early Days of New France*. Toronto: University of Toronto Press, 1986.

Jones, J.R. *Britain and Europe in the Seventeenth Century*. London: Edward Arnold, 1966.

Judges, A.V. "Philip Burlamachi: A Financier of the Thirty Years' War," *Economica*, 18. (Nov., 1926): 285–300.

Kingsley, Charles, ed., *Westward Ho: The Voyages and Adventures of Sir Amyas Leigh*. Boston, 1885.

Kirke, Henry. *The First English Conquest of Canada*. London: Sampson, Low, Marston & Co., Ltd., 1908 (2nd ed.).

Kishlansky, Mark. *A Monarchy Transformed: Britain 1603–1714*. London: Penguin, 1996.

Kupperman, Karen Ordahl, ed. *America in European Consciousness 1493–1750*. Chapel Hill: University of North Carolina Press, 1995.

Kurlansky, Mark. *Cod: A Biography of the Fish That Changed the World*. New York: Penguin, 1997.

Laing, David, ed., *Royal Letters, Charters and Tracts Relating to the Colonization of New Scotland*. Edinburgh: Bannatyne Club, 1867.

Landsman, Ned C. ed., *Nation and Province in the First British Empire: Scotland and the Americas, 1600–1800*. Lewisburg, Pennsylvania: Bucknell University Press, 2001).

Laud, William. *Works of the Most Reverend Father in God, William Laud*. 7 vols. Oxford: Oxford University Press, 1860.

Lee, Maurice. "James VI's government of Scotland," *Scottish Historical Review* 54 (1975).

– *Government by Pen: Scotland under James VI*. Urbana: University of Illinois Press, 1980.Ro

– *The Road to Revolution: Scotland under Charles I, 1625–37*. Urbana: University of Illinois Press, 1985.

– *Great Britain's Solomon: King James VI and I in His Three Kingdoms*. Urbana: University of Illinois Press, 1990.

Lenman, Bruce. *England's Colonial Wars, 1550–1688*. Harlow: Pearson Education Ltd., 2001.

Levine, Philippa, ed., *Gender and Empire*. Oxford: Oxford University Press, 2004.

Litalien, Raymond and Denis Vaugeois, eds. *Champlain: The Birth of French America* (trans. Käthe Roth). Montreal: McGill-Queen's University Press, 2004.

Loades, David. *England's Maritime Empire: Seapower, Commerce and Policy, 1490–1690*. Harlow: Pearson Education Ltd., 2000.

Lockyer, Roger. *Buckingham: The Life and Political Career of George Villiers, First Duke of Buckingham, 1592–1628*. London: Longman, 1982.

– *The Early Stuarts*. London: Longman, 1989.

Lublinskaya, A.D. *French Absolutism: The Crucial Phase, 1620–1629*. Cambridge: Cambridge University Press, 1968.

Lucas, Paul. *American Odyssey 1607–1789*. Englewood Cliffs, New Jersey: Prentice-Hall, 1984.

Macdougall, A.J., ed. *The Huron Relation of 1635 by Jean de Brébeuf*. Midland, Ontario: Martyrs' Shrine, 1973.

Macinnes, Allan I. *Charles I and the Making of the Covenanting Movement*. Edinburgh: John Donald, 1991.

– *Clanship, Commerce and the House of Stuart, 1603–1788*. East Linton: Tuckwell Press, 1996.

– and Arthur H. Williamson, eds. *Shaping the Stuart World 1603–1714*. Leiden: Brill, 2006.

Maidment, John. ed. *State Papers and Miscellaneous Correspondence of Thomas, Earl of Melros*. Edinburgh: Abbotsford Club, 1837. 2 vols.

Mancke, Elizabeth, and Carole Shammas, eds. *The Creation of the British Atlantic World*. Baltimore: Johns Hopkins University Press, 2005.

Martin, Colin, and Geoffrey Parker, *The Spanish Armada*. London, 1988.

Mason, Roger, ed., *Scots and Britons: Scottish Political Thought and the Union of 1603* (Cambridge: Cambridge University Press, 1994).

McGrail, Thomas H. *Sir William Alexander, First Earl of Stirling: A Biographical Study*. Edinburgh: Oliver and Boyd, 1940.

Mcllwain, C.H., ed., *The Political Works of James I*. New York: Russell and Russell, 1965.

M'Crie, Thomas. *The Life of Andrew Melville, Containing Illustrations of Ecclesiastical and Literary History*. London: T. Cadell, 1824.

Mithun, Marianne. "The Synchronic and Diachronic Behavior of Plops, Squeaks, Croaks, Sighs, and Moans," *International Journal of American Linguistics*, Vol. 48, No. 1 (Jan., 1982), 49–58; and "Untangling the Huron and the Iroquois," ibid., Vol. 51, No. 4 (Oct. 1985), 504–7.

Morgan, Edmund S. "The Labor Problem at Jamestown, 1607–18," *American Historical Review* 76 (1971): 595–612.

Morison, Samuel Eliot. *Samuel de Champlain: Father of New France*. Boston: Little, Brown and Company, 1972.

Morrill, John, ed. *The Oxford Illustrated History of Tudor and Stuart Britain*. Oxford: Oxford University Press, 1996.

Morrin, James, ed. *Calendar of Patent and Close Rolls of Chancery in Ireland, Charles I*. London: HMSO, 1863.

Nicholls, Andrew, D. *The Jacobean Union: A Reconsideration of British Civil Policies Under the Early Stuarts*. Westport: Greenwood Press, 1999.

– "Showdown at Fort Rosemar: *The Beaver*, June/July, 2004, 30–4.

– "The purpois is honorabill, and my conduce to the good of our service": Lord Ochiltree and the Cape Breton Colony, 1629–1631," *Acadiensis*, XXXIV, 2 (Spring, 2005), 109–23.

Nichols, John, ed. *The Progresses, Processions, and Magnificent Festivities of King James the First*. London: Printer to the Society of Antiquaries, 1828.

Ohlmeyer, Jane. "Seventeenth-Century Ireland and the New British and Atlantic Histories," *American Historical Review* 104, no. 2 (April, 1999): 446.

Parker, Geoffrey, ed. *The Thirty Years' War*. Totawa, New Jersey: Barnes and Noble, 1987.

Parkman, Francis. *Pioneers of France in the New World*. Boston: Little, Brown, and Company, 1885.

Parry, J.H. *The Age of Reconnaissance: Discovery, Exploration and Settlement 1450 to 1650*. Berkeley and Los Angeles: University of California Press, 1981.

Perceval-Maxwell, Michael . *The Scottish Migration to Ulster in the Reign of James VI*. London: Routledge and Kegan Paul, 1975.

Pestana, Carla Gardina. *The English Atlantic in an Age of Revolution, 1640–1661*. Cambridge Massachusetts: Harvard University Press, 2004.

Pocock, J.G.A. "British History: A Plea for a New Subject," *Journal of Modern History* 47 (Dec. 1975): 601–24.

– "The New British History in Atlantic Perspective: An Antipodean Commentary," *The American Historical Review* 104, no. 2 (April, 1999): 490–500.

Pope, Peter. "Adventures in the Sack Trade: London Merchants in the Canada and Newfoundland Trades, 1627–1648," *Northern Mariner*, 6: No. 1 (January 1996).

– *Fish into Wine: The Newfoundland Plantation in the Seventeenth Century*. Chapel Hill: University of North Carolina Press, 2004.

Pratt, Edwin John. *E.J. Pratt on His Life and Poetry*. Toronto: University of Toronto Press, 1983.

Quinn, D.B. *England and the Discovery of America, 1481–1620*. New York: Allen and Unwin, 1974.

Rabb, Theodore A. *Enterprise and Empire, 1575–1630*. New Haven: Yale University Press, 1967.

Rae, T.I., *The Administration of the Scottish Frontier 1513–1603*.

Reid, John G. "The Scots Crown and the Restitution of Port Royal, 1629–1632," *Acadiensis*, 6: 2 (spring 1977).

– *Acadia, Maine, and New Scotland: Marginal Colonies in the Seventeenth Century*. Toronto: University of Toronto Press, 1981.

– *Sir William Alexander and North American Colonization: A Reappraisal*. Edinburgh: University of Edinburgh, 1990.

– J.H. Stewart, Kenneth McNaught, and Harry S. Crowe, eds. *A Source-book of Canadian History*. Toronto: Holt, Rinehart and Winston, 1959.

Rodger, N.A.M. *The Safeguard of the Sea: A Naval History of Britain 660–1649*. New York: Norton, 1999.

Rogers, Charles, ed. *The Earl of Stirling's Register of Royal Letters Relative to Scotland and Nova Scotia*. Edinburgh, 1885.

Rubinstein, Hilary L. *Captain Luckless: James, First Duke of Hamilton, 1606–1649*, Totowa, New Jersey: Rowan and Littlefield, 1976.

Russell, Charles and John Prendergast, eds. *Calendar of State Papers Ireland*, James I, Vol. 5: 1615–1625. London: PRO, 1880.

Russell, Conrad. *The Causes of the English Civil War*. Oxford: Oxford University Press, 1990.

– *The Fall of the British Monarchies 1637–1642*. Oxford: Oxford University Press, 1991.

Sacks, David Harris. *The Widening Gate: Bristol and the Atlantic Economy, 1450–1700*. Berkeley: University of California Press, 1991.

Sagard, Gabriel. *The Long Journey to the Country of the Hurons*. George Wrong, ed. Toronto: Champlain Society, 1939.

Sainsbury, W. Noel, *Calendar of State Papers, Colonial Series, 1574–1660*. London: HMSO, 1860.

Schuster, Carl. "Into the Great Bay: Henry Hudson's Mysterious Final Voyage," *The Beaver*, August/September, 1999, 8–15.

Scott, W., D. Laing, and T. Thomson, eds. *The Bannatyne Miscellany*. Edinburgh: Bannatyne Club, 1827.

Scott, Walter, ed. *A Collection of Scarce and Valuable Tracts Particularly That of the Late Lord Somers*. 13 vols., New York: AMS Press, 1965.

Sharpe, Kevin. *The Personal Rule of Charles I*. New Haven: Yale University Press, 1992.

Slafter, E.F., ed. *Sir William Alexander and American Colonization, Including Three Royal Charters*. Boston: Prince Society, 1873.

Smith, David L. *The Stuart Parliaments 1603–1689*. London: Arnold, 1999.

Spottiswood, John. *The History of the Church and State of Scotland to 1625*. London, 1677.

Stevenson, David. *Highland Warrior: Alasdair Mac Colla and the Civil Wars*. Edinburgh: Saltire Society, 1994.

Swinton, Archibald, ed., *Report of the Trial of Alexander Humphreys or Alexander Claiming the Title of Earl of Stirling Before the High Court of Justiciary at Edinburgh for the Crime of Forgery*. Edinburgh, 1839.

Taylor, E.G.R. "Master Hore's Voyage of 1536," *Geographical Journal*, Vol. 77, No. 5, May 1931.

Thwaites, Reuben Gold, ed., *The Jesuit Relations and Allied Documents*. 73 vols. Cleveland: Burrows Brothers Company, 1896–1901.

Tooker, Elizabeth. *Ethnography of the Huron Indians, 1615–1649*. Washington: U.S. Government Printing Office, 1964

Trigger, Bruce G. *Huron Farmers of the North*. New York: Holt, Rinehart, and Winston, 1969.

– *The Children of Aataensic: A History of the Huron People to 1660*. Montreal: McGill-Queen's Press, 1976.

– *Natives and Newcomers: Canada's "Heroic Age" Reconsidered*. Montreal: McGill-Queen's University Press, 1985.

Trudel, Marcel. *The Beginnings of New France*. Toronto: McClelland & Stewart, 1973.

Ware, Horace E. "An Incident in Winthrop's Voyage to New England," *Publications of the Colonial Society of Massachusetts 12: Transactions 1908–1909*, 107.

Wernham, R.B. *The Making of Elizabethan Foreign Policy 1558–1603*. Berkeley: University of California Press, 1980.

Williamson, J.A., ed. *The Cabot Voyages and Bristol Discovery under Henry VII*. London: Hakluyt Society, 2nd. Ser. 120, 1962.

Index